"This book captures the relatability so ⟨...⟩ adult children struggling with mental ill⟨...⟩ ⟨...⟩ messages of hope around reclaiming your life and not fixing your child. This is a truly courageous work that will be an aid to many mothers in the 'storm.'"

—**Angela Berra,** LMSW, MA
Director of Programs, NAMI Saint Louis

"Linda Hoff does an extraordinary job describing the reality and complexity of caring for an adult child with severe mental illness. My sister had her first psychotic break at the age of fifteen, more than fifty years ago. My mother had virtually no support and was extremely embarrassed. How she would have loved to read this book and know that she had *Sisters in the Storm!* Thank you, Linda!"

—**Barb Mecker**
Sibling of sister diagnosed with Schizoaffective Disorder
Retired Special Education Teacher
NAMI F2F Facilitator

"I appreciate Linda Hoff for putting pen to paper and sharing her story and knowledge of mental illness. *Sisters in the Storm* is a very enlightening and educational. I learned more about mental illness and can relate to what she shared. It's nice to know I'm not alone."

—**Dorinda Wright**
Mother of son with undiagnosed MI and addiction

"*Sisters in the Storm* is a heartbreaking and heartwarming book of the struggles many of us live with daily. I learned so much reading this book and enjoyed the honest and real portrayal of what mothers of MIACs experience. Linda's presentation of her life was very relatable. I recommend book this to not only the moms of MIACs, but fathers as well."

—**Lucinda Brown**
Mother of son with anxiety and depression,
additional undiagnosed MI, and addiction

"I pray that families touched by mental illness find hope and encouragement in *Sisters in the Storm*. May they know that they aren't alone on this harrowing journey."

—**Megan Manning**
Sibling of brother diagnosed with paranoid schizophrenia
Director and Teacher of Mighty Kingdom Academy, Hermann MO

"*Sisters in the Storm* is a raw, no-holds-barred account of life with a mentally ill adult child. This book fearlessly and unapologetically tackles the pain and stigma of mental illness. The author's journey through the grief, volatility, despair, fear, guilt, resentment, and shame are well written and relatable for anyone who loves a mentally ill person. With knowledge comes understanding and acceptance, and *Sisters in the Storm* has a lot to offer in the way of education, practical tools, strategies, and resources. Ms. Hoff ultimately found her way to peace and healing, and this inspiring, compassionate, and therapeutic book can help anyone in a similar situation do the same."

—**M.S.**
Mom: child with Bipolar II and/or
Borderline Personality Disorder (BPD);
Sister: sibling with Bipolar II, Generalized Anxiety Disorder (GAD), and Post-Traumatic Stress Disorder (PTSD);
Niece: Persisted Depressive Disorder (PDD), Social Anxiety Disorder, and Attention-Deficit/ Hyperactivity Disorder (ADHD).
Previously diagnosed Bipolar II, Post-Traumatic Stress Disorder (PTSD), and Reactive Attachment Disorder (RAD)

"Linda Hoff tells the story of her mentally ill son, sharing some of the challenges and heartbreak that a mother faces with a MIAC (mentally ill adult child.)

She explores the importance of stepping away from the madness, even if it's just for a little while. Linda facilitates a broader perspective, upholding personal boundaries, and creating a daily self-care routine that so many struggling moms need.

You'll learn how to love your MIAC by accepting what is, how to advocate for your MIAC, and how to continue to fight the stigma, the criminal justice system, and the mental health care system for better options of care.

Sisters in the Storm reminds every mother that they're not alone in the fight to help their MIAC."

—**Sandy Samaniego**
Mother of a son who's been diagnosed with Schizoaffective Disorder, Anxiety, OCD, and Depression. He also struggles with addiction, homelessness, & incarceration.
NAMI Family Support Group Facilitator
NAMI Help Line Volunteer
Administrator of Private Face Book Group,
Mothers of Adult Children Who Suffer with a Mental Illness/Addiction

"Linda has shared her deepest, heartfelt thoughts to benefit mothers with mentally ill adult children (MIAC). There's a good chance you will cry—and maybe even laugh a little—at your life while reading *Sisters in the Storm*. One thing is for certain: you will learn more than you expected. Take advantage of the tools and advice offered, and you'll undoubtably become a stronger sister in the storm for its reading."

—**Trisha Munger**
Mother of son diagnosed with schizophrenia
NAMI F2F Facilitator

Sisters in the Storm

Sisters in the Storm

FOR MOMS OF MENTALLY ILL ADULT CHILDREN

LINDA HOFF

Stonebrook Publishing
Saint Louis, Missouri

A STONEBROOK PUBLISHING BOOK
©2022 Linda Hoff

This book was guided in development and
edited by Nancy L. Erickson, The Book Professor®
TheBookProfessor.com

All rights reserved. Published in the United States by Stonebrook Publishing,
a division of Stonebrook Enterprises, LLC, Saint Louis, Missouri.
No part of this book may be reproduced, scanned, or distributed in any
printed or electronic form without written permission from the author.

Please do not participate in or encourage piracy of copyrighted materials in
violation of the author's rights.

Library of Congress Control Number: 2021925601

Paperback ISBN: 978-1-955711-09-8
Ebook ISBN: 978-1-955711-10-4

www.stonebrookpublishing.net

PRINTED IN THE UNITED STATES OF AMERICA

Dedication

This book is dedicated to my son B. Your courage and determination to live each day to the best of your ability is an example of fearlessness and hope. With humor and compassion, you've inspired me to be a better person. Your desire to live on your own terms, despite severe mental illness, is a reminder to cherish every minute of every day. I wouldn't be half the person I am today if not for your illness.

As we traverse this storm together,
from my heart to yours with love always,
Mom

Contents

Dedication ix
Preface. xiii
To the Mothers xix
1. Make Peace with Your Grief 1
2. Coming to Grips with MI. 27
3. Defeated Mom to Badass Warrior 67
4. Climbing Out of the Rabbit Hole. 101
5. From Helpless Victim to Conscious Chooser 129
6. Expectations are Planned Resentments 165
7. Is It Yours to Carry?. 195
8. Inner Peace Begins When You Let Go 227
9. Self-care Isn't Selfish; It's Survival 249
10. Courage in the Face of Fear. 281
11. Find Happiness in Acceptance. 295
12. Pull Yourself from the Rubble 319
13. Joy Is an Inside Job 337
Resources 373
Acknowledgments. 375
About the Author 377

Preface

And once the storm is over, you won't remember how you made it through, how you managed to survive. You won't even be sure, whether the storm is really over.
But one thing is certain. When you come out of the storm, you won't be the same person who walked in.
That's what the storm's all about.

~ Haruki Murakami

The storm that came on that bright, sunny August afternoon wasn't forecasted. The sky was a brilliant blue with just a handful of innocent, fluffy clouds. If only I'd paid attention to the ominous rumbles of thunder in the distance, the occasional sharp crack of lightning. If I'd known the severity of the impending storm, maybe I would have taken cover. Instead, I assumed it would pass, and I wasn't prepared when it hit with gale-force winds—ferocious, merciless, and torrential. It was adverse and violent, severe and unreasonable, pitiless and invisible. This angry turbulence knocked me flat. Chaotic, destructive, unnatural—an unbridled menace. It left me battered and broken amidst the wreckage.

Mental illness is, indeed, a storm. A storm of epic proportion; a storm that not only damages but also destroys; a storm that changes the terrain and trajectory of lives; a storm that claims its place in history; a storm that divides before and after; a storm that washes away all you dreamed was possible and forces you to rebuild from the ground up.

LINDA HOFF

We Are Sisters . . .

We are sisters
Bound together
By ill children
By refusal to give up hope
By determination to find answers

We are sisters
From every part of the world
From every walk of life
From every economic background

We are sisters
We share an eternal love for our child
We share the same struggles
We share the unimaginable

We are sisters
Forged together
By pain, by misery, by loss
By a tragedy nobody understands
By a nightmare with no end, no answer, no resolution

We are sisters
So different, but the same
Tied to each other by disease
Tied to each other by stories
Tied to each other by torment

We are sisters
Frightened and alone
Frustrated and disheartened
We fight to survive, to thrive

SISTERS IN THE STORM

We are sisters
Lost in our child's illness
Lost in darkness
Lost in an unsympathetic world

We are sisters
Every story different
Every child unique
Every struggle the same

We are sisters
We cry silent tears
We cry brokenhearted tears
We cry angry tears at a society that doesn't see us

We are sisters
We share a journey
A journey of despair
A journey of tragedy
A journey of unfathomable destruction

We are sisters
Together we're stronger
Together we survive
Together we move forward

We are sisters
We share sorrow and emptiness
We share empathy and compassion
We share hopes and dreams

We are sisters
We hold each other in our hearts
We honor each other's path
We celebrate each other's wisdom

LINDA HOFF

We are sisters
Born to climb mountains
Born to bear unimaginable misfortune
Born to carry our burden in silence
No more

We are sisters
Together we have power
Together we make a difference
Together we show the world who we are
Together we find help for our children

We are sisters
United in grief
United in misery
United in the desire to create change

We are sisters
And we're done
Done with stigma
Done with discrimination
Done with shame

We are sisters
We are sisters with Mentally Ill Adult Children
We are sisters with a voice
We are sisters with a mission

We are sisters
We move through battle together
We move forward together
We move on with our lives

SISTERS IN THE STORM

We are sisters
With love in our hearts
With hope and prayers
With happiness and peace

We are sisters
We are the unspoken warriors
Our lives are linked
Our hands are linked
Our hearts are linked

It's time
We have work to do

We are sisters.

To the Mothers

This book is a way to honor your journey as the mother of a mentally ill adult child (MIAC). As a mom, you entered parenthood wearing blinders, assured that all would be well, and if not, you'd have the knowledge and perseverance to figure it out. How bad could things get? Horrific accidents and traumatic diseases happen to other people but not your family, not your child.

If you're here now, you know horrible things can and do happen to everyone. Things that others whisper about. Things that lurk in the recessed shadows of the mind. Things that nobody wants to bring into the light of day.

It didn't happen overnight, but that beautiful baby you brought home morphed and changed into someone unrecognizable. That small child with the bright smile and twinkle of mischief in his eye, that girl who loved to snuggle and read books, who rode her bike and played sports—that person faded away. In place of your happy child is one who's sullen, angry, and unapproachable. Is this just being a teenager? You hoped he'd outgrow this phase.

Then high school was over, and things headed downhill fast. No thoughts of college, he jumped from job to job, unable to have any perspective on life. She was past teenage angst and into drugs, alcohol, irrational behaviors, and unreasonable demands. You talked, pleaded, and begged. Ragged and raw, you berated yourself for your bad parenting skills, sure that you were a terrible mother because you couldn't help your child.

Something unknown and unbidden snuck in and snatched your child's mind. There's a stealth and darkness to what has come. All that remains are the memories of what could have been, what should have been. In its place are irrational rants, incoherent actions, aggression, anger, and delusional thoughts. Personal hygiene, normal dietary habits, and sleep have vanished. Instead, you hear about grandiose money schemes, see the hours spent in isolation, tolerate his nasty moods, become the brunt of everything wrong in her life, and you watch your child's unrelenting need to self-medicate. Everything unravels. How much worse can this get?

Something unknown and unbidden snuck in and snatched your child's mind.

Unfortunately for me, we hadn't yet hit bottom. I was convinced that it couldn't get any worse. He didn't eat, insisted the neighbors were conspiring to harm him, and collected hundreds of bits of paper with license plate numbers, dates, and secret messages. I couldn't deny it any longer. These weren't the normal woes that all young adults experience. Something was gravely wrong, and I didn't have the skills to deal with whatever this was.

For my son, it took the police and two involuntary psychiatric hospitalizations to receive a definitive and grievous mental illness diagnosis. Praying that drug addiction had induced his bizarre behaviors, I harbored foolish thoughts that all could be fixed with the proper medication, and I held on to the illusion that normal was still within reach. My real child would reemerge, and our lives would pick up where they'd left off. Gone would be this disturbed imposter who wreaked havoc and turned life into a daytime nightmare. Gone would be the shell that looked like my child but was actually a stranger.

This book is a compilation of the journey I took to hell and back—of the storm I weathered—as I grappled with caring for my mentally ill adult child (MIAC). The lessons learned and insights gained came over a period of several years. Not a single moment of wisdom, but instead a spiral of increasing awareness and a release of harmful thoughts and beliefs until everything no longer useful was stripped away. I was in and out of the light and dark, over and over again, exposed and vulnerable until I wondered if anyone would recognize what remained. How much more would I need to let go of? In the end, what emerged was a deeper perception and acceptance of what couldn't be changed—the creation of a new reality for both my MIAC and me.

> *In the end, what emerged was a deeper perception and acceptance of what couldn't be changed—the creation of a new reality for both my MIAC and me.*

This book is written for you as you emerge from the storm and trudge through the day-to-day struggles, chaos, and attempts to cope with a MIAC. You won't find answers about how to change or fix your child. Instead, this will be your journey of exploration and expansion. Each chapter is designed to help you reclaim your life.

You may not feel ready to take this path of self-discovery, but I urge you to take the first step. Rest assured that this material will push you beyond your comfort zone. You might agree with parts of this book and disagree with others, but wherever you are on this journey, I honor you for the love, commitment, and support you have for your child. May you experience increased joy and balance as you navigate toward a better life.

The inspiration for this book came as I struggled to find support and advice. The insightful Iyanla Vanzant says, "It's important that we share our experiences with other people. Your story will heal you, and your story will heal someone else. When you tell your story, you free yourself and give other people permission to acknowledge their own story."

I make no claims to be a professional other than through my war-weary experiences. My story will be different from yours. But the journey is the same, the one you're about to launch to reclaim your life, your purpose, your joy. Remember that you're not alone, you're stronger than you know, and there's a light in the storm.

If you're ready, let's walk out of this storm together. Let's begin the journey of discovery, redemption, and liberation. Thousands of women walk this path alongside us. They, too, seek answers, want to be understood, and are desperate for support. As you read, imagine yourself surrounded by these women—your sisters—each of us here to offer you encouragement, acceptance, and love.

As Buddha advises, "Pain is certain; suffering is optional."

We are sisters
Tied to each other by our trauma
Lost in the midst of a child's illness
We share a journey of tragedy
We're united in our grief
We long to reclaim our lives
Together we survive
Together we flourish
Together we find joy
We are the mothers of a mentally ill adult child

Make Peace with Your Grief

We are sisters
Bound by heartache
Adrift in a sea of despair
We grieve a lost child
We share a mother's pain
We are sisters

It's 9:00 p.m. The phone rings. My heart skips a beat. My breath catches. It's been four days since I committed my son to a locked psych ward. "I'm B's doctor," the caller says, "and I've diagnosed him with chronic paranoid schizophrenia. You should seek legal guardianship as soon as possible. Your child will never be well."

"What?" I ask. "Are you sure? What does that mean?"

"Call the hospital social worker in the morning, and she'll give you the name of an attorney," the doctor said. "Good night."

Click. Silence. My heart pounds in my ears as I drop to the couch, dazed. A cloud of darkness and impending doom surrounds me as I grapple with this dismal prediction.

This is a nightmare. My vision goes dark, and I drop my head between my knees as tears drip onto the carpet. I need to do something, but what? My ears buzz. My stomach lurches. I'm lost. There's nothing to do until morning . . . except worry. Adrift in a vortex of pain, I can't breathe, I can't speak, I can't think, I can't comprehend what this will mean for B and my family over the next few weeks, months, and years.

I open my eyes. Everything looks normal, but it's not, and I know in the depths of my soul that nothing will ever be the same. I'm not the same person who answered the phone five short minutes ago. Life is forever divided into before and after.

Mind too muddled to even Google schizophrenia, I'm sucked into the center of a mental health catastrophe. No time to eat or sleep. I need to find an attorney, become my child's legal guardian, and learn as much as I can about this brain-snatching illness.

Everything seems impossible. Shock and disbelief hold me under. I'd hoped against hope that his bizarre behaviors were induced by illicit drug use. My life as I know has ended. A line has been drawn in the sand. Like a kaleidoscope, my perspective tilts, and the world becomes unrecognizable, broken pieces of glass.

It remained this way for a long, long time. Each spare minute over the next few years was filled with decisions of what to do next, how to help this lost child, find resources, and get appointments with psych doctors in less than six months.

The Roller Coaster of Grief

What is grief? Why doesn't it look and feel the same for everyone? Is it possible to grieve someone who's still alive? You expect to grieve a loved one lost to old age or accident, but how do you grieve a loved one lost to mental illness (MI)? A child who's still very much alive but is creating chaos and upheaval in the family? How do you make time to grieve what's gone while you're in the trenches of everyday crises?

When your child is diagnosed with a severe mental illness, you face fears you never knew existed and discover strengths you never knew you had. Only in hindsight will you realize your true resilience.

Many won't understand how it feels to lose your child and have him replaced by an angry, out-of-control, irrational, delusional imposter. "What's there to grieve?" they ask. "Your child didn't die. He's still with you. What's all the heartache about?"

Until you have a MIAC, you can't understand the pain of watching your child lose his very identity, his dreams, his future, his dignity, his personality, and his mind. Your child was healthy one minute, and the next, he's replaced with a distorted fun-house version of his former self. Gone are any chances of a normal life. He's now an adult with minimal ability to make rational decisions, who can't handle finances, can't maintain personal hygiene, can't find or keep a job, and has limited capacity to self-regulate his emotions and actions.

When your child is diagnosed with a severe mental illness, you face fears you never knew existed and discover strengths you never knew you had.

Not only has your child's life undergone profound changes, but your life is now unrecognizable. You expected your child to grow, mature, and one day become self-sufficient as he moved into adulthood. This isn't what you signed up for when you decided to become a parent. This isn't a disabled child. Yes, mental illness causes disability, but it manifests as poor behaviors and brings with it a multitude of additional problems.

Elisabeth Kubler-Ross and David Kessler in *On Grief & Grieving: Finding the Meaning of Grief Through the Five Stages of Loss* present the way most people deal with loss. There's a predictable progression when you lose a loved one: you deny, you become angry, you attempt to bargain, you settle into depression, and you end with acceptance. Everyone moves through these stages at their own pace. There's no set time frame; each experience is unique. What's similar in cases of significant loss and mental illness is that someone very much loved is gone forever.

However, with severe mental illness, your beloved child is still very much alive, while at the same time, everything about him is different. The stages of grief replay over and over. After you move into acceptance, your MIAC can and will relapse, and the grief starts all over again. The difficulty you face trying to mourn the loss of your child and deal with the day-to-day challenges of caring for him, your family, and yourself is unimaginable.

How do you come to terms with this calamitous change when every interaction with your MIAC is a reminder of what's gone? It becomes impossible to remember him as capable and whole before the storm of mental illness destroyed his once-healthy mind. Every encounter is a reminder of what can never be. Whenever the open wound in your heart begins to heal, something else happens to rip off the scab. Each day is a rerun of pain and heartache, loss and ruin.

Most ailments and diseases show up as physical limitations or mental delays. No other disease manifests as a willful disregard of appropriate behavior. MI symptoms can include the use of illegal drugs, acts of self-harm, violence, destruction of property, criminal activities, promiscuous sex, irrational communication, homelessness, financial irresponsibility, lack of personal hygiene, the inability to keep a job, volatile relationships, and/or threats or attempts of suicide. No other disease impacts so many facets of life.

> *No other disease manifests as a willful disregard of appropriate behavior.*

The National Alliance on Mental Health (NAMI) has compiled a list of the stages of emotional responses to ongoing mental health crises:

1. First, you DEAL with the catastrophic event, which leads to shock, denial, and hope against hope.

2. Next, you LEARN to cope or "go through the mill," which ushers in anger, guilt, resentment, recognition, grief, denial, anger, bargaining, and depression.
3. Last, you MOVE into understanding, which fosters acceptance, advocacy, and action.

Your response to your child's mental health diagnosis is so much more complex than the simple grief of a loss. With MI, it's possible to move from acceptance to shock and denial to anger—in one day. There's no finish line as the emotions shift back and forth until you take the time to work through this diagnosis and loss. Some days or weeks will be a roller coaster of emotions.

Even when you've worked through things and come to a place of balance, there will be times you feel like you're back at day one again. So, you pick yourself up and begin the work again. Even though it feels like you start over each time, you're actually making great progress as you work to process this loss.

One day, like me, you'll be in a place you never thought possible. When someone asks, "How can you be so calm and joyful?" I tell them, "It's taken years of personal development and many, many tears."

Painful beyond imagination, those early days required a strength I didn't know I had. Sometimes I wanted to give up, curl into a fetal position, and never leave the bed. Everything felt so difficult. Over time, it became easier to breathe, and the world seemed a little brighter. Hope allowed me to move forward, and you can too. The end result makes all the work worth the struggle.

I searched online and found a NAMI Family-to-Family (F2F) class nearby. It was my lifeline in those early weeks as my world was torn apart by a tornado of grief. The class offered so much information that I compared it to expecting rain and, instead, being caught in a flood. So much to learn and try to comprehend. I'm forever grateful for the information, support, and camaraderie that I gained from that class. While it touched on just the tip of the iceberg, it was a place to start, a place to begin to learn, accept, and heal.

I was disappointed to learn that, for many people, medications don't eradicate the symptoms of serious mental illness. It seemed reasonable to assume that once my son, who I refer to as B, started medication, life could return to normal, and we'd both pick up where we left off. But not all prayers get answered. If I'd known what a long journey this would be for us, I might have chosen to give up. Mental illness doesn't follow a regular path of crisis, diagnosis, treatment, and recovery. Nobody makes it back to normal.

> *Mental illness doesn't follow a regular path of crisis, diagnosis, treatment, and recovery. Nobody makes it back to normal.*

What is Recovery?

Let's take a hard look at what actual recovery looks like in cases of serious mental illnesses. After my child's initial diagnosis, I didn't understand what severe MI does to the brain. I naively thought that once my son was medicated, he'd become a normal adult again. Medication doesn't fix the damage; it simply puts a Band-Aid over the bleeding. But the wound never heals. The psychosis may stop, but the brain never recovers. With severe mental illness, medication takes away some of the psychosis, delusions, thought disturbances, and hallucinations, but it doesn't return motivation, clarity, critical thinking skills, or rationality.

Lives do not pick up where they left off.

Mental illness is the equivalent of a train wreck. Imagine your child was hit by a locomotive. Because of the physical damage, he'd spend the rest of his life in a wheelchair, unable to do the most basic things for himself. Special accommodations would be required. You wouldn't expect much of him when it came to a job, self-care, or doing anything productive. You'd understand that every activity would exhaust him, and to just sit in a chair and look out the window might be all he's able to handle.

Your MIAC has a similar injury. His body looks like it's intact because the real devastation is concealed within his mind. If you visualize your child's brain as being in a wheelchair, it becomes much easier to see his behaviors as symptoms of the wreckage mental illness causes. Your child may recover from the initial crisis, but he'll never return to his former level of functioning.

Medical professionals say that it takes two to three years for your child's symptoms to stabilize after a break from reality—and ten years before a new baseline of behavior is achieved. Recovery really means creating a new normal after the initial diagnosis. The brain is a very complex and delicate organ. With each psychotic episode, levels of ability are reduced. It can take years to see moderate improvement, with no resumption of prior normal activity.

> *Recovery really means creating a new normal after the initial diagnosis.*

The NAMI F2F class started my journey toward healing. While I learned everything possible about the brain and MI, it also became a path of self-discovery, inner exploration, and the opportunity to rebuild my life. At times, a darkness consumed me as I grappled and struggled to create a new identity. I felt overwhelmed as I let go of what no longer served me, created new beliefs, and accepted current realities. Each shift in awareness left me walking on a tightrope of uncertainty. My new normal was to feel unsteady and vulnerable. Some days it felt like all my skin had been stripped off, and I'd been left raw and exposed. Every time it seemed there was no more to surrender, I'd circled around to another layer that needed to shift and change.

Identifying Emotions

I figured out that I needed to create a list of the possible reasons for the emotions that rose up in me. Understanding what and why I felt a certain way offered tremendous relief. It gave me a sense of control over my feelings and why they occurred. Asking myself questions helped me to explore, clarify, and move toward a more positive outlook of the situation.

As I worked through and released unwarranted emotions, I was able to focus on what needed to be addressed. Holding on tightly only created emotional, mental, and physical overload. Piled-up feelings seemed insurmountable. But if I dealt with the emotions as they came up, I found a neutral space to work through what had occurred.

It's less complicated to handle situations from ground zero rather than from atop a mountain of emotional baggage.

It's less complicated to handle situations from ground zero rather than from atop a mountain of emotional baggage.

Emotional Responses	Reasons Why	What's Behind It
Anger	Things not going your way	Fear you can't fix it
Frustration	Your MIAC won't listen	Fear your MIAC can't do…
Sadness	Recognize what's lost	Still can't believe
Disgust	Unrealistic expectations	Unwillingness to accept
Embarrassment	Want to cut association	Uncomfortable with reality
Contempt	Want to distance yourself	Want to blame and shame
Fear	Feel lack of control	Grief for child and self
Resentful	Put upon by your MIAC	Attempt to drag your child
Righteous	Your way or the highway	Dead set on control
Demanding	You want it your way	You play guilt card
Irritable	Stressed and tired	Lack of self-care
Anxious	Unsure of the outcome	You worry about…
Overwhelmed	Codependency	You need boundaries
Guilty	Want to fix your child	You compensate with stuff
Burdened	Doing too much	You need to stop

Grief will manifest as countless other emotions, and each one masks your inability to come to terms with your child's MI diagnosis. Until you accept your MIAC's reality, it's impossible to grieve what you and your child have lost. Instead, you continue to bury the truth under a pile of emotions, each a distraction from what you must deal with—a mental illness that won't go away. Every emotion is caused by a symptom of the disease and your child's inability to change his behaviors and thought processes. To deny your grief, you push away your MIAC's prognosis and continue to perpetuate your delusion that all is well, that your child is capable of change, and that you can control the outcome.

It's normal to feel all these emotions, but it's important to figure out why you try to hide from them. The bigger the pile, the longer it takes to get to the core issues. Ask yourself why you feel the way you do, if what you feel is valid for the circumstances, and if your MIAC can change his behaviors.

Just when I think most of the grief is past, I'm reminded of what's gone. The simplest activity can cause heartache. For instance, when my MIAC needed a haircut, it took six months to coax my son into agreement. He looked like Medusa with a head of wild, dirty curls. I whispered a prayer that the young girl who cut his hair wouldn't find any bugs.

He sits calm and quiet and explains the cut he wants to the stylist and even asks about her day. He almost sounds like any other thirty-year-old as he makes small talk, but he doesn't look like one. With his stained clothes and disheveled appearance, he looks homeless. As I watch through tears, I remember him at the barbershop as a small boy. The promise of a positive future still hung in the air. His eyes shone with energy and excitement. Today his eyes are dull from the meds, and there's no expectation of any future.

"Thanks," B says, always polite. As I pay the girl, he adds, "Mom, she worked hard with my hair. Give her a big tip." He looks nothing like the unkempt young man who walked in the door a few minutes ago. I look up at my handsome MIAC and imagine him healthy. He should be able to pay for his own haircut and then head off to be with a girlfriend. Instead, he gets in my car, and I drive him back to the residential care facility where he now lives. A haircut seems like such a simple activity that everyone should be capable of doing, until it's not. Today my heart hurts.

What's Lost

Until you've experienced what it's like to live with a MIAC, you can't comprehend the degree of ruin the disease can cause. The entire family can be slaughtered by the destruction. It's as if a hurricane picked up your life, spun it around, then hurled it back to the ground, broken and scattered.

What's been lost with a MI diagnosis? Your child is still very much alive, but so much of what makes him who he is has vanished. Mental illness sucks out the positive qualities and deposits negative behaviors. What's left is a unique hybrid of who your child used to be: A shattered brain hidden within a healthy body; an adult who looks normal but, in fact, needs the care and structured environment of a much younger child.

Severe MI carries many layers of grief that continue to unfold as the disease progresses—and to the degree to which your child is affected. Each loss is another stone added to the pile that lies heavily in your heart. You need to assess what's changed, what he's capable of doing now, and what will never be.

It's difficult to understand what appears to be a healthy young adult who behaves in the most inappropriate ways. To many, especially parents, his behavior seems like a matter of laziness. Here's someone who used to work, drive, pay bills, hang out with friends, and initiate and carry on rational conversations. Where did all that go? How does the simplest personal care routine just vanish? What became of the capable child you raised? It's as if a hole's been burned into the "adulting" part of your MIAC's brain. The skills haven't been lost, but his ability to follow through has vanished. His life now is focused on how to reduce or eliminate his symptoms, with no regard for future consequences.

Put yourself in his place and consider how you'd function if you had to deal with the same symptoms. Would your decisions be any better? Would you want to give up on everything? Are the choices your MIAC makes unreasonable when you consider his altered brain function?

Here's a truth I hold in my heart: Everyone is doing the very best they can every single day based on their level of ability. Nobody wakes up and decides to be the shittiest version of themselves. Whatever they are or aren't able to do, it's their best. If you also believe that, you'll be able to look at your MIAC as doing his best. With so many random, bizarre thoughts that enter his head, on some days, all he can do is sit in a chair or take a nap. It makes sense that he'd be on edge and unable to control his moods. Look for what's left instead of what's gone. Don't dwell on the loss but choose to focus on the parts of your child that are still intact. Accept his limitations with compassion.

> *Nobody wakes up and decides to be the shittiest version of themselves.*

After you grasp and grieve what your MIAC has lost, take stock of what remains. No, it's not a better version of your child, but it's the one that's here to stay. Try to enjoy the person your MIAC is now. If you can't see him for who he is, how detrimental is it to his overall mental health? What happens if you always push and pull him to be more of this or less of that? You'll send a message that he's not good enough, isn't lovable enough just as he is. This is what unconditional love looks like: letting go of the expectations that he can't live up to.

Love your MIAC enough to see past what he lost and embrace and encourage the strengths and characteristics that remain. My son has a wicked sense of humor, loves puns, and is able to pull them out to diffuse even the most tragic situations. Honesty, politeness, and integrity are also qualities B displays, even when his illness is relentless. Compassion for others, superior intelligence, and a good moral compass round out his personality. Do I see these all the time? No, but I look for them and am reminded that my child is still in there, trapped behind an atrocious disease. If he can show up every day and do his best, then I have no excuse not to do the same.

A friend asks, "How often do you visit B in the hospital?"

"Once a week and sometimes less when he's psychotic."

I'm sure she doesn't understand my answer, but this is not a normal illness or a normal hospital. At a psych hospital, the main entrance is locked, and you have to be buzzed in by a security guard. You sign in, get a name badge, and stuff all your personal items into a tiny locker. Then you're checked for weapons.

Sometimes B sits, and sometimes he paces. Sometimes he recognizes me, and sometimes he insists, "You're not my mom."

Sometimes he's mute, sometimes he talks in foreign tongues, and sometimes he tells me, "Mom, I brought my roommate back from the dead."

Sometimes he refuses to come out of his room at all. Sometimes this is all too much for my fragile heart, and I stay home. There are no real conversations, no rational talks, no normal catching up. It's a crapshoot, and I wonder what the experience will be each time. Even when he's not hospitalized, visits with my son don't approach normal.

When rational thought isn't possible, time spent together is a challenge. Words need to be measured, plans need to be short and stress-free, and we have to be flexible. Car rides induce anxiety; busy restaurants cause panic; noisy, bright stores produce paranoia; and a question asked and misheard can lead to a slew of curse words. A peaceful visit can turn on a dime into demands for money or cigarettes. Sane one minute, it's not uncommon for B to insist that people in the next room are plotting to harm him a moment later. A shared story about cousins can be interrupted by the insistence that he has a tracking device implanted in his head.

So, when asked, I respond, "I visit my son once a week."

To see a young couple share dinner or play with a small child at the park is heartbreaking. To talk with a friend who shares a story about her grown children is heartbreaking. When I explain to my son that seeing twelve-foot spiders is a symptom of his disease, it's heartbreaking. Handling my son's finances, being present at doctor appointments, and cleaning up his messes is heartbreaking. As I watch others give my son strange looks, as I see parents hold their children closer when we pass, as I hear discriminatory comments from family and friends—all of it is heartbreaking. Family and friends believe medicines should fix the problem, so it's understandable why you and I still feel so much sadness.

Demands for money, the inability to maintain a clean home, violent mood swings, aversions to certain foods, aggressive conversations, never changing clothes, refusals to bathe, the list goes on and on. Everyday tasks become a battleground of misunderstandings and twisted words.

Those with MI can't always hear the actual words we say, and sometimes B responds with accusations of lies, says his thoughts are being messed with, his stuff is being moved, or people are breaking into his apartment. Irrational ideas are the norm rather than the exception.

These are the sorrows of my son's mental illness. It exhausts me, and I'm heartbroken to have a full-grown adult who has the mental capacity of a teenager. When the disease moved in and took over, he could no longer make decisions on his own behalf.

Isn't that enough to lose? But no, so much more has disappeared. The ability to make friends, to attend social activities—even family events—to find and hold a job, to show emotions, to handle his finances, to recognize that he's sick, to know when something will be harmful, to have a simple rational conversation about his disease. That part of him is gone.

When all your responses come from grief, you're unable to connect with your MIAC with positivity and love. The grief stands in the way of accepting your child as he is now, post diagnosis. We all need to go through the time of grieving what's lost. But to remain attached to the sorrow and to choose to suffer serves no one.

Your child is very perceptive of your emotions, and he recognizes when you struggle. By refusing to let go of your regret, you make your MIAC feel a sense of guilt and responsibility for your emotions. This isn't to say that you won't experience brief moments of sadness that pop in out of the blue, but you need to move past the bereavement phase.

> *By refusing to let go of your regret, you make your MIAC feel a sense of guilt and responsibility for your emotions.*

It's impossible to move on in your own life if you're still attached to your MIAC by a cord of disappointment and loss, and it hinders your child's ability to create a new normal for himself. There comes a time when it's no longer necessary to grab and hold tight to the feelings that come up; you'll be able to let them wash through you. With no need to get emotional yourself, you can respond to your MIAC's emotions instead of his demands. You can sympathize with how he feels and his struggles and also know when no amount of discussion will be productive.

When you've decided to let go of what life should have looked like, you'll begin to enjoy small moments of joy. When you let go of the grief over what's gone, it permits you to appreciate what's still here. Even if your child refuses all help and lives what you consider a frightful lifestyle, it's important to release your need to try to fix it. It's critical to honor your MIAC's choices if you want to have peaceful interactions. You don't have to agree with or condone the behavior to love your child.

Even if your child refuses all help and lives what you consider a frightful lifestyle, it's important to release your need to try to fix it.

The problem occurs when you try to change reality. You can't go back, and to go forward can seem impossible and scary. But if you stay stuck, it'll consume you. Just because your child will never have the life you or he expected doesn't mean your life has to be miserable. Who does it serve to deny yourself pleasure? To live a tragic, abject life won't change anything. In effect, you'll be holding him hostage with your misery. How can your MIAC begin to heal himself when he knows he's the cause of your despair?

Love your child enough to accept him where he is without making him responsible for your happiness or unhappiness. Love your MIAC enough to grant him as much sovereignty as possible while you allow for his unique limitations. Love your child enough to work on your own personal growth instead of trying to fix him. Love your MIAC enough to let him figure things out for himself.

The Time Conundrum

As a mom, you might think that the worst possible scenario is for your child to die before you do. In reality, some situations can leave you more than heartbroken. In traditional grief, you get to take as much time and space as you need to transition through the stages of acceptance. But when you deal with the daily turmoil of your MIAC's behaviors, it seems impossible to work through your grief. You struggle just to keep your head above water and handle the daily emotional upheavals. It's like you're in a rowboat, trying to stay afloat, bracing yourself against the next irrational wave or surge of aggression. It's impossible to carve out quiet personal time to deal with the loss. You can't find the time or energy to take a breath and feel into the emotions of your MIAC's diagnosis. Grief is a luxury that's out of reach.

And yet, you need quiet time to work through these changes. You need time to grieve for the adult your child will never be. You need time to process your sadness and pain, time to come to terms with your new reality, time to understand the truth of this diagnosis, time to let go of what might have been. But there's always another crisis to manage, another decision to make, another doctor appointment, another phone call, another argument, another emergency trip to the pharmacy, another irrational discussion, another visit to the ER, another psychotic break with a call to the police for assistance, another hole in the wall to repair, another demand for money, another day that you need to care for your MIAC.

It goes on and on, the endless list of things that need immediate attention. Nothing can wait; each problem requires a decision *right now.* How will you ever have time to grieve the loss of your intelligent, imaginative, funny child when all your time is consumed by the turmoil created by his disease? How do you mourn the loss when you feel angry, annoyed, and overwhelmed by the pandemonium his illness creates? How do you find the time when every minute is spent putting out fires and running interference?

In death, a child is remembered with love and affection. With MI, it's the death of potential, masked in the rages and screams of the out-of-control nightmare that your child has become. How do you grieve the child who resorts to verbal or physical attacks? Is it possible to separate the lost child from the one you have now? You want to mourn what your child could have been, the loss of a normal life, the loss of an easy life, the loss of rational conversations, the loss of friends and family, the loss of community support, the loss of what was. You also need to mourn what your child has become: this perverse, irrational, delusional, paranoid, anxiety-ridden imposter who masquerades as your child with flippant disregard. The dichotomy of the situation makes it seem impossible.

But you can do it.

The Practice

Set aside time each day, even fifteen minutes, to sit with your feelings. This allows you to sort, experience, and release the pain. Step one is to accept that your MIAC will never get better. Step two is to face all the aspects of life that are forever changed for both of you. Take baby steps. Looking at everything that's been lost is too much to bear at one time. Tiny bits of grief released a little here and a little there is easier.

You can't speed through grief. It requires time and a readiness to feel your emotions in order to release the pain. Be gentle with yourself and allow things to unfold in a natural rhythm. This is a personal journey, a quest to find your innate inner fortitude. It requires courage, awareness, and resolution to reconnect with who you used to be. You need to *want* a better life for yourself, to have a deep desire to do whatever it takes to live your best life in spite of your child's illness. Brief moments of mourning over weeks and months will provide immeasurable peace.

The more you learn about mental illness, the more pain you'll feel for your child. The prognosis for severe MI is more than dismal; it discourages even the strongest mother. There's not much material available to families of MIACs, and nobody addresses the grief that accompanies such a grim diagnosis.

> *You need to want a better life for yourself, to have a deep desire to do whatever it takes to live your best life in spite of your child's illness.*

I was able to acknowledge my grief and begin to mend my own broken heart by becoming a facilitator for the NAMI F2F classes. As I listened to others' stories and offered them comfort, that, in turn, comforted me. The grief still comes in waves and never leaves altogether, but over the years, I've been able to move past sorrow and into happiness. Carrying grief spoils and sours your life. This isn't what your child wants.

When things at home are quiet, begin your inner journey of self-reflection. Work on yourself; it's all you can control. That's where you begin. It's scary to face your emotions head-on.

You'll want to hide behind your facade, your brick wall of "I'm fine. Everything's okay." If your veneer cracks, you fear you'll be uncovered and vulnerable, and you don't know if you can handle being raw and exposed. How can you protect your MIAC if you're unmasked in all your unhealed mess?

But what if you acknowledge your feelings as they come up, and that dissipates the strength and energy behind them?

The key is to recognize what stage of grief you're in, know that it's temporary, and move through this phase. You'll move back and forth between the stages each time something happens with your child—understand that. But you'll find that you're not pulled into the grief and crisis stages as often, and you'll spend most of your time rooted in acceptance and advocacy as you deepen into self-growth.

Each time your MIAC experiences another acute episode, it will throw you back into earlier moments of grief and despair. Take time to be with your pain; otherwise, it will build and paralyze you. Stuffing your feelings will undermine your well-being. If you're a shattered jumble of emotions, you can't support your child.

Releasing this grief is a continual process, just as the circumstances that cause the grief are ongoing. But you have a choice regarding how you feel each day. You can choose joy or misery. If you choose misery, it doesn't change anything about your child's illness. It just affects your life. Choose wisely. Choose joy.

My nephew's wedding and reception is a magical time. A wonderful memory-making family experience, but I'm heartbroken. As everyone else rejoices and celebrates the newlyweds, I sit in the shadows—alone—and cry.

It's been two months since B's initial diagnosis. Still raw and confused, my world doesn't make sense, doesn't seem real. I have the horrible realization that B will never marry, and I know I'll be denied a similar beautiful event because of his MI. I don't share my sadness with anyone because I won't be understood, and I don't want to dampen the festivities. Although we can't predict if our children will marry, it hurts to know that B very much wants this experience, but he'll never have it.

Everyone knows B's not well, was hospitalized just a couple months ago, diagnosed with a chronic illness, but only one person asks how he is or if I'm okay. Is it because nobody cares, because they don't know what to say, or because they believe that MI is a problem of self-control or an indication of laziness? I don't have an answer, but I do know that if B's diagnosis was cancer, many would have asked about him.

I carry the burden of lost friends, critical family members, and a society that chooses to ignore us both. Maybe this tragedy feels too close to home, makes others feel too vulnerable, or maybe they just don't know what to say. Those who haven't walked this path have no clue what's lost with a severe MI diagnosis, and it hinders their ability to understand or be supportive.

Hidden Grief

Being the mother of a MIAC is a grief you hide because it's so misunderstood. You need a sympathetic environment where your sorrow is acknowledged and accepted. Support groups offer a shared camaraderie, but in my opinion, they don't allow you to heal and recover. You need a place to air your pain and a community of wise women to show you how to move through the heartache and continue with your life. A place where each holds space for you to accept, grow, and expand past your MIAC's diagnosis.

> *You need a place to air your pain and a community of wise women to show you how to move through the heartache and continue with your life.*

Don't hide your struggle. Began to initiate conversations about MI. When someone asks about your child, explain that he has a mental illness. If people are curious, answer their questions and help expand their knowledge of the disease. Even if family and friends don't ask, let them know what your MIAC is up to and how you are. When you open up, you'll find many others are challenged with similar struggles. Speak up. It allows others the opportunity to share their own heartache. Being witness to another's grief helps both of you heal.

Don't Make Yourself Sick

I wanted my son to be as independent as possible, so a few years after his diagnosis, I moved him into the condo next door to mine. It seemed a good solution because he'd have supervision and also a degree of autonomy. Over the next few months, it became apparent that he needed extensive support to manage the most basic daily skills. B made friends with others in the area who had similar issues. I was thankful that he had friends, but those friends brought more opportunities to make poor choices. I often felt like the director of my own mini-psych ward.

Less than a month after B moved in, I began to have extreme pain in my right hand, and it became impossible for me to work. This might not have been an issue except that I'm self-employed. For the next three months, I visited doctors, suffered through weeks of physical therapy, endured painful cortisone injections, and wore a plaster cast. None of it helped. In the end, I resorted to stem cell therapy because it was less invasive than hand surgery. Nine months later, I started to feel some relief.

When I looked back on this time, I realized that the stress and anxiety of being a full-time caregiver had caused my hand problem. It took a toll on my physical, mental, and emotional well-being. The pain was a warning sign that said I wasn't equipped to handle the day-to-day care my son required. If I'd listened to what my body had tried to tell me, I could have avoided so much discomfort. Even after I recognized that my emotions were the cause of my physical issues, it still took me another year to make the conscious choice to find a better solution for my son. I had a hard time considering my own health as important as B's. Deciding that he needed more support than I could provide was, to me, admitting defeat.

Unacknowledged grief can and does impact your overall health. When you hold on to heartache, the effect will always be negative—on every level. That doesn't mean you shouldn't feel your emotions. As a mom to a MIAC, you cling to your grief as if it's the very child you've lost. You hold on for dear life in an attempt to regain what's gone. And you suffer so much when you remain stuck.

Emotions that are trapped in your body can manifest as physical, mental, and emotional illnesses. Sometimes you hold on until you become so sick you're forced to let go to focus on yourself. Your illness serves nobody. It won't make your MIAC healthy again, it impairs your ability to be a strong advocate, and it degrades your quality of life. You don't need to become ill just because your child is. It makes everything you experience more of a challenge, disrupts family dynamics, and makes everyday life miserable.

You don't need to become ill just because your child is.

Unhealthy Distractions

When B was first diagnosed, I used unhealthy distractions as a way to avoid my feelings that seemed too big to face. I ate junk food, drank alcohol (which wasn't normal for me), zoned out in front of the TV, and isolated myself from social activities. I could have used my time more effectively, but I was incapable of pulling myself out of the muck. I couldn't think of healthier ways to navigate the daily struggles of caring for my son, so I floundered, lost in a sea of despair and defeat. That was okay for a while, but I didn't want to continue like that.

You may wallow in denial, self-pity, and anger for a long time. You may gain weight, sleep poorly, or develop a physical ailment before you begin to recognize the toll your child's illness is taking. Physical problems elicit empathy and understanding, whereas mental health concerns cause people to distance themselves. Did you know that becoming sick can be an unconscious attempt to find much-needed support? You may be so desperate for connection that you'll do anything to get it. Now that you recognize what's going on, you need to realize that you're the only one who's going to take care of you.

It's time to take back your health and your life. Time to pay attention to your choices. Your MIAC's illness shouldn't put you in an early grave.

Did you know that becoming sick can be an unconscious attempt to find much-needed support?

My solution was to make better food choices, stop ordering drinks, and start walking the neighborhood again. I learned to meditate, turned off mind-numbing TV, and began to reconnect with my love of books and knowledge. I made the decision to become the best version of myself. After all, who would be there for my MIAC if I became ill?

Whenever I experience a physical, mental, or emotional problem now, I ask myself if it could be related to how I'm dealing with B's illness. Am I out of alignment with what I should be doing for myself? What choices have I made that don't work for me?

I learned more about how body parts correlate to different emotions and create imbalances, which, in turn, cause illness. The familiar saying, "We drown in grief," is an indication that, in times of loss, illnesses can manifest in the lungs. Hands and fingers correlate to how we deal with the details of life. The left hand relates to emotions and what we receive from others. The right hand is tied to how we deal with practical aspects and day-to-day challenges. Once I started to release more grief and my need to handle all my child's care on my own, my hand healed. You can find out more about how emotions cause illness in Louise Hay's book *Heal Your Body*.

It's up to us to heal ourselves, so we can lift up those moms who are still treading water. When we share our stories, triumphs, and failures, we help others walk the same path. As we hold hands and hearts in support, we heal ourselves further.

Remember, drama drains you. Guard your energy and stay above the fray. You can't control the drama that happens around you, but you can decide whether to give it space in your mind and soul.

It's time to learn as much as possible about mental illness and how it impacts your MIAC's life.

Visualization Journey

Sit in a comfortable, quiet place. Close your eyes. Breathe in and out slowly to the count of three several times until you feel yourself begin to relax.

Picture yourself in a meadow, feel the sunshine warm on your shoulders, smell the scent of wildflowers as they blow in the breeze. All is peaceful and calm. Walk through the tall grass. Feel it brush softly against your legs.

You cross the meadow and enter into a forest. The trees block the sun; it's cool, quiet, and dark. Your eyes adjust, and you follow a path deep into the woods. You hear birds call to one another, leaves rustle, and the smell of damp earth is in the air.

The path winds deeper and deeper into the trees. You come to a small cave with a door. It has three locks. You remove three keys from your pocket. The bottom lock represents your willingness to have an open mind. You use the brass key to open the bottom lock. The middle lock represents your desire to let go of your suffering. You use the silver key to open the middle lock. The top lock represents your ability to receive healing. You use the gold key to open the top lock.

The door opens, and you walk into a small passageway. Candles flicker on the walls, and the floor is covered in sand. Take off your shoes and leave them outside the door.

Walking slowly, you feel the sand between your toes as you enter a small chamber. The room is warm and inviting, filled with soft pillows, dim pink lights, and soft music. You close the door and get comfortable as you sit or lean against the pillows. The smell of rose is in the air.

You have entered into a sacred space. It represents your heart space, where all your broken dreams, heartaches, and grief are stored. Look around. Is anyone else in the chamber with you? Have your guides, ancestors, or angels come to help? Your heart space asks you to do some house cleaning. New hopes, dreams, and love can't enter if your heart's filled with pain and suffering.

Take three deep breaths. Ask your heart to show you what it's ready to let go of today. You may see or hear one answer or several. Next, ask your heart what it needs to help you release your pain. There are no wrong answers. Is there anything you aren't ready to release? Ask again what is needed to help you let go of your sorrow. Trust whatever answers come. Your heart is wise and knows what's best for you. When you feel complete, come back into yourself. Stop and journal your answers.

Thank your heart space for the assistance in releasing your pain. Thank any guides or angels that came to help you with the process. Bid farewell until you meet again. Rise and make your way to the door, open it, and feel the cool breeze of the passageway. The chill is a healing balm against your warm body. Walk back to the outer door of the cave.

Retrieve your shoes and re-lock the entrance. This is your sacred cave. You are the only one who may enter. You can visit any time you feel the need. Walk down the path toward the sunlight and into the meadow. When you get to the far side, take one last deep cleansing breath and thank Mother Earth for her beauty and comforting presence.

Open your eyes and journal any additional messages you received. You may want to purchase a special heart-shaped key to keep with you as a reminder of this healing exercise.

Coming to Grips with MI

We are sisters
Blindsided by mental illness
Confused by symptoms
Overwhelmed by the chaos
We look for our child beneath the disease
We are sisters

Hopefully, this chapter will help you understand that most of your MIAC's behaviors aren't willful misconduct but ways to cope with a debilitating brain disease. Most antisocial behaviors are symptoms of serious brain illness, not moral wrongdoing. Gaining more knowledge may help you understand the ways your child deals with life.

If you don't know how to handle the unique symptoms and realities of MI, you aren't alone. Mental illness is unlike any other disease. There's no blood test to flag a problem; diagnosis is based solely on behavioral interpretations. Some classify MI as a disease and others as a disorder, but what really matters is the impact mental illness has on every area of your child's life and the lives of those who love him. The fact that it manifests as aberrant, bizarre, and sometimes dangerous behaviors is what makes it so difficult to diagnose and understand. Add to that the contrast between how physical vs. mental illness is viewed and treated, and you'll begin to see why you struggle as much as your child.

> *... what really matters is the impact mental illness has on every area of your child's life and the lives of those who love him.*

MI Hurdles

The World Health Organization (WHO) states that one in four people are affected by mental or neurological disorders. These numbers indicate that mental illness is more prevalent than all physical diseases, including cancer, heart disease, and diabetes, but it isn't treated with the same attitude and compassion. The medical community is far behind on research, treatments, doctor availability, and facilities to effectively treat mental health and addiction disorders. Below is a long list of ways mental illness differs from physical illness and why your MIAC refuses or is unable to find the treatment needed.

- **Blame vs. Treatment**—A physical illness is viewed as a defective organ or body system, but with mental illness, your child is seen as defective because of his inability to control his behaviors, words, or actions.
- **Attitudes about seeking help**—Your MIAC isn't concerned about the way he'll be perceived when he seeks professional help for a physical ailment, but with a mental illness, he feels a need for privacy and is concerned about what others might think, how it will affect his job, his relationships, and his life.
- **Insurance coverage**—While there's supposed parity laws in place to assure that physical and mental conditions are covered equally, in many cities and states, insurance companies find loopholes to deny or shorten mental health hospital stays and outpatient treatment programs, making it difficult for your child to receive the help he needs.
- **Missing work or school**—With a physical disease, doctors give a release order to remain at home until healed, but with

MI, there are no orders prescribing rest. Most companies and schools don't accept mental health time off the same way they do for physical ailments.
- **Public perception**—Unfortunately, many consider physical illness as being beyond a person's control, but they see mental illness as something your child should be able to control if he could just get himself together.
- **No scientific tests**—Would it be viewed differently if there were tests to diagnose a mental illness? Would concrete evidence of a biological abnormality make MI more legitimate? Most don't believe what they can't see, and that includes your MIAC.
- **Societal views**—If diagnosed with a physical illness, there are plenty of offers of help, support, and empathy, but with MI, people tend to avoid the MIAC, think he doesn't try hard enough, or judge his irrationality.
- **Discrimination/Stigma**—MIACs are discriminated against in the workplace, when looking for housing, trying to secure disability benefits, or seeking treatment. Being treated for MI leaves a stain of disgrace upon your child. He feels humiliated and dishonored.
- **Lack of research and funding**—Research and funding for brain illnesses fall far behind the effort for cancer, diabetes, heart disease, and many other physical illnesses. Mainstream brain illnesses, such as autism and Down syndrome, receive more funding because these aren't perceived as frightening or as uncontrollable as bipolar disorder or schizophrenia.
- **Family members' opinions**—Families usually don't learn anything about mental illness until someone they know becomes ill, so many parents view MI as a behavior or attitude problem, and they judge and criticize their sick child. Lack of societal education and discussion about MI leads to poor understanding when dealing with your MIAC. Certain ethnic groups have an even harder time accepting a mental illness diagnosis.

- **Lack of available information**—It seems that everywhere you turn, you find information about prevention or treatment for a physical illness, but hospitals, primary care physicians, and psychiatric offices provide very little information about long-term solutions for the mentally ill or their families.
- **Understanding symptoms**—Because open conversation about MI is limited, most people are in the dark when symptoms first appear. Lack of understanding leads to the belief that what occurs is within your child's ability to control.
- **Medication side effects and noncompliance**—The side effects of medications for mental illness can be brutal and debilitating, which causes your child to be noncompliant. Some side effects can cause increased and/or additional permanent disability. Your MIAC may also refuse meds because he doesn't recognize that he's sick, so staying med-compliant once released from care can be a problem.
- **Dual diagnosis**—Addiction often goes hand in hand with MI. Why? Because your MIAC desperately wants to feel better, so when traditional medications don't offer relief, he turns to illegal drugs and alcohol to medicate himself. It's my belief that the majority of addicted individuals also have a mental illness.
- **Resource availability**—There aren't enough hospitals, doctors, outpatient services, or case managers available to treat the numbers of people who suffer from MI. Your child may be turned away or have to wait months to see a doctor because of the lack of available services in your community.
- **Ease of receiving treatment**—As soon as your child is no longer a threat to himself or someone else, he'll be released from the hospital. But he'll still be too irrational to seek follow-up care. He may be released too soon, so a bed can be made available for someone else. Or he may be denied admittance because his symptoms aren't serious enough to indicate that he's in danger.

- **Long-term care options**—Finding a care facility for someone who needs 24/7 support is like finding a needle in a haystack. There's no way for families to search for such facilities, there aren't enough government-funded beds available, and there's not much discussion by medical professionals about these care options. Long-term care is seen as a last resort, and many families have to beg to get their MIACs appropriate placement.
- **Workplace support**—While businesses will work with physical illness modifications, they rarely want to deal with mental health issues. It's difficult to find a job if you have MI, and if you're hired without disclosing a diagnosis, a relapse could lead to termination.
- **HIPAA laws create problems**—The Health Insurance Portability and Accountability Act (HIPAA) was designed to provide privacy and protection for patient medical records and other health information. Because this law was enacted to protect, it can inhibit the family's ability to get help for or be informed about the care being provided to their MIAC.
- **Limited federal funding**—National Institute of Health (NIH) states funding for mental health is less than half of what it is for cancer. More funds are appropriated for the less stigmatizing mental illnesses. For example, autism receives more funding than eating disorders, even though more individuals die from untreated, chronic eating disorders.
- **Bad press/media coverage**—Due to the media attention after a mass shooting and the misconception that all mentally ill individuals pose a violent threat to society, your child may be less inclined to seek treatment. The truth is that the mentally ill are much more likely to be victims of violence, not perpetrators.
- **Nobody wants to discuss MI**—Until we can all feel comfortable having conversations about mental illness, nothing will change. We need to address the elephant in the room.

Chronic, acute, untreated mental illness can cause disturbances in mental, physical, and emotional health. Strong and/or multiple medications can add even more debilitating symptoms. Most psych medications are designed to take away the negative symptoms of an illness, but they do little or nothing about the behaviors the illness invokes. Example: A medication might make a schizophrenic's voices quieter, but it does nothing to address his inability to recognize he has an illness. Further, brain medications aren't targeted to the area of damage. Instead, they affect the entire brain. While the meds might take away delusions and hallucinations, they don't reestablish critical thinking, motivation, or reduce paranoia.

Symptoms of MI

The following is an overview of potential symptoms experienced by those who suffer from a mental illness. Your MIAC may have one or two of these symptoms or most of them. MI is a spectrum illness, which means that those with less severe symptoms are more likely to seek treatment and be helped by medications and therapy. Those with a more serious MI diagnosis are less likely to seek out support.

- Impaired awareness of illness (anosognosia)
- Irrational cognition, the inability to respond to words
- Flat affect or inappropriate emotional responses
- Living in his head, can't discern what's real
- Delusions, hallucinations, paranoia, anxiety, depression
- Inability to formulate and hold on to organized thoughts
- Issues with language, jumping topics, disordered sentences
- No motivation, inability to move forward with life
- Aggressive, hostile, violent behaviors
- Over-acute or blunted perceptions
- Slow motor responses
- Withdrawal from family and/or friends
- Eccentric, bizarre behaviors
- Lack of insight into ways to find help

- Addiction to alcohol, drugs, sex, food, compulsive spending, gambling
- Self-harming behaviors, cutting, eating disorders
- Lack of personal hygiene
- Financially irresponsible
- Inability to get or keep a job
- Poor choice of acquaintances
- Criminal activity, stealing, selling drugs, violence

Because MI manifests as socially unacceptable behaviors, it affects every area of life. It's difficult for families to determine what's caused by the illness and what's manipulation, laziness, or lack of personal responsibility. I choose to believe that my MIAC is doing the very best he can every day based on how his brain functions, and if he tries to manipulate me, it's because his disease impairs his ability to make wise choices. Most times, his manipulation involves efforts to get money to buy alcohol, so he can reduce his symptoms. His entire motivation in life is to feel better, quiet the voices, calm the anxiety, and get rid of the hallucinations. Everything he does or doesn't do is geared toward symptom relief.

No other illness causes people to do almost anything to feel better. Most diseases or chronic illnesses have only a handful of symptoms, whereas severe mental illness has an entire encyclopedia. This is frustrating for the MIAC, families, and the medical community.

I'm so frustrated when my son's doctor and case manager discuss things he can do when he feels stressed, anxious, or hears voices, and he won't even try their suggestions. He spent twelve months in an intensive day program and can tell you exactly what he learned, but he's unable to implement any of those skills.

At my wit's end, I want to scream at him, "Just get up and do something, anything! All you do is lay around all day, every day. Come on; you have to be capable of more than smoking and listening to music. You've been out of the hospital for months."

I ask myself, Is he being lazy and manipulating me so he doesn't have to work or pay his own bills, or is his brain really that broken? During his last psych visit, the social worker said he was on track and doing what he should be at this point.

"How is that possible? Why didn't anybody tell me his progress would be snail slow? Wouldn't it help as his parent to know what to expect, instead of second-guessing my son all the time?"

If I push B to go out and run errands with me, he's unable to get out of bed for the next two days. This sure doesn't look like manipulation, and it doesn't look like he's playing me. It looks like an inability to function normally.

Lack of Motivation

As time went on, I began to understand what severe mental illness does to a person's ability to take initiative. I learned that apathy is a symptom of MI. There's so much going on in B's head that it's impossible for him to take learned information and put it into action. Some days, he doesn't even know which world is real: the one I live in or the one in his head.

He says, "Mom, I want so much more out of life. I want a job, a girlfriend, a family, a house. I want the voices to stop."

When he says this, all I want to do is cry ugly heartbroken tears for this wonderful young man who will never have the life he wants. The symptoms of MI have taken away almost every aspect of what makes life good. How is he able to keep going when he has so little to live for? I think one of the reasons he gets up each day is that I accept him in spite of his limitations. My love for him is unconditional, even if all he does is lie in bed all day.

> *I think one of the reasons he gets up each day is that*
> *I accept him in spite of his limitations.*

One of the most frustrating things when caring for a MIAC is his inability to do anything to make himself feel better. It doesn't matter how much you talk, explain, plead, or argue; he resists any attempts to change his circumstances or behaviors and refuses to make different choices. This lack of motivation can be misconstrued as simply not caring, but in reality, it's a symptom of a serious thought disorder. Many who struggle with mental illness may look fairly normal but live with brains that have extensive damage.

Lack of motivation, also called *avolition*, makes it nearly impossible for those with chronic MI to move forward after the initial crisis phase has ended. The fact that your MIAC doesn't recognize that he's sick decreases the likelihood that he'll change his behavior or accept advice from others. This is common in many severe mental illnesses, such as bipolar disorder, schizophrenia, persistent depressive disorder, PTSD, traumatic brain injury, and Alzheimer's disease, and it can also be a side effect of certain medications. This condition affects your child's ability to groom himself, show up to work, be involved in social activities, regulate his moods, use appropriate coping skills, or act responsibly.

Some antipsychotic medications have even been shown to increase the lack of motivation. Antidepressants can sometimes help, as well as cognitive behavior therapy, but many times, there's no answer to this troubling symptom. Just like weight gain and neuropathy can be ongoing symptoms of treated diabetes, avolition and lethargy are ever-present symptoms of severe mental illness. Psychosis and serious thought disturbances damage the delicate brain tissue and cause irreversible devastation. If you could see the deterioration in the brain, you might better understand and accept the limitations your MIAC exhibits. Chronic, severe mental disorders are like train wrecks of the mind; the damage is catastrophic and changes the person and their capacity to regain prior functioning.

Once I understood the physical and biological reasons for my MIAC's inability to move ahead with his life, I began to show more empathy and compassion for what he'd lost. Instead of continuing to harp on what I think he needs to accomplish, I allow him to choose what he feels like doing. Life isn't always about how much you get done in a day, but more about living each day to the best of your ability. I wouldn't expect someone with a broken leg to get a lot done, so why do I think my son should be able to do any better?

Your child is not his disease, his limitations, or his inabilities. He's who the disease has left behind. He's the spark of God hidden behind the illness, desperate for connection and love.

My MIAC's disease has stalled his mental capacity, prevented emotional maturity, and taken away his potential to continue with his prior life, but he has retained his sense of humor, gentle nature, creativity, and interest in chemistry and biology. What he does or doesn't do each day isn't who he is. Your child is not his disease, his limitations, or his inabilities. He's who the disease has left behind. He's the spark of God hidden behind the illness, desperate for connection and love. How I choose to see my son's lack of motivation has everything to do with my ability to recognize his disease and accept his abilities as they are now.

"Mom, I gave up smoking," B says.
"That's great news. I'm glad you made that choice."
Ten minutes later, "Mom, I need money for cigarettes."
"Didn't you just tell me you quit?"
"Yes, but I need something to take the edge off."
We replay a version of this conversation every week. I fought tooth and nail to keep my son from smoking. It's such a smelly, unhealthy habit. I haven't been successful in getting

him to quit. I feel discouraged, I feel like a terrible mom for funding his habit, but I feel lost in how to help him any other way. I feel angry that the medications available don't alleviate his suffering. I feel his pain and anguish.

Unhealthy Behaviors

We all have nicotine receptors in our brains, and nicotine helps people with MI. For those who hear voices, it creates a gating action in the brain, which mutes—or quiets—the symptoms. Nicotine reduces anxiety and relaxes the body. This is why up to 75 percent of MIACs smoke. Never in my life did I think I would willingly buy cigarettes for my child. Now I see it as a lesser evil compared to other types of self-medication. Cigarettes may not add to the quantity of his life, but they do add to the quality. I would rather my son have twenty-five decent years as opposed to thirty-five miserable ones.

Do you think smoking and a poor diet are ruining your MIAC's physical health, but you're unable to change these destructive behaviors? Research suggests that a mental and physical diagnosis is more than a coincidence. There's a physiological reason for poor habits, such as eating junk food, smoking, illicit drug use, lack of exercise, or poor sleep habits. Studies show that mental illness impacts physical health, creates inflammation, changes heart rate and circulation, causes metabolic changes, and increases stress hormones that can influence physical health. National Institute of Mental Health (NIMH) research suggests that people with mental and physical illness tend to have more severe symptoms in both.

Why doesn't your MIAC take better care of himself? Doesn't he understand that it would be beneficial? When mental health is poor, you may be at greater risk for poor physical health and disease. Mayoclinic.org states, "Alterations in thinking, mood, or behavior, or a combination, is associated with impaired functioning in all areas of health." When your brain doesn't work properly, it inhibits your ability to make good choices about other aspects of your life. Your MIAC uses junk food, alcohol, illegal drugs, cigarettes, and risky behaviors as a distraction, a way to avoid thinking about the limits his illness creates. The more serious the thought disorder, the less likely a MIAC is to take proper care of his overall health. Poor physical health habits are a good indication that someone may suffer from an undiagnosed mental illness.

For the last six months, my MIAC won't eat any animal products. He insists they mess with his brain. Last week he decided that's no longer true, so now he eats only fried hamburgers, cheese, and white bread. I have no clue what next week will bring. No matter how hard I try to make sure he eats a healthy diet, he never sticks with it.

A functional medicine doctor prescribed high dose vitamins, fish oil, and nutritional supplements and recommended that B eat six to nine servings of fruits and vegetables a day. That regime lasted for about two weeks before he became unable to follow through, even with reminders.

Sometimes he eats the same bad food for days on end, some days he just eats meat, other days chips and salsa, and some days he doesn't eat at all, and only drinks cup after cup of coffee. Other times, he gorges until he vomits. I have zero control over his bizarre eating habits.

B tells me he has a headache. "Have you eaten today?" I ask. Later, he complains of a stomachache. I try to educate him on why it's so important to eat regular, balanced meals, but he can't follow through. It's not that he can't hear what I say, and it's not that he doesn't understand. It's that his disease prevents him from making good choices in the moment. Then there are the days where he insists all food is poisoned and I'm trying to kill him.

My son doesn't do anything to care for himself on a regular basis. This used to bother me because a mental illness is enough to deal with. I don't want him to have to fight a physical illness, too. Eventually, I let go of this idea because I can't and won't monitor his every action. He needs to be able to make some choices for himself, even if they're poor choices. Many people smoke, eat poorly, drink, don't exercise, and still have relatively long healthy lives, so I let go of the thought that I could control his health and wellness habits. If he gets sick, I'll deal with it then. If it makes him happier to choose how he treats his body, I have to honor the choices he makes because he didn't get a choice when he became mentally ill.

Lack of Personal Hygiene

What about your MIAC's lack of personal hygiene? Mental illness thwarts even the most mundane ministrations such as showering, brushing your teeth, combing your hair, and changing your clothes. It's not a sign of laziness but an indication of brain disfunction. When the brain is so tied up in its disease, there isn't enough energy left to take care of personal cleanliness. Poor hygiene is a sign of self-neglect and often accompanies severe mental disorders. Unfortunately, as a society, we tend to shame or humiliate individuals who don't adhere to a certain standard of personal self-care.

Why should you continue to encourage your MIAC when it comes to hygiene? If he doesn't have good hygiene habits, problems can arise, such as tooth decay, pimples and rashes, bacterial viruses, athlete's foot, urinary infections, lice, hookworms, hepatitis A, and staph infections. That's a formidable list of potential ailments that can occur due to poor hygiene.

So how do you persuade your MIAC to perform certain hygiene tasks? Here's another question: Why are you so concerned? It's probably because bathing is an indicator of recovery and normality. "The impact of forcing or coercing someone to bathe is well known, and research suggests doing so can cause relapses in mental health," states the *Journal of Psychosocial Rehabilitation and Mental Health*.

Nobody seems to have any real suggestions about how to persuade a MIAC to take better care of his body. Asking for compliance doesn't work. Withholding something will occasionally work, but in the long run, when someone has a brain disorder, bathing is not at the top of the priority list. Actually, it's not on the list at all. Surviving each day is what your MIAC focuses on.

Do you love him any less when he's dirty, unshaven, has slimy teeth? Does it change his brain functioning when he's clean? What do you really want when you ask him to clean up? Aren't you just asking him to get better? He would if he could. *He would if he could.*

"B, do you think it's time for a shower and some clean clothes?"

"No, Mom. Nobody else showers or changes clothes, so I'm good."

It's a constant battle to get him to bathe once a week and to stop wearing the same soiled clothes day after day. His hair is greasy, stringy, and sticks up in all directions; his teeth have a scummy film on them; and I don't want to take a deep breath when I'm around him.

"Mom, look at this rash on my legs."

"I see it. Do you think maybe you should shower more? Washing off all the bacteria and dead skin might make you feel better."

When he smells particularly ripe, I withhold things until he agrees to shower. Even when he does shower, he refuses to wash his hair and insists the poison water will make it fall out. Haircuts are a once or twice a year occurrence, saved for special occasions.

During his latest hospitalization, he only bathed three times in four months. No amount of coercion could convince him the water wouldn't hurt him. The staff tried everything, but no amount of encouragement would change his mind. B was also afraid that they would plant listening devices in his clothes.

At that point, I realized nobody's ever died from being dirty. My focus became his brain health, not his hygiene.

If bathing made his mind better, I'd force showers, but unfortunately, recovery isn't that simple.

I now ask about showering and clothing changes but rarely make him do either. I address issues as they arise and don't worry about the rest. Having a clean body and fresh clothes feels great to me and you but is too much for him to handle. I spend time with him, not his body or clothes choices. The rule is that if he chooses to go out with me, his clothes need to be reasonably clean, teeth brushed, and if his hair isn't brushed, it's a hat day. Most days are hat days. I don't know what it takes for my son just to make it through each day, so I'm willing to let his hygiene slide.

FYI, I carry peppermint essential oil in my purse. It works great placed under my nose when we're in close quarters, such as the car.

Living in a Mess

Why do so many MIACs live in squalid conditions? Perhaps a chaotic living environment is a reflection of a chaotic brain. It's an external example of the disorder that my MIAC experiences internally. There's a difference between being a slob and living in a deranged mess. A slob chooses to ignore organization, whereas mental illness creates too much noise in your MIAC's mind for him to have a choice.

Unfortunately, when you live in a filthy environment, it can make mental illness symptoms worse. Clutter has a detrimental effect on the brain, makes it harder to focus, decreases productivity, is linked to poor dietary habits and an impaired ability to process information, can lead to a more pessimistic attitude, and increases stress and anxiety. It feels too stressful to clean up, so your MIAC continues to add to the mess. This procrastination leads to increased depression and social isolation.

Neurosis, obsessions, and compulsive behaviors also contribute to living in a dirty, neglected environment. Your MIAC's mind is so filled with irrational thoughts and delusions that he's unable to perform the most basic household tasks. What's interesting is that many with MI are motivated to clean up when offered help or an incentive. Money is a strong motivator. It's fascinating that with the right reward, MIACs are able to perform household chores—not perfectly, not even well—but the bare minimum can be accomplished. I think it has something to do with triggering the feel-good/reward area of the brain.

Your MIAC's goal every day is to feel better. So, anything that can potentially make him feel good for a few minutes offers motivation. He looks for distractions from the inner turmoil and the confusion he struggles with. That's why incentives sometimes can push him to clean up. At other times, nothing will work because his brain is in survival mode and can't deal with anything beyond making it through the day. Think of it this way: if your life depended on you climbing a mountain, you would attempt to climb it, but you won't be concerned with picking up litter along the way.

"Yuck! What happened in here? I thought you said you would clean up."

B looks at me and says, "Mom, it is clean. See my clothes folded in neat piles?"

"Yes, I do see that, but don't you want to put them away in your closet or dresser? What about that smelly pile in the corner?"

"I'm going to wash them later," B says. "There's clothes in the washer and dryer, and I'll move them tomorrow. I'm too tired today."

I sigh and walk away in frustration. "How do you help the elderly woman next door vacuum, take out trash, clean litter boxes, and wash dishes, but don't even see that the same things need to be done in your own house?"

Even though he promises to clean his place and wants the chance to do it on his own, it never happens. I end up cleaning his condo, complaining and resenting it the entire time. He stands by, uselessly hovering and getting in my way when I ask for help.

I dread each month when it comes time to clean up his mess. The sink is full of moldy dishes, the stovetop and skillets caked with grease, stinky and stained bedsheets. It's too much!

"I'm done!"

I hire my sister-in-law to clean every couple of weeks. It's the best money I've ever spent and the best decision for my peace of mind—until B starts to think that she's the devil and won't allow her into his house without me being there.

"Really! I'm so over how ridiculous this has become," I tell B. "If you don't want her here, then I'll hire a company to do it."

Then the sh*t really hits the fan, his paranoia sets in, and he threatens to barricade the door. All of this drama over cleaning.

"Why? Why do I have to have this fight with you every month? Why can't you help? Don't you care how you live? You have a nice place and are in the process of destroying it with all the filth."

He slams the door, locking me out.

I'm a firm believer that living in a clean, somewhat organized space improves your mental health, but I have no clue how to make this happen without doing it myself or hiring help. I also believe that your thought processes are clearer when you live in an orderly home. It's a catch-22. MI causes the mess, and the mess contributes to perpetuating or increasing the mental illness. Again, mental health professionals don't have any answers to this nasty dilemma. They give goals, checklists, and offer life-skills classes, but if your MIAC has a severe brain disorder, these likely won't change his behavior.

Your choices are limited, but they do exist. You can help your MIAC clean, do the cleaning yourself, hire outside help, or move your child out of your house. If they live independently, you can stop cleaning up their mess, find placement for them in a care facility, or accept that this is what severe MI looks like. The choice is yours.

I know that if my MIAC was well, he wouldn't be living in squalor. As a child, he was neat and orderly, with a little bit of mess thrown in. But there was no filth. I try to look at the issue with compassion and understanding instead of blaming or shaming him for his lack of competence. I know he wants to do better, to make me proud, to be a capable adult. And it breaks my heart that he isn't able to do so.

Inability to Handle Money

Many people who experience psychological stress also experience financial stress. It's no coincidence that financial issues and mental illness go hand in hand. All MI includes some sort of thought disorder. The degree to which the mind is affected is directly related to the severity of the illness. Those disorders that involve delusions or mania tend to cause more irrational thoughts, but even anxiety and depression can contribute to poor financial choices.

Just like people who are well, the mentally ill spend money as a way to boost their mood. The problem is they don't know when to stop. MIACs may also buy gifts for others in an attempt to be liked and raise their self-esteem. They are desperate for friends. Furthermore, they have poor impulse control. The idea that you need something, and you need it *right now*, is common with mental illness and causes impulsive, irrational decisions around spending.

We all purchase things we really don't need, but MIACs don't have the reasoning power to look at what they've done and decide not to do it again. Spending money is almost like a drug. It allows them to distract themselves from what's going on with their disease. For just a moment, they can step away from their circumstances and feel happy. Of course, the feeling doesn't last, so they want to spend more and more.

A MIAC's brain can't rationalize through the many reasons why this could be a problem. If they have money, they have a visceral need to spend it. I believe this inability to control or monitor spending is a reliable symptom of serious mental illness. Every family I've encountered has described their MIAC's irresponsible spending as a major problem, not only for their child but also for the entire family, as parents usually supplement their child's irrational spending habits.

> *I believe this inability to control or monitor spending is a reliable symptom of serious mental illness.*

There are many programs and therapies available that offer help for irresponsible financial habits, but rarely do they work with someone who has severe MI. These services teach strategies to help you recognize triggers, create checks and balances, and show how to live on a budget. Unfortunately, you need to be capable of rational thinking in order to grasp and follow these lessons.

Those with severe mental impairment simply don't have the critical thinking skills needed to make wise choices with money. Thought disorders change how the brain perceives what's important. MIACs live in the moment, with no thought of the next minute, next hour, or next day, and can't appreciate the long-term consequence of their actions.

My MIAC receives an extra $83 a month for personal expenses. The rest of his social security check goes to pay for his room and board at a residential care facility. Most of his roommates get a check each month. His extra money comes to me, and I purchase the things he needs and wants. Bottled water, cigarettes, snacks, and soda. He gets no spending money because he's shown that he's not capable of making wise choices. That doesn't mean he doesn't sell cigarettes and soda for cash. He has a handful of change and a couple dollars but has nowhere or way to spend it. Having the money makes him feel safe. I don't like that I have to monitor my MIAC's spending, but the alternative led to several hospitalizations. I'm now totally clear: he isn't able to handle his finances and never will be.

Being my MIAC's legal guardian and payee makes it easier for me to handle his finances, but I realize that everyone isn't in that position. My suggestion, in cases of severe, chronic MI, is to either become or hire a service to be your child's payee. I understand that many times your MIAC doesn't want you to have anything to do with his life, even when he makes terrible decisions.

This may sound harsh, but it's important for your child, for you, and for the rest of your family to stop giving him money. By giving him money, you may think you're helping him purchase necessities, but the truth is that you're enabling his continued poor choices. You're not giving him an opportunity to learn from his bad decisions and make better choices next time. If you don't stop funding your child's disease-induced spending, it will financially bankrupt you.

If you don't stop funding your child's disease-induced spending, it will financially bankrupt you.

There are government services available for those unable to take care of their own financial needs, but sometimes your MIAC needs to hit bottom in order to receive those services. Your child needs to understand that you won't be there to bail him out. Even those with severe mental disorders have a natural instinct to survive. You can't change how they handle their finances, but you can accept that doing what you've always done hasn't helped. You don't control your MIAC's actions or choices, but allowing him to fail either shows he needs a guardian or POA (power of attorney), or it will allow him to qualify for government assistance.

I think everyone should be allowed a few chances to make better choices, but if your child shows he's incapable, then it may become necessary to step in and take over. It will take perseverance and time to make that happen, but it's possible. For your own health and happiness, you need to draw a line in the sand. Even if you don't handle your MIAC's finances, you can stop giving him money.

Dual Diagnosis/Addiction & Mental Illness

According to the National Survey on Drug Use and Health in 2018, "Approximately 9.2 million people experienced both mental illness and a substance abuse disorder." It's impossible to know what came first, as many self-medicate to reduce symptoms of an undiagnosed mental illness. Studies show that alcohol and drug use make mental health disorders worse, not better. The more a person uses illicit substances, the more mental illness symptoms they experience—and the more the disease manifests, the more they use. It's a self-perpetuating behavior that requires intense therapy and better medications to treat the most prevalent symptoms of MI.

The following story is shared with permission from a close friend who was blindsided by her son's relapse.

Since high school, H has been unable to move forward with his life. Racked with anxiety and depression, he gravitates toward other young men who also struggle to find their way. He sits at the dinner table; his head bobs in a feeble attempt to stay upright in his chair.

"H, what's wrong with you?" I ask, sure I already know the answer.

He mumbles, "I'm just tired. I need you to buy me cigarettes."

A few days later, I send him three hours away to a treatment program. I worry incessantly that he won't have what he needs, that he will try to run away, that I don't know what's going to happen to him. Is it enabling if I mail him cigarettes and snacks, I wonder?

When he gets out, he looks good for the first time in ages. Gone is the gaunt boy with the lifeless eyes, and in his place is a healthy-looking young man with a bounce to his step. He looks so good. My heart soars! Now maybe he'll get his life on track.

H decides to move several states away, and within a month, he has a couple jobs and a small apartment. Did I notice that he never seemed to have enough money? Did I notice that he always had severe respiratory allergies? Did I notice that he was unable to handle making arrangements to come visit without me doing it for him? I continued to send him care packages of food, restaurant coupons, household items, and of course, money. Did I stop and think about what was really going on?

I chose to believe him when he told me everything was fine and that he liked the jobs he had. Then his apartment was broken into and his paycheck stolen. A month later, H came to visit and spent most of the time in his room. When he came out, he was too tired to stay awake. It was a disappointing visit.

Alarm bells should have been going off in my head, but I wanted so desperately for him to pull his life together that I didn't see all the signs that it never had been, and now his carefully constructed facade was crumpling. Within a month, he was fired from both jobs but refused to come home. At this point, I become frantic. I begged him to come back and sent more and more money to keep him afloat.

Still no warning bells. I have my head buried so far in the sand that I can barely breathe. A friend and I fly down to get him, rent a truck, and bring him home.

"H, get out here and help us pack your stuff."

I'm frustrated by his lackadaisical mood. It takes him three hours to get up and get ready.

"What's going on with you?"

H confides that he's taking an RX prescribed by his therapist. The bottle is a couple years old. Still no warning bells.

Two days after our return home, a friend of his says to me, "You know he's snorting heroin, don't you?"

H then tells me he's been doing it for two years. It feels like I've been physically punched in the gut. How did I not see what was under my nose all along? I'm angry at myself and at him. I feel defeated, I feel deceived, and I feel that any trust I had for my son is gone.

As a society, we need to recognize the connection between these two seemingly different disorders—mental illness and substance abuse—and treat the person as having one disease—a brain disease. I think mental illness comes first because nobody in their right mind would choose to become an addict. Intellectually, your child knows that self-medicating is wrong, but his mind is incapable of logical thinking and can't foresee the long-term consequences of his poor choices. Your child looks for a quick fix, something he can do right now to feel better, with no thought to tomorrow.

I like to call this the "Jonesing Gene," the need to find a distraction, any distraction, to stop how he feels inside. Of course, when that doesn't work long term, then your MIAC tries harder drugs, uses more alcohol, and spends excessively—whatever he can do to make the pain go away. This showcases the underdeveloped emotional and mental maturity that are hallmarks of MI.

Unable to apply logic or rationality, MIACs choose the path of least resistance. This may sound controversial, but if I experienced just a handful of the symptoms our children go through, I would likely make similar choices. I would try anything to get rid of the pain.

My son says he drinks until he passes out because it's the only way to stop the voices in his head. He knows this could have dire consequences when mixed with his six medications, but he's willing to risk it to have a few minutes of quiet. He says he doesn't want to die and isn't trying to kill himself when he drinks like this, but he's unable to make the choice to abstain. What he fails to consider is that he could die from alcohol poisoning, fall and hit his head, or even develop pancreatitis. When he's unable to drink, he finds another distraction, anything to take him out of his reality for a few minutes. Nothing works in the long run, so he always wants to purchase a new video game, new herbal supplement, anything new. Unfortunately, there's nothing out there to take away his symptoms, so it's a constant circle of symptom, distraction, addiction, symptom.

Addiction comes in many shapes and sizes but is considered to be any behavior that diverts the mind or disrupts symptoms. There are addictive behaviors and addictions to substances; both work in the same way to interrupt life as it is, with the hope of making it better or more tolerable, even if only for a few hours.

Addictions can take many forms: illegal drug use, misuse of prescription drugs, alcoholism, compulsive shopping, over-eating, binge-watching TV, video games, and overuse of social media. Sex can become an addiction, pornography, gambling, smoking cigarettes or weed, or excessively drinking coffee, energy drinks, and espresso shots are also candidates. Working excessively can also be considered an addiction when it takes over your life.

How many times have you used some of the same coping strategies when you've had a particularly bad day? The difference is that your brain isn't damaged by illness, so you know when to stop. I'm not saying it's any better when you resort to these behaviors, but you go into them knowing what you're doing. That's why so many people with mental illness end up with some kind of addiction, simply because their mind is unable to exercise control. Damaged and dysfunctional brains make incredibly misguided choices.

I choose to see addiction as another symptom of mental illness instead of a separate disorder. The mental illness must be addressed first before any success can be achieved with controlling the addiction.

If you choose to allow your MIAC to use drugs in your home, you're subconsciously condoning his addictive behavior. And if his form of seeking relief is using drugs, do you want to be considered an accomplice when he overdoses?

My MIAC spends hours researching alternative herbs to alleviate his symptoms. If one pill is recommended, he'll take four. Whatever he ingests, more is always better. There's no self-reflection regarding the harm he might cause himself.

Interestingly, my dad had the same tendencies; he did everything to excess. My son spends hours researching CBD and hemp buds. He wants to roll his own hemp cigarettes, which leads to many arguments because I won't buy any of this for him. In his care facility, he can't have any contraband in his room, and thankfully anything that isn't prescribed by a doctor, even vitamins, is prohibited.

The Truth About Self-Harm

Thankfully, my MIAC doesn't self-harm unless you consider drinking to excess self-injury. The following story was shared by an acquaintance whose daughter struggles with an undiagnosed mental illness. I tell it to you with permission.

Dinner isn't going well. R is antagonistic and defensive.

I ask, "How was your day? Did you fill out any job applications?"

R throws down her fork, splashing spaghetti sauce everywhere. "You're always on my case. Can't you just leave me alone?"

I yell back, "Can't you just sit at the table and eat dinner? Does everything have to be a fight?"

This is how most of our meals end up; yelling, screaming, and R throwing something. I'm so tired of walking on eggshells, never knowing what will set her off, afraid of what she might do to herself. R slams back her chair and stomps off to her room. For a moment, I'm relieved, but I push my plate away, no longer hungry.

I feel lost and defeated. I just don't know what to do with her anymore. She doesn't want to go to school, can't put forth the effort to find a job, and is always on edge, ready to lash out at anyone who questions her behaviors or moods. I listen to R slamming around in her room, apparently throwing things at the door. Eventually, she stops, and I sit for a minute and soak in the silence. I give her a few minutes to calm herself, then knock on her door. No answer. Is she ignoring me? I give her a few more minutes and then come back and knock again. Still no answer. Now I begin to feel the fear snaking up my back, the hair on my arms stands on end. I knock more frantically, yelling, "R, open the door now!" I push at the door, but it won't budge. I look for something to jimmy the lock.

It seems like hours before I manage to get the door open. R is lying on her bed, covered in blood. A box cutter in hand, she has made several deep cuts in her thigh. I race to the phone and dial 911, sobbing to the dispatcher, "My daughter has cut herself again, and this time it's really bad. She's unconscious."

There's so much blood. I can't breathe and drop my head between my knees to keep myself from passing out as I wait for the ambulance.

In the ER, the doctor pulls me aside and asks, "How long has your daughter been self-harming?"

"I'm not sure," I tell him. "This is the second time I've had to call for an ambulance in the last three months."

The doctor transfers R to the psych ward, and my relief is palpable. I think, Maybe now we'll find an answer. Maybe now we'll get a diagnosis. Maybe now she'll be put on medication. I hope this will be the last time I have to call 911.

Self-harm, also known as self-injury, is defined as an intentional injury done without the intent to commit suicide. Reasons for self-harming behaviors include:

- The desire to ease emotional distress
- A deficiency in emotional regulation skills
- A need to get rid of bad feelings
- The urge to feel more alive instead of numb

If your MIAC uses self-harm, self-mutilation, or self-abusive behaviors, you're not alone. The prevalence of self-harm is much higher in MI adolescents and young adults and much lower for older MI patients. Self-harming behaviors are seen more in certain mental illnesses, including BPD (Borderline Personality Disorder), Dissociative Disorder, MDD (Major Depressive Disorder), and eating disorders. It's believed that people self-harm to reduce negative feelings, anxiety, or stress. It can also be linked to using pain as a relief valve when unable to express emotions, as self-punishment, or as suicide avoidance.

Threats, negative consequences, and/or bribery are not effective long term in creating positive behavior changes. If your MIAC was thinking logically, he wouldn't express his anguish with risky behaviors. Unfortunately, many times your child will hide his actions because he doesn't want to be ridiculed, shamed, or confronted. It's scary to be trapped in a mind that can't handle frightening or painful situations and overwhelming or uncontrollable emotions. It isn't usually apparent to your MIAC that others don't share his struggles and that it's possible to learn more appropriate ways to handle his problems. Confused reasoning leads to poor choices, lying, and manipulation.

In my opinion, self-harm is similar to addiction in that it's a distraction from the pain a MIAC suffers. Mood dysregulation, inadequate coping skills, ineffective medications, and/or an improper diagnosis all factor into these risky behaviors. Your child is no more able to stop cutting than he's able to stop drinking. Brain immaturity, irrational thought patterns, and delusional judgment all play a part in why MIACs choose to hurt themselves rather than seek more appropriate ways to handle distressing situations and emotions.

Treatment most often starts by addressing the underlying mental illness. Understanding what triggers your child to self-harm can help him avoid the situations or learn ways to manage them differently. It's important to introduce more benign coping skills before self-harm can be dealt with. For cases of continual or serious self-harm, it's best to involve a doctor or therapist—and when necessary, call 911 for assistance.

Mentalhealth.org states, "Some of the ways MIAC's cause injury to themselves is by cutting, burning, biting, scratching, punching, head banging, gnawing on fingers until bloody and damaged, or taking life-threatening risks. In more severe cases bone-breaking, self-amputation, or permanent eye damage can occur."

It's sad to think that your child is so distressed that he believes he needs to harm himself to get relief. I believe this is an attempt to feel some sense of control in a body that struggles with an out-of-control brain. Just like anorexia and bulimia, controlling what happens to your body when your mind experiences chaos seems rational to the person injuring themselves. Your child doesn't want to die; he just desperately needs the agony to stop. Self-harming is a cry for help, a message that something is seriously wrong and that professional treatment is needed. Those who self-harm won't stop on their own. Intervention is required to create healthier coping skills.

Safe Ways to Handle Aggressive or Violent Behaviors

An article in ncbi.nlm.nih.gov states, "Most stable mental health patients don't present an increased risk of violence," although there is an increased risk of aggressive behavior or violence with the more severe mental illnesses, such as schizophrenia, schizoaffective, and bipolar disorder, due to symptoms of psychosis, delusions, and hallucinations. If the individual has a co-occurring substance abuse disorder, then the probability of violence increases. While the news reports suggest that most mass shootings are committed by the mentally ill, studies show that only about 3 percent of the MI population is violent and dangerous.

What are the reasons for aggression and violence in your MIAC? An inability to self-regulate moods, a mind filled with irrational and chaotic thoughts, and a lack of appropriate coping skills make it more likely that your child will become overwhelmed and lash out. This can take the form of derogatory intimidation, threats of violence if he doesn't get his way, throwing or breaking things, hitting or punching, menacing others with a weapon, shooting, or stabbing someone. The more disorganized and aberrant his thinking, the more likely your MIAC may resort to threatening behavior. The more unstable your MIAC's thinking, the more disturbed his actions may become.

Not everyone with a serious mental illness will become violent, but most will exhibit increased agitation and decompensation when their delusions and paranoia are challenged. The sinister voices in your MIAC's head make him fearful and uncertain and can lead to defensive reactions to seemingly innocent circumstances. When you consider he's living in an imaginary reality of demons and giant spiders, it makes it easier to understand why your child responds with hostility and belligerence and feels the need to be on high alert at all times. We would likely approach anyone who discounted our reality with combativeness, too. Most violence committed by mentally ill people is done in a residential setting, meaning a family member is more likely to be the victim. Substance abuse increases the incidence of violent and aggressive behaviors, another reason not to allow your child to use drugs in your home.

Aggressiveness is simply another symptom of a complex brain disorder and should be viewed as an expression of your child's illness, not as a willful act of violence. It may look like his actions are intentional, but they come from a disordered brain and not his heart. With that being said, it's not okay to allow your MIAC to threaten, assault, or harm you in any way. Even if he isn't in his right mind, you still need to enforce respectable behaviors. To maintain an assurance of safety in your home, rules should be put in place with associated consequences. The police should be called to intervene before situations become dangerous or lethal. I don't care how much you love your MIAC; he should never be allowed to harm you or destroy property. Sometimes the only way for your child to learn a different way is to be forced to accept the consequences for inappropriate actions. You should never accept abuse from your child.

The following are examples of aggressive or violent behavior. Notice that some seem rather mild compared to others, but they're all forms of abuse.

- Foul language aimed at you
- Yelling, screaming, insulting you
- Slamming doors, throwing things, destroying property
- Pushing, hitting, punching, or kicking you
- Threatening to harm you, using a weapon to coerce or hurt you
- Trying to kill you

None of these behaviors are acceptable, regardless of the degree of illness. You may understand that your MIAC isn't in control of his actions, but you must take the necessary steps to ensure your safety. The time to have a conversation is when he's calm, and you can discuss unacceptable behavior and consequences for breaking the rules. If this isn't possible, write down the information so your child can review it privately.

It doesn't matter if he likes or agrees with your rules. It matters that you consistently enforce the consequences. If your MIAC uses physical violence as a means to get his way, it's imperative that you call the police, file a report, press charges, and/or file for a restraining order. If your child is living with you, the authorities need to know that can't continue. If your MIAC is taken to a psych unit, the doctors and social workers need to be made aware of your safety concerns. Many times, if you explain that your child has nowhere to go, no money, etc., then social services will step in and look for housing and long-term care options.

As hard as it is to turn your child out, it does neither of you any good to continue in a cycle of abuse, aggression, and violence. Nobody has the right to harm you, not even your child. Unfortunately, your MIAC's brain disorder is not a valid reason to let him hurt you, destroy your property, or ruin your peace of mind. In your home, you make the rules, and if they aren't followed, then your child needs to find other accommodations. You may not like this choice, but you aren't here to be your child's doormat.

These decisions are some of the most difficult you'll ever make, but there's no chance of things getting better if you don't make different choices. Many of us don't have our MIACs living with us for various reasons. Mental illness is a gruesome disease, but it's not your responsibility to be held hostage by your out-of-control MIAC.

The following story was shared by a mom who started an online support group for mothers of adult children with mental illness and addiction. Her story covers so many of the areas we all worry about: homelessness, addiction, incarceration, and victimization. It's a perfect example of what happens when a loved one falls through the cracks of a broken mental healthcare system, a broken judicial system, and a broken society that still sees mental illness as a controllable behavior.

"I wish my son could be home with me. I pray daily for his safety," S says. "Doctors blame his drug addiction for causing his mental health diagnosis. The experience of living with him when he's using is so stressful that, at times, I can't function. That's why he's homeless. If only he would listen to reason, if only he could stay clean, if only he would take his meds, if only I could have my son back."

Sleepless nights, fear, sadness, guilt, and anger have all contributed to my own depression and anxiety. I try to keep my days full to avoid having to dwell on my son walking the streets and slowly killing himself. Painting is a lifesaver for me. When I pull out my watercolors, I feel the rest of my life fall away, and I'm transported to a place of calmness and joy.

My life has been a living hell, with brief moments of relief. When he's sober, he begins taking his meds and seems okay. Then he stops, and he's back on the street. Every day I wonder if today will be the day that I receive the call every parent fears, the one that tells me my son is dead.

Driving to the hospital, tears streaming down my cheeks, I pray that my son is alive.

His case manager called and said, "Your son was found on the ground. He's been stabbed in several places, has lost a lot of blood, and is being rushed to the ER."

Stabbed in the eye, face, stomach, neck, and buttocks. "Mom, I got into a fight with another man, and he pulled out something sharp. I was fighting with the devil."

Detectives and doctors can't agree on whether he's been attacked or has done this to himself, so the case is closed. Not well enough, my son refuses to pursue the issue.

With this incident, my concern for his safety is constant. "Please, Lord, watch over my son. I place him in your hands," I pray.

He's been in jail fifteen to twenty times, arrested for being under the influence or for probation violations, and admitted to the only psych hospital in our area at least ten times. He panhandles for money, and occasionally, strangers buy him food. I'm heartbroken, remembering this young man, a star football player with so much promise, who's struggled with social phobia, addiction, anxiety, and depression for over eighteen years. The court system hasn't heeded my requests to admit him to a treatment program but instead dumps him back onto the streets.

My son is broken, our mental healthcare system is broken, and our justice system is broken. I know my son is in there somewhere, and I will continue to fight for him. I just want him back—the son I remember before this nightmare began.

ScienceDaily.com reports, "The mentally ill are much more likely to be victims of violent crimes than to be the perpetrators. Almost one-third of MIACs are likely to be victims of violence, and those that have been a victim are more likely to commit a violent act themselves."

The more severe the mental illness, the more at risk that person is of becoming a victim. Poor social and problem-solving skills, irrational thinking, impulsivity, substance abuse, and homelessness all compromise your MIAC's ability to protect himself.

Homelessness

While most research states that approximately 25 percent of the homeless population is mentally ill, I find that number hard to believe. Other studies estimate over 60 percent of the homeless population have problems with addiction. If you put those two numbers together, that means the majority of those who are homeless struggle with a mental health disorder. Obviously, we as a society have a serious problem if the majority of our homeless are a vulnerable subset of the population. Unfortunately, it's not illegal to be homeless, even if you've been diagnosed with a mental illness.

Why is this such a huge problem? Back in the 1960s, the government programs that funded state-run mental institutions decided to close them due to budget cuts. Federally funded community mental health centers were supposed to replace these asylums. "As a result, 2.2 million severely mentally ill individuals stopped receiving psychiatric treatment," states Kimberly Amadeo in her article "Deinstitutionalization, Its Causes, Effects, Pros and Cons."

She continues, "There are three times as many seriously mentally ill people in jails and prisons, due to a shortage of psychiatric hospital beds. In 2009, states cut $4.35 billion in mental health spending over three years." Add to this the fact that the HIPAA laws make it almost impossible to place someone in a psych hospital against their will, and it's easy to see why the homeless population is primarily composed of people with mental illness and substance abuse issues.

Another reason for the high incidence of homelessness in the mentally ill is due to some of the symptoms of the disease. The inability to recognize that they're sick, medication noncompliance, or behaviors that force families to refuse them a place in the home all contribute to the problem. Lack of available housing for this demographic, lack of mental health centers, lack of doctors, lack of funding in communities also cause many MIACs to fall through the cracks. As insane as it sounds to us, many of them choose to live on the streets rather than conform to requests to seek treatment, stay sober, or admit they have a problem. Lack of insight limits their ability to make rational choices, and privacy laws limit our ability as their parents to make better choices for their care and safety. The government believes everyone, as long as they aren't a threat to themselves or someone else, has a right to decide where they live, how they live, and whether they take medication.

Criminal Activity and Incarceration

Psyom.net says, "Experts say jails and prisons have become the nation's largest psychiatric facilities. Mass incarceration, poverty, and a drug epidemic—coupled with lack of access to treatment—have resulted in criminalization of the mentally ill in a system often unprepared to properly deal with the problem."

There are three times more seriously mentally ill people in jails and prisons than in hospitals in the US. This is because, during a mental health crisis, people are more likely to encounter police than get medical help. Not violent criminals, but without resources, they spend time in jail for minor crimes instead of being transferred for psych evaluation and treatment. NAMI.org states, "At least 83 percent of jail inmates with a mental illness don't have access to adequate treatment."

Mentalillnesspolicy.org, by Dr. E. Fuller Torrey, states, "Nowhere in our society is the debacle of deinstitutionalization felt more than in our criminal justice system. Jails in over three thousand counties have more severely psychotic individuals than any other facility in those counties. Many ill individuals are held with no charges against them while waiting for psych evaluation, hospital bed availability, or transportation to a psych hospital." This same study found the majority of US jails don't provide adequate psychiatric services. Most MIACs are arrested on misdemeanors such as trespassing, intoxication, vagrancy, and disorderly conduct.

While jail can seem like the last place you want your psychotic MIAC to be, it's sometimes the easiest way to get your child the social services and disability benefits he needs. Priority for psychiatric services is given to those with criminal charges pending. Because of the symptoms of severe brain disorders, most incarcerated individuals usually end up with increased psychiatric symptoms due to the trauma of the experience. On rare occasions, people report jail time as a positive experience because it enabled them to get much-needed help.

A mother I met in a NAMI F2F class pressed charges against her schizophrenic son when he attempted to murder his father. After several years in prison, her son was released into subsidized housing, has a job, a small apartment, and his own car. He credits his time in prison for helping him to gain control of his behaviors, adhere to medication schedules, and learn better coping skills to deal with his illness.

Unfortunately, our healthcare system is unable to keep up with mental health treatment demands, so the penal system has been forced to pick up the slack, with dire consequences. Underfunded, untrained, and overcrowded jails are the worst place for a seriously mentally ill individual. Mental health courts link offenders to long-term community-based treatment. Since 1997, the number of mental health courts has grown from four to over three hundred, with programs in almost every state. There are eligibility criteria for participation based on diagnosis, established treatments, and severity of the infraction.

Samhsa.gov has developed an extensive database of mental health courts in the US. These courts can improve the lives of offenders, reduce recidivism, and reduce costs, but the downside of the system is forced treatment/medication, lack of available services, longer sentences, and admittance of guilt. Mentally ill offenders have ongoing monitoring to address their needs and maintain public safety. "The goal of mental health court," we learn from npr.org, "is to identify people with serious MI and get them treatment earlier."

Crisis Intervention Training is a police mental health collaborative program. The CIT program teaches officers the best ways to respond to a mental illness call. "There are more than 2,700 communities nationwide with CIT programs," says NAMI.org. "These programs reduce arrests of the mentally ill and increase the likelihood they will receive mental health services. CIT community programs give the police more tools to do their job safely, keep law enforcement's focus on crime, and produce cost savings."

When your MIAC is in crisis, and you feel the need to have police intervention, it's best to ask for a certified CIT team or officer. If your city doesn't have one, advocate for the importance of training.

> I've called the police several times for help to get my severely psychotic MIAC to the hospital for treatment. Luckily, our city officers are CIT trained. They show up without lights or sirens and meet me in the driveway to find out more details of our crisis.

"My son is psychotic and has refused food and water for several days. He thinks everything is poison and has an eating disorder related to his mental illness. He has a diagnosis of schizophrenia," I tell the officers.

"Is he armed or dangerous?" they ask.

I'm shaking and tearful, but thankful I can respond, "No, he's not violent, but very delusional."

I hate when I have to do this. I know my son will be mad and scream at me but will go with the officers and get in the ambulance. He desperately needs treatment.

At the hospital, I'm required to fill out an affidavit explaining why I believe my MIAC needs treatment. If I can't convince them that he's a threat to himself, the hospital can refuse to admit him. I walk in and sit by his bed.

"Who are you? Get out! You're not my mom. My mom wouldn't treat me this way."

My heart breaks because he's too irrational to understand that this is for his own good. He's six feet four inches tall and weighs only one hundred and ten pounds. He looks like a concentration camp prisoner. I sit in my chair trembling and wish there was a better way to get my son the care he needs. I say a silent prayer, *Please, God, let them see that he needs to be here. Please don't make me have to take him home in this condition.*

I wonder if he'll ever be better, if he'll ever understand the difficult choices I've made to keep him safe, if he'll remember what he's said to me. Even if he doesn't, I will. And his words tear a hole in my heart.

Suicide

For all of us with a MIAC, one of, if not our biggest fear, is death by suicide. Twenty-five percent of MIACs with schizophrenia will end their lives by suicide.

Initially, it's a constant, nagging fear, like a rock in my shoe. The thought is sharp, painful, and always there, rolling around, biting into my psyche. I wasn't sure if I'd be able to handle my son's death. The thought made my heart break. After years of observing what my son struggles with on a daily basis, I realized that as gut-wrenching as it is for me to watch him suffer, what he lives with on a daily basis is unimaginably horrific.

NAMI.org shares these signs that warn of suicide. If your child shows any of the following, pay attention. All these signs should be taken seriously, as they are an indication of severe inner turmoil and suffering. Each one is an outward demonstration of your MIAC's desire to remove himself from his inner demons.

- Aggressive behavior
- Increased alcohol and drug use
- Withdrawal from friends, family, and community
- Dramatic mood swings
- Impulsive or reckless behavior
- Collecting or saving pills
- Buying a weapon
- Giving away possessions, organizing personal papers, or paying off debts
- Saying goodbye to friends and family
- Voicing threats of suicide

Suicidal behaviors and/or talking about suicide are both psychiatric emergencies and require professional intervention. I wonder: If there was access to better treatments and to more effective medications and if it was easier to be hospitalized during a crisis and society viewed mental illness as a biological disease instead of misbehavior, would fewer MIACs choose suicide? How tormented must you be for suicide to seem like your best choice? How sad and disheartening that we have so little to offer in the way of relief and recovery for those who have suffered from ongoing mental illness for decades.

It's important to have these conversations with your MIAC when he's calm and before he voices a desire to end his life. Shying away from this sensitive topic won't stop it from happening. That's why my son and I periodically have these hard conversations. It lets my son know that I care enough to ask what he wants. Asking him to continue to battle demons just so I won't lose him is selfish. No loving mother would want her child to continue to struggle with no end in sight. I need him to know that if a time comes when he feels like it's too much, I will allow him to choose for himself. I don't want him to stay just for me. I show my unconditional love for him by allowing him to have a choice.

We occasionally have talks about life and death. My MIAC has made it clear to me, at this time, that he very much wants to live. So that's why I step in to keep him safe from his poor choices. If that changes in the future, I will honor his decision to end his life. This is not easy, but he deserves to make that choice for himself, and I will be at peace, knowing that he is finally at peace.

This is a very personal decision on my part to honor his wishes, and that may not be your choice. But it's a discussion you need to have with your child. It shows you care about his struggles, his opinions, and his choices. Even if you don't agree with him, it's your responsibility as his parent to listen and share your views.

I believe that death isn't the end—just a shift into another dimension of being. Spirituality has taught me to believe that we go to a better place when we leave our human body, so I'll accept my son's choice to move on if he decides that his time here is too difficult.

Understanding mental illness is just the beginning. It's imperative that you gain skills to navigate the unbridled fear this disease causes not only to your heart but also to your soul. Don't get stuck in the despair. You need the information to move ahead with courage and determination.

It's up to us to heal ourselves, so we can lift up those moms who are still treading water. When we share our stories, triumphs, and failures, we help others walk the same path. As we hold hands and hearts in support, we heal ourselves further.

Come along, and let's work together as we restore our lives. Are you ready to become a badass warrior?

Visualization Journey

Sit in a comfortable, quiet place. Close your eyes.

Breathe in and out slowly to the count of three several times until you feel your mind and body begin to relax.

Visualize yourself as you walk down an unfamiliar path. It's twisty, dimly lit, and littered with rocks. You feel uncertain, unsteady, and slightly frightened.

Around the next bend, you see a friendly face, your beloved grandmother. She gives you a warm, welcoming hug and takes your hand firmly in hers. You breathe a sigh of relief and already feel stronger and more courageous. She quietly tells you, "I'll be with you on this path to offer support, encouragement, and insight."

You continue to walk and encounter a group of people. You feel frightened. They appear disheveled, dirty, and confused. Some mumble, some shout, and some appear angry. A few wander aimlessly in circles, a few appear homeless, and a few seem to be intoxicated. One wears prison garb, one cuts himself, and another tries to start a fight.

You're glad to have your grandmother with you on this journey. She reminds you that this is the mental illness path and that you need to look closer at those you've encountered.

Upon inspection, you see that everyone in the group wears a mask. The masks are scary, hideous, and distort reality.

Grandmother urges you to step forward, and you begin to remove each person's mask, and what you find changes your perceptions.

Under each mask, you see the truth and recognize the struggle each person is going through. Your heart hurts for these ailing individuals.

Hidden under the masks, you find fear, confusion, and self-loathing. Some cover panic, pain, sadness, and depression. Others hide anxiety, anger, and distorted realities. And a few others cover up grief, loneliness, and unworthiness.

Each individual is trapped in a world of irrational thoughts, haunted by demons only they can see and hear.

You offer each one love, understanding, and a prayer for peace. You wish them well.

You and Grandmother turn and head home, saddened by what these individuals are forced to endure, saddened by the fact that they must wear masks to feel safe, saddened that there is nothing you can do to help them.

Before Grandmother leaves, she whispers a reminder, "Don't forget to look beneath the outer emotions and appearances to find the true struggles each person faces."

Slowly walk home.

When ready, open your eyes and journal any messages, words, or symbols you received. What masks do you wear to protect your vulnerability?

Defeated Mom to Badass Warrior

We are sisters
Bound by defeat
Low on self-worth
We look for answers
We take back our power
We are sisters

In the lockdown psych ward, I visit with B for the first time since he was involuntarily committed three days ago. He's never been hospitalized before. He screams, curses, and rants about irrational conspiracy theories.

"Who do you think you are having me locked up? You're the one that's crazy! It's going to be on the f*ing news! Then you'll feel bad for what you've done."

I've never seen him act this way. He won't listen to reason and lunges over the table at me. My breath catches. I shake. I'm afraid. I've never been afraid of my son before today.

Just then, a burly staff member comes in and reminds B, "Settle down, or your visitor will need to leave," he says.

But there's no way to stop the tirade of vehement swearing that comes from B's unsound mind.

The attendant catches my eye. "Leave. You don't need to subject yourself to his disrespect."

On wobbly legs, I stand.

B looks me in the eye and screams, "You're not my mother! My mother wouldn't leave me in this place!"

I'm escorted to the door and told, "Give him a few days to cool off before your next visit."

The door closes, and I'm alone in the deserted hallway.

The ability to feel like a competent mom is fleeting when faced with a mentally ill adult child. My resolve crumbles as the voices in my head begin. I remember the things my mother used to say: what will the neighbors think; it's bad to be too emotional; don't forget our family's no-talk-no-tell rule; you must do whatever to keep the peace.

Doubts of my self-worth swirl through my head. My value is tied to my child's well-being. If he's sick, then I must be a terrible mom. He's called my skills into question. Who else will?

The objectives of mothering are to nurture, protect, empower, and launch. When babies are born, they're dependent on their mothers for all their needs. A tight bond is created to ensure the child is cared for and feels loved. As children grow, the cords of connection loosen, and they're given more freedom to explore and mature. This continues until the child grows into an independent adult. At that point, both mother and child become autonomous unless something happens to prevent separation.

A health crisis can cause moms to reattach. With a chronic mental health diagnosis, the fight-or-flight response is activated, and Mom latches back on to her child in an attempt to rescue, protect, and save him.

While this may be necessary in the initial stages of illness, it can be detrimental to both you and your child if you don't attempt to rebalance personal accountability. It's terribly difficult for most moms to let go after an MI diagnosis. When you're plunged back into the role of caring for every aspect of your child's life, fear makes you hold tighter and tighter in an attempt to regain the functional adult the disease has consumed. You become so enmeshed in your MIAC's recovery that you give up your own life. When the boundaries between you and your child become blurred, relationships deteriorate.

> *You become so enmeshed in your MIAC's recovery that you give up your own life.*

None of us are infallible. We all make mistakes. That's part of our human experience. But life can be much smoother if you evaluate your attitudes about being a mother, about what, why, and how you expect things to look, and then adjust to reflect your perspective. It can be a real eye-opener to delve into the reasons behind your actions.

To change the way interactions unfold between you and your MIAC, you need to change your views about what a good mother should do. It's not within your power to change him, but you can make positive adjustments regarding how you approach difficulties. Transformation happens when you challenge the ways you think and come from a place of authenticity and love within a structure that supports everyone.

Sometimes you don't realize you're drowning in your attempts to be the life preserver for your MIAC. It's futile to make changes as a mom if you don't know the hidden beliefs that created your choices. Your beliefs are the framework that structures your decisions and actions. If you feel you're an abysmal failure as a mother, then there's a disconnect between your inner philosophy and the invisible rules you try to live up to.

Society perpetuates impossible standards for mothers to uphold. No matter what you do or how good you are, you're doomed to failure. So, sit down and write a list of the qualities *you* believe a good mother should possess. When I reviewed my own list, I realized how ridiculous most of my rules were. Instead of subconscious background noise, they were in charge of the show. Just because I'd always done something a certain way didn't make it a realistic option in my current circumstances.

I reviewed my list and considered each belief, then I thought about where I'd learned those principles. Did they come from my mom, grandma, society, other women, media, or books? Were they valid or attainable? I asked myself what I hoped to accomplish by holding myself to these strict standards. Finally, I wrote a revised list that reflected how I felt after this exercise. What could I live with? What seemed possible for me to achieve when considering everyone's needs? I found that most of my limited, harmful behaviors came from my inability to feel worthy without the approval or acceptance of others.

After that, I took my original list and revised it to reflect my improved values. In the statements below, I show my new values in italics. Take a look:

- I must do everything I can within my power to help my child *as long as it doesn't hurt me.*
- I must seek out and explore every option to find treatment for my MIAC *within reason—as long as it doesn't consume me or drain my finances.*
- I must provide for my MIAC's needs and wants *within my abilities and not out of a sense of guilt.*
- I must do what makes my MIAC happy so he doesn't get angry or upset and stop loving me. *It's my responsibility to make sure my MIAC is safe and cared for, regardless of whether he professes his love. It's his choice to take my help or not. Loving myself is my responsibility. I can't make anyone else happy.*
- I must take into account the opinions and advice of others. *I know what's best for my child and don't need to take advice from anyone who hasn't experienced what I'm dealing with. I use learned knowledge, doctor recommendations, and my intuition to make choices that are good for my family.*
- I must be available 24/7 and put my needs on hold for my child. *I will set aside time to be available for my MIAC but will also make time for my own life. Clear boundaries are important.*

- I must put up with my MIAC's disrespect because that's what moms do—offer unconditional love. *I will hold my MIAC to normal rules of courtesy and respect or else I'll remove myself from the situation. I deserve to be treated well and will not allow myself to be abused. I won't allow any behaviors from my MIAC that I wouldn't allow from a stranger.*
- I must listen and do what doctors advise because they know best. *I will take the advice of doctors into consideration but will make my own decisions based on all the information I have, what's best for my child, and my family.*
- I must put myself last. *I must put myself first, so I can be a good advocate.*

How you feel about the way your mother treated you has an enormous influence on how you raise your own children. The choices you make and the way you want to be perceived are all byproducts of your childhood. For example, if you felt unworthy as a child, as a mother, you may choose to give your children everything they ask for. If your parents expected you to be the perfect child in order to receive love, you might allow your child to get away with poor behavior. When you attempt to live up to unrealistic ideals of being the perfect mother, when you strive to be what society and your own misguided beliefs deem acceptable, you'll always fall short.

The choices and decisions I made about my MIAC's care didn't produce the results I'd hoped for or expected. We were both miserable, and I teetered on the brink of illness. That's when a friend shared an article about how to heal "the mother wound." I was intrigued, and the more I read, the more I realized that it related to my own struggles.

Until you heal your own mother wounds, the article said, you can't parent your MIAC in an effective way and still meet your own needs. Your beliefs about being a mother have been skewed by your childhood experiences, and in an effort to make up for what you didn't receive, you make dysfunctional choices with your own children.

> *When you attempt to live up to unrealistic ideals of being the perfect mother . . . you'll always fall short.*

That was true for me. I didn't feel like I measured up in my mom's eyes as a child, and it caused me to go overboard when parenting my own children. My attempts to be the perfect mom and to gain the acceptance I never received as a child created many problems.

It never works when you try to live up to someone else's standards. This applies to every woman who attempts to live up to unattainable ideals. The harder you try, the more you feel like a failure. Perhaps you live your life based on someone else's idea of who you should be and how you should act, and you do what's important to others with no thought about what you believe. You have no idea where your beliefs came from or if they resonate with you. You don't question if your approach is yours or if it creates the desired outcome you want for your child and yourself.

If you model your mothering style on how you were raised, what you wanted but didn't receive from your own mom, and what society promotes as appropriate behavior, you'll be miserable. Without evaluating yourself, you'll follow the crowd, won't take time to contemplate your choices, and will end up repeating your mother's mistakes.

Your mother did her best to nurture and love you, but your relationship with her may still be fused with undercurrents of shame, guilt, or obligation. You may continue to carry unresolved grief, fear, disappointment, and resentment toward her long after you're grown.

How does this show up? Many dysfunctions stem from your inability to release and heal the pain of your childhood. It's time to give up the dream that your mother will someday be who you want her to be. If you want to create a life independent of her and find your own inner source of unconditional love, you have to let this idea go.

Can you relate to any of these unhealthy behaviors?

- Constant comparison or competition with other moms
- Self-sabotaging your own happiness

- Weak boundaries or the inability to say no
- The subconscious belief that there's something wrong with you
- A pattern of codependency in all your relationships
- The inability to speak with authenticity or express your emotions
- Sacrificing your dreams and desires for others

We all fall into these dysfunctional patterns once in a while, but if they become habits, it's time to take a hard look at the hidden reasons you continue to express these unhealthy behaviors.

When you understand more about the mother wound, it leads you toward the concept of *feminine empowerment*. If you explore your beliefs about motherhood (what's expected of mothers vs. fathers, how the medical community blames mothers for their children's mental illnesses, and how your own mother and grandmothers shaped your view of who you should be as a mom), you'll understand why you've continued to struggle. Recognize that you can recreate your own mother identity that aligns with your beliefs and values. Empowerment means that you choose for yourself what values, beliefs, and standards of conduct you want to live by.

When you reclaim your voice, you'll feel stronger in the decisions you make for yourself and your child. You can step into your authenticity because you no longer adhere to outdated ideals. When you're the one who decides what fits with your moral code, you'll make decisions from personal integrity. To stand in your own power permits you to take action in good faith, even in times that stress or challenge you. When you know you're making the best choices for yourself and your MIAC, much of the drama and struggle is dissipated.

When you know you're making the best choices for yourself and your MIAC, much of the drama and struggle is dissipated.

What qualities do you feel a good mom should possess? Make a list. Then evaluate the validity of each item. These qualities should align with your beliefs about what constitutes good parenting, what types of support you'll offer your MIAC, how you'll express compassion, and how to show love to your child—while honoring your humanness and your own needs and wants. Work to make decisions that don't include a hidden agenda or go against your personal convictions. In each situation, list the options available that are in line with your values, weigh the pros and cons, and make a thoughtful choice. Life with your MIAC will be so much easier when you stop second-guessing your decisions. When you choose the direction you want to head and let go of unrealistic expectations, you become more comfortable with your parenting skills and can see more options to help your child.

Guilt

Guilt eats deep into my psyche. It throbs in my chest, a cold, wet blanket wrapped around my heart. Every time I look at my son, I feel the guilt of not being able to fix him. No matter how hard I try, I don't have the power to make him well again. I laid awake last night, staring up at the dark ceiling, wondering what I should do next. What could I do to make his life better? These thoughts rolled through my mind:

He needs a hobby. I'll buy him a drone, a new video game, markers, and a sketch pad.

"Mom, I'm bored."

"Play a game, watch a movie, draw something," I suggest.

"No, not today. I'm tired."

He needs to socialize more. I'll sign him up to volunteer at the food bank. I'll take him to family functions. I'll have him attend a day program.

"I need to go home right now," B tells me.

"We've only been here half an hour," I counter.

"I'm having side effects. I can't stay."

He needs more exercise. I'll get him a gym membership. I'll walk with him every day. I'll buy him an exercise machine.

"I'm bored," B states for the tenth time today.

"Let's go for a walk," I say.

"No, I don't want to do that. I'm tired. I'm going to take a nap."

He needs to be happy. I'll buy him a new TV. I'll cook for him. I'll let him rescue a cat.

"Hey B, when was the last time you cleaned the litter box?" I ask.

"A few days ago, I think."

"You begged for a cat and said you would care for it," I say, trying not to inhale too deeply. "This place smells awful."

"I'll do it tomorrow. I'm tired."

He needs to be well. That's not the entire truth. The reality is I need him to be well to feel good about myself. He's hated every single thing I've tried to do for him, except the cat, but now he's not taking care of it. He loves all his new possessions for about a week, and then the novelty wears off.

I've spent countless hours and thousands of dollars trying to make a difference for B. I gave in to his every whim and demand, and he's no better than the day he received his diagnosis. There are small changes, but none of the things I did created those. Let me repeat that. **None of the things done out of guilt—the money spent that I didn't have, giving in to unreasonable requests, or the investment of huge amounts of time made any difference in my son's prognosis.**

It all caused more harm than good. It made me resentful, angry, and tired. So tired! A physical, mental, and emotional tired. A deep-down-in-my-soul tired. I allowed our relationship to become one based on manipulation, threats, and misguided optimism. My son became tired, too. Tired of trying to act normal, tired of failing, tired of being unable to do what other adults can do with ease, tired of my expectations that he get well.

Guilt is a double-edged sword. When your adult child is sick, it takes you back to the days of being a new parent. You become more attached and preoccupied with your child's care, and you feel the need to safeguard him in the face of an unknown adversary. An MI diagnosis is like a foreign invader, and you feel it's your duty to make it better. When no solution can be found, and your child's impairment is permanent, you have a profound sense of guilt and liability.

To release the guilt, you have to admit that you have no control over this ruthless disease. When you surrender to the fact that you have no power over the course of your child's mental illness, only then will your feelings of responsibility lessen.

> *To release the guilt, you have to admit that you have no control over this ruthless disease.*

How do you pull yourself out of despair and heartache to make the best choices for your MIAC? How do you stay strong in your beliefs when everyone implies that you're the cause? It's difficult to be an effective advocate for your child's care when you don't have the answers, aren't sure where to find them, and are accused of being the reason for this tragedy.

The guilt will suffocate you. You're held hostage by the belief that it's your responsibility to find a way to make your child better. Your inability to effect positive changes in your MIAC's life causes an endless loop of blame, criticism, and guilt.

After you exhaust every avenue of treatment—in addition to your energy and finances—you'll hit a wall. It's finally time to face the fact that you can't fix your child, to admit that you don't have all the answers, and to start learning how to navigate this new life.

You've probably read books that were written by people who live with MI, and they function at near-normal levels. But others say that recovery isn't possible for those with severe MI. Admit it: your child doesn't fit into the first category.

That recognition hit me like a tidal wave as I reviewed my son's progress since his diagnosis. His condition had not improved since we started this MI journey—and that made me question my guilt. If nothing could change this dreadful diagnosis, then I needed to recognize that I couldn't control the outcome. When I became more knowledgeable about the spectrums of MI, the guilt let go of me. As mothers of MIACs, we're only guilty of one thing: we want the best outcome for our children.

So, what can you control? You can control your attitude and the way you interact with your MIAC. You can choose to feel guilty, or you can choose to set yourself free. Hanging on to guilt hurts you, and it sure doesn't help either you or your MIAC lead more productive lives.

Your guilt is just another layer of grief. Save the guilt for when you act in a way that doesn't match your principles. The challenges of caring for a MIAC give you plenty of opportunities to feel legitimate guilt from time to time, but don't take on the emotion unless it's warranted.

Your guilt is just another layer of grief.

When you step away from the guilt, you're able to open the door to greater happiness and freedom. When you admit you're powerless to change your child, then you create the possibility for transformation to occur.

Erratic behaviors for more than a year. Poor choices, experimenting with drugs to get high, no plans to go to college, three menial part-time jobs in the last year, and hanging out with marginal friends. Last night was the last straw. He calls.

"Mom, I totaled my car. I'm at the hospital."

I blurt out, "Were you drunk or high?" I didn't ask if he was okay or if anyone else was hurt.

Eventually, I did ask if he was okay, but initially, I was too angry with him for making yet another poor choice.

That night I felt a deep sense of shame because my first thought wasn't to ask about my child's well-being. I immediately jumped into accusations. I could excuse myself by saying that because he'd been involved in so many escapades recently and had come out unfazed every time that he seemed impervious to any harm. But that doesn't excuse me for not considering his health first. This was just one of many times that I reacted in an unsupportive and demeaning way toward my child.

Days later, we talked about the incident.

"The accident wasn't my fault. The road was slick."

B insists he isn't to blame, he wasn't drunk, blah, blah, blah. I don't believe anything he says anymore. I'm frustrated with trying to reason with him and his inability to understand how his poor choices could harm him.

I snap and say, "If you want to kill yourself, just do it and get it over with because I can't keep having this same conversation over and over!"

I regret the words as soon as they leave my mouth. I want to yank them back, but there they are, hanging in the air like a toxic cloud—the culmination of months of pent-up emotions that explode from the depths of my heart, a volcano of frustration, disappointment, exasperation, confusion, sadness, and despair.

Shame

You may feel profound shame for the misguided choices you made for your child before his or her diagnosis. You're embarrassed and ashamed by the litany of blame, accusations, judgments, and threats you threw at your MIAC before you understood. You had no idea that MI was involved, but you still feel contrite for the injustices you heaped upon your child at a time when love and support should have been offered. How do you let go of the shame and forgive yourself?

Shame can have many causes. It can come from failure to live up to your own ideals or standards, which makes you feel flawed at the core level. It appears when you feel inadequate in your ability to unconditionally love your child. But the first step to releasing the gridlock of shame is to own your negative actions toward your MIAC. You can't move forward until you acknowledge your misguided choices and choose to do better.

It's painful to look at your own inadequacies, and doing so will make you feel exposed and vulnerable. But remember that at the time of your actions, you had limited knowledge.

It takes time to break down the self-defeating thoughts that fester in the back of your mind. Many of those old messages come from your parents. If they didn't know what mental illness looked like, then you couldn't know what you'd never been taught. Be gentle with yourself as you learn about the disease and what appropriate responses look like. The steps below will help you along the way:

- Accept that you have a lot to learn about severe mental illness.
- When you know better, do better.
- Trust that it will take time to implement the knowledge you've gained.
- Try something different, and don't let fear stop you.
- Make notes, talk to a friend, or rehearse your new responses before you engage with your MIAC. Practice until you feel comfortable.
- If you don't feel you did your best, remember a time when your choices created a better result. Use this experience as a lesson for what doesn't work and try something else next time.
- Be gentle with yourself. New skills take time and practice to master.
- Have a positive attitude. You can do it. Changes for the better take time.

Because of the nature of severe MI, your experiences with your MIAC may not change much, even after you've learned appropriate responses to his behaviors. But this isn't about making changes to his actions or words; it's about modifying your responses. When you approach interactions with your MIAC with love and awareness for the challenges he faces, you'll be able to react with calmness and integrity. And when you don't, offer yourself grace.

When you free yourself from the unwanted shame, it gives you a better perspective and allows your MIAC the opportunity to stop being so defensive. Hurled threats and scornful words hurt everyone and create a barrier to trust, honesty, and cooperation. Decide to offer your child patience, emotional support, and compassion, regardless of his behavior. Of course, that doesn't mean you condone or allow violence or abuse.

Navigating MI

I was disgusted by my actions and the way I spoke to my son prior to his diagnosis. His erratic moods and irrational behaviors provoked me to lash out and hurl threats and ultimatums. I'm ashamed and appalled at most of what I said and did in my attempt to get B to conform and modify his actions. When he denied his illness, then I assumed his poor choices were deliberate. His disrespect, constant profanity, and use of alcohol and illegal drugs seemed perverse and within his control.

As your child moves from adolescence into young adulthood, you expect and demand a higher level of maturity and accountability. You foresee a few incidents of inappropriate behavior but assume your child will learn from those mistakes. What you least expect is the deterioration of rational judgment as your child heads into young adulthood. Unable to interpret your child's behaviors, you ignore the first ominous signs of his disintegrating mental health. Blatant disregard for rules or acceptable conduct, an inability to hold a job or attend college, a fascination with more and more risky behaviors regardless of discipline or natural consequences, your child could now be described as a delinquent.

Unable to interpret your child's behaviors, you ignore the first ominous signs of his disintegrating mental health.

My son's diagnosis of severe mental illness landed like a swift punch in the stomach. I was blindsided, broken. All the cruel and callous words I'd flung at him over the years came back in a flood of regret and remorse.

At last, there was a reason for all the insanity. Now I needed to up my game and make better choices with my responses. His disease controlled him, but it didn't need to control my behavior. Even with that awareness, frustration still got the better of me many times as I strove to learn the depth of his limitations.

Why didn't the psychiatrists explain how damaged his brain was or tell me what to expect? Better yet, what *not* to expect? This new reality felt like navigating a minefield while wearing a blindfold.

I didn't have the experience to do it gracefully, and neither do you. So, consider asking your MIAC for forgiveness. It'll boost the trust and acceptance between you and your child.

His disease controlled him, but it didn't need to control my behavior.

As you learn more, your responses will be much different. Look underneath the disease and search for your child that's hidden amidst the rubble of his damaged brain. The only thing you should expect from your MIAC is respect. Not every situation requires a response or an agreement from you. Learn to walk away when there's no chance of a rational conversation. It isn't your child who attacks or threatens you; it's his disease/addiction. Hold yourself to a higher level of personal integrity. You now understand that when you humiliate your child, you also shame yourself.

Change Your Awareness

Now that you know your child's diagnosis, it's time to move from unconscious incompetence to conscious competence. When you can see through a new lens, you'll be able to offer empathy, kindness, and sensitivity. Be patient with yourself. It takes time and practice to feel comfortable making mindful choices rather than knee-jerk reactions. Where are you on the competence scale described below?

Unconscious Incompetence

Everyone begins here. This is when you don't know what you don't know. You don't have information about how mental illness makes your child act, so you don't know your MIAC can't choose his behaviors. And you can't make different choices because you don't know there's a better way.

Conscious Incompetence

You realize there are things that you don't know. You've learned about mental illness, but now you need to learn how to respond to your MIAC in a new way. You'll continue to learn as much as you can about MI.

Unconscious Competence

You're learning to do the right things, and you know some better approaches to interacting with your MIAC. Sometimes you do it right, but not all the time. It's hit or miss regarding compassion toward your child.

Conscious Competence

You know what's best, and you also know how to go about it. You understand MI and the ways it presents itself: erratic behaviors, odd mannerisms, bizarre ideology, paranoia, delusions, irrational thoughts. Now you're able to respond in a calm, empathetic way. You realize what your MIAC is and isn't capable of doing, and you know the most effective ways to respond.

Reactions vs. Responses

When I started moving up the scale toward conscious competence, I noticed that I'd changed the way that I asked B questions. I was bringing more respect and dignity to my fact-finding, and my tone and inflection were transformed from making accusations to authentic inquiry. Here are some examples:

Reactions	Responses
What's your problem?	Tell me why you're doing that.
Why don't you listen?	What keeps you from hearing what I say?
Where's your logic?	Tell me why you chose to do that.
How can you possibly think that's okay?	Explain your reasoning.
When are you going to get a job?	What prevents you from working?
I can never trust you.	I have a difficult time believing what you say.
Stop arguing with me.	What would you like to do?
Have you lost your mind?	Your choices don't seem very rational. Can I offer some input?
Your room is a pigsty.	Why is it so difficult to stay on top of chores?
I can't believe you got fired again.	Why is it so hard for you to keep a job?
Get the f… out of my house!	I need you to leave, or I may need to call 911.

I shift nervously from foot to foot as I stand in the empty hallway and wait for my son to emerge from the locked psych unit. He was involuntarily committed nineteen days ago, and the doctor decided he's well enough to come home.

I'm not sure what to expect, but the person who comes through that door is far from well. He's wearing the same clothes he arrived in, he's unwashed and unshaven, he carries his clean clothes in a trash bag. It's been over a month since he's bathed or brushed his teeth. Talking in rhythms and codes, he has no idea how long he's been hospitalized. This is better?

The nurse hands over a release form to sign and a one-page sheet of information, which includes his diagnosis, a note to follow up with a psychiatrist, and a one-month supply of psych meds. That's all. No doctor recommendations, no suggestions for what to do if he becomes psychotic again—nothing.

What's supposed to happen now? Inpatient treatment was supposed to make him better, and this isn't better. I worked so hard to get him into the hospital and to keep him in there long enough for me to obtain guardianship, but now what? He's just as sick as the day he went in. The only difference is that I'm now legally responsible for his care. I've just paid fifteen hundred dollars for the right to make my son's decisions for him and have no idea where to turn for help or what choices to make for him to receive the care he desperately needs.

I pick up the trash bag of clean clothes, and we head for the car.

Personal Power

If you continually see yourself as a victim of circumstance, you'll be stuck, powerless, and reluctant to stand up for what's in your best interest. The first step to changing a miserable situation is to recognize that you can make different choices. Of course, you feel overwhelmed when you're thrown headfirst into the dismal abyss of MI, but to continue to do the same thing over and over and expect a different outcome is the definition of insanity. You feel so overwhelmed, so confused, and so heartbroken that inertia sets in, and because you don't know which direction you want to go, you don't move at all. How can you make changes when your MIAC refuses help?

As you take back your personal power, you can begin to make more effective decisions. You'll be able to create a happier life for yourself when you embrace your inner warrior.

Some days it feels like the quicksand of your child's irrationality may pull you under. You aren't able to make effective choices for yourself or your child. It seems easier to stay stuck than to put forth the effort necessary to take control of your life. What if you make the wrong decisions? What if things get worse? Yes, you're miserable, but it's become a comfortable place. Change feels too scary when your world is filled with catastrophe. You want to cling to what you know, even if it's unhealthy and dysfunctional. Every day there's another fire to put out, another obstacle blocking your progress.

You want to cling to what you know, even if it's unhealthy and dysfunctional.

You may feel too overwhelmed to add one more item to your to-do list. To take that step back and evaluate your choices boggles your mind. But the longer you stay stuck, the more effort it takes to pull yourself out. It may take a total collapse to bring you to your senses, perhaps a financial crisis, a decline of your physical or mental health, or problems in a relationship to finally cause you to wake and realize you need to start making better choices.

If it seems like climbing Mount Everest to get to the changes you want, break it into small steps. Don't fret about how long it will take to reach the top, just take one new step each day. If you've always said or done (*fill in the blank*) in a particular situation, now do (*fill in the blank*) instead. It will feel scary as hell, and you may want to procrastinate, but I promise that if you take no action, in a year, you'll still be miserable.

Don't be surprised if your new choices cause your MIAC to push back. That's expected. Following through is so important. If your child knows you'll buckle under pressure, then your new choices won't stick. Change is hard—for everyone—but it's the only way to create a different, better reality for you and your MIAC.

You'll have to shift the way you look at things before you can change the way you react. When you follow old belief patterns, you *react* to a situation rather than *respond*. When you react, you do so without forethought, conscious evaluation, or circumspection. But when you respond to circumstances, you take time to pause, consider, and weigh your words and actions. A mindful response allows you to step outside the incident and choose the best way to reply. It gives you an outsider's perspective and offers you the opportunity to remove your emotions from the situation.

When you change the way you address issues, you create space for your MIAC to make better choices. Your changed responses compel your ill child to do the same, although at first, you may receive a backlash of anger and resentment. This is a good thing because it means you've gotten his attention. If he has the capacity to recognize the change and have a negative reaction, then it also means he may have the capacity to adopt more positive behaviors.

A mindful response allows you to step outside the incident and choose the best way to reply. It gives you an outsider's perspective and offers you the opportunity to remove your emotions from the situation.

The best way to diffuse, alter, or manage the outcome is to control the situation. This isn't manipulation; it's redirection. Similar to a train diverted to a different track to avoid a head-on collision, you alter your responses to affect a change in your MIAC. Most important is that even if your child doesn't change at all, the way you see the situation and the way you handle it will. That's the ultimate outcome, to view your child's actions differently and realize you have choices.

You're the only one who keeps yourself stuck. Nobody else controls your choices, attitudes, or responses. Once more, *you're the only one who controls you.* If you allow your MIAC's actions or words to influence you, then you're choosing to let him have power over you. You still make the choice, but you blame it on your child. If you're stuck and unable to change your behaviors, it's because you choose to use your child and his illness as an excuse to stay miserable.

As much as you'd like to, you can't control another person's actions. You'd love to wake up tomorrow and have your MIAC make good choices, behave in appropriate ways, and lead a happy, fulfilled life, but that's outside your control. Will you choose to stay miserable simply because you can't fix your child's life? Or will you choose to live your life to the fullest to honor what your MIAC has lost?

If you're stuck and unable to change your behaviors, it's because you choose to use your child and his illness as an excuse to stay miserable.

It feels awesome to know that you control what happens in your life. You don't control what someone else does, but you do control how you respond, or even if a response is necessary. Once you own your power over your life, everything changes for the better. You stop waiting for your MIAC to get it together.

I bolt upright, awake to a sound in the house. My neck hairs are on alert as I decide what to do. I sneak into the kitchen.
"It's only me," B whispers, as I let loose a scream.

"You scared me! What are you doing in here? It's 3:30 in the morning."

He squints as I turn the light on and says, "I was looking for a snack."

B has no sense of boundaries and will enter my condo any time he needs something, even with constant reminders to call me first. The locked door isn't a deterrent. If I ask for thirty minutes of quiet, he knocks or calls until I answer. It never ends, this constant need for him to be in my space. I can't go on like this and need to make changes to build in personal time and space for myself.

Back to the drawing board for more ideas on how to make this work for both of us.

Neglecting my physical, emotional, and mental health, I couldn't sleep, ate junk, and made no time for relaxation or fun. It didn't take long to feel the effects of these unhealthy habits, but I continued to ignore the signs. Struggle and misery started to feel normal, and I didn't consider there could be another way. If I attended to my needs, that would mean stepping away from the drama and turmoil of my child's illness. That felt like a betrayal of my mother code of ethics.

One day I simply couldn't do anymore. In terrible shape, every area of my life in decline, I was in a free fall. How was it possible that I hadn't hit bottom yet? I'd spent so much time, energy, and money to no avail. My child is still ill, and now I'm headed toward a breakdown myself. I've wasted years of my life trying to make my MIAC well. Was the price I paid worth it?

B's delusions and paranoia around food and water make this an ongoing battle. At times, he refuses to eat what they fix at the home where he now lives and won't even consider drinking tap water. It's been building for a while, me delivering food and cases of water. Today he decides he needs a particular brand of water from a specific store, and I lose it.

"I'm done!" I scream, giving him a tongue lashing. I give him some money and tell him to figure it out.

"You won't see me for two weeks. I'm taking a break."

"I can't even call you?" he asks.

"Nope. I'm done with your delusions. You can have them, but they don't need to be mine. I'm done being at your beck and call, giving in to all your demands."

As I drive home, I think about how poorly I handled that. This is what happens when you ignore your own needs. The stress builds until, one day, you pop your lid and scream at your MIAC.

When it comes down to either your care or your child's, you must choose yourself. If you don't, you'll do what I did and lose it over a simple request for bottled water. You need to be healthy in order to be an effective caregiver for your MIAC—and to be a decent person.

Try creating a list of the causes of your poor health, and then add in small positive changes.

- More healthy meals, less fast food
- More water, less soda and alcohol
- More movement, less mindless TV and social media
- More sleep, less foggy thoughts
- More quiet time/meditation, decreased anxiety
- More connection to a higher power, less loneliness and helplessness
- Save more money, worry less about bills
- More play, less misery
- More time with friends and family, less isolation

Making one simple change each day will add up to massive change over time. Now and then, you'll fall back into the old habits, and that's okay. Just acknowledge that your choices aren't the best today, be gentle with yourself, and do better tomorrow.

When you stop trying so hard, it forces your MIAC to be accountable for his own behavior and health. Focus on yourself; it compels your child to take ownership for his words and actions. At first, you may feel guilty for not doing more, but remind yourself that the things you gave up didn't work and won't change your child's disease. If something significantly enhances your MIAC's health, then do it if possible. Otherwise, you're just trying to soothe your own feelings of loss and inadequacy. If you put yourself first, it will strengthen your relationships and give you back your life.

Inappropriate Behavior

> We're in the ER. All the psych treatment rooms are full. We sit under the harsh lights in a narrow hallway. For safety, it's mandatory that each patient change into scrubs and turn over their clothes and personal possessions to the security guard. Because of his paranoia, my son thinks there might be a spy cam in the bathroom, so he decided that it's better to change right where he stands. I turn to see him naked in the crowded hallway.
>
> "What are you doing? Go into the bathroom."
>
> But he won't listen to reason. The staff pays no attention, but I feel uncomfortable and exposed amongst all these strangers. I tell myself, *Breathe. This isn't the worst experience I'll have with my son.*
>
> I want to close my eyes and wake up in a normal world, away from the glaring lights, stark hallways, and grotesque abnormalities of mental illness.

It took a long time to grasp the full spectrum of symptoms associated with a severe mental disease. I vacillated between embarrassment for myself and feeling embarrassed for my son. While many things seemed within his control, I had to understand that wasn't always true. Yes, he could sometimes pull things together for a few minutes or even an hour, but that's an illusion of normality that he couldn't maintain because I wanted him to. I had to see his behaviors as they were—symptoms of a catastrophic brain disease.

I struggled with embarrassment whenever we were in public together. He would talk to himself, try to convince me he was being followed, or behave in bizarre, irrational ways. Because he had no personal hygiene, he looked like a homeless person I'd picked up off the side of the road. What would others think if I allowed him to act out and behave this way? Sometimes people would shy away from us, pull their children closer, or simply shoot a look of disgust in our direction. While I'm sure some of that condemnation was pure fabrication on my part, there were many people who judged us. I wanted to reprimand him for acting out, wanted to be invisible, wanted to stop the "crazy" bus and get off.

The ability to pull things together for a few minutes or even an hour is an illusion of normality that can't be maintained by desire alone.

And yet, my MIAC has never shown any embarrassment over his disheveled clothes; dirty and uncut hair; or random, disjointed speech. Due to the severity of his MI, he may be completely unaware of how he's perceived. He certainly doesn't understand that he may frighten or make others ill at ease.

I've never stopped going out in public with my son, but many times I've felt the need to explain his odd appearance and behaviors to strangers. I told myself I did this to protect him, but if I'm being completely honest, I did it for me. It reduced my own feelings of discomfort.

Now, instead of trying to make excuses for him, I focus on how he interacts with others. He's always polite and friendly, always offers a hello, and says thanks to everyone. Instead of trying to make him be someone he isn't, I applaud his courage and ability to go out in public even though he's different. I rarely notice how other people react. My attention is focused on my son, and I appreciate our time together.

Your MIAC's capacity to be out in the world may change from day to day. Just like you don't always feel the same every day, neither does he. Some days you may be more tired, feel a little anxious, or be angry about something. It's the same for MIACs. To expect perfect compliance and best behavior every day is ridiculous. Look for the glimmer of your child hidden under the disease and offer empathy.

If your MIAC is aggressive, violent, or seems to have no redemptive qualities, it may be a challenge to embrace this attitude. I urge you to look for the small glimpses of the child you remember. If you can't find any, recognize that the distressing symptoms you see are a manifestation of the disease and remember your child struggles daily beneath the burden of severe MI. Is it possible to love the tortured soul from a distance? While you may not condone his behaviors, are you still able to distinguish between your child and the disease and offer compassion and sympathy?

Refuse to be embarrassed by your MIAC. It's the only way to stop stigma. It has to begin with you and me. If we, the mothers of MIACS, remain strong in the face of discrimination, then others will begin to learn from our example. It takes a village to raise a child, and it takes an army of empowered moms to make changes in how mental illness is viewed and treated. Change begins with the way *we* see our children and how *we* feel about our role in their care and treatment. While our MIACs aren't always able to conduct themselves appropriately, we have control over how we choose to respond. Let's act on behalf of our ill children and begin to remove the misperceptions of MI. Let's become badass warriors.

Refuse to be embarrassed by your MIAC.
It's the only way to stop stigma.

We're at a family get-together, and B says he wants to live with me. I explain the house rules.

"No drugs, no illegal herbs, and no alcohol if you want to live in my house. And if that's not okay with you, find another place to live."

My other adult child insists, "Mom, you can't say that because he has nowhere to go and will end up homeless."

It's her opinion that I need to make him follow the rules. Ha, again! How do you make an irrational adult follow the rules?

My response is, "Can you make your two-year-old go potty on the toilet? You have less control than you realize. Besides, I know B. He's resourceful and will find somewhere to crash."

Earlier, I talked about how my relationship with my mother—or lack thereof—affected how I mothered my own children. Outdated parenting beliefs can color your perspective and decisions about your MIAC's care, too. You probably react with behavior habits learned from your parents, giving no thought to the validity of the ideals you were raised with. That is, until life goes sideways and you're forced to reevaluate your parenting principles.

What beliefs, values, and morals did your parents instill in you? While these can vary from family to family, there are many shared parenting rules. Society dictates certain appropriate behaviors, and individual families may add what they consider acceptable. Some rules are very clear and concise, while others can be subject to interpretation. You tend to follow in your parents' footsteps and mother your children the way you've been raised, even if you didn't like your parents' attempts to control or modify your behaviors.

Cultural differences also come into play when you dole out discipline. In some cultures, physical punishment is acceptable. Other parents may resort to more covert penalties. They may withhold love and affection, withdraw privileges, or use public shame. What types of discipline did your parents impose upon you as a child?

I've listed some ways that parents attempt to force appropriate behavior on their children. Some spank, slap, whip, yell, scream, make accusations of family betrayal, ground from activities and friends, humiliate in public or private, take away allowance or privileges, give the silent treatment, make the child feel invisible, threaten to remove the child from the house, use physical or emotional intimidation, or withhold affection. Many of these are dysfunctional and create further problems. Were any of these punishments effective in changing your misbehavior? How did being punished make you feel? How did it impact your relationship with your parents? How many of these tactics do you use with your children and continue to use as they reach adulthood? Have any punishments worked with your MIAC's inappropriate behaviors, or have they led to more problems?

It's impossible to manage an irrational adult's conduct. When that adult has a teenage mentality, the process can be a daunting fiasco. Most of the behavior modifications you can use with healthy brains do not affect a MIAC. That's why you must evaluate your parenting techniques and decide if they need to be updated. It's essential to figure out if what you've always done still serves you and your family.

> *Most of the behavior modifications you can use with healthy brains do not affect a MIAC.*

Arguments, threats, or coercion won't make a significant change. Praise doesn't work; neither does intimidation. Nothing in your standard parenting toolbox is effective. How do you get through to someone who's paranoid, delusional, aggressive, or irrational? It's possible to do so, but it takes effort on your part to change the old patterns and form new ones. You must release your limited mindset in order to gain a new perspective.

In the beginning, when I was in public with my MIAC, I felt like the main act at a circus sideshow. All I wanted was to hide under the nearest rock. This led to feeling unworthy. At my wit's end, none of my efforts to reduce my son's aberrant behaviors worked.

It never dawned on me that I needed to rethink my choices. Why didn't I see that I couldn't reason with a mentally ill adult sooner? What made me think I could ever control his behavior, especially since he had a diagnosed thought disorder? Maybe I was the delusional one.

Ask yourself if your inherited parenting rules line up with your personal values. Do you really care what others think? Does it matter? What behavior guidelines are important to you and your family? When you take an honest look, it all seems ludicrous. It takes strength and forgiveness to look at the way your parents raised you, see the limitations they learned from their parents, accept that they did their best, and decide to put aside those rules and learn better ways to communicate with your child.

You don't need to think your parents were wrong. You can believe they did the best they could, and every choice they made was because they loved you. When you change generational patterns, other family members may feel challenged. You may feel alone in your desire to learn different parenting skills. When you break cycles of dysfunctional communication, it stirs up emotions, resistance, and defenses. Even unhealthy ways can feel more comfortable than attempts to try new, untested strategies.

There's a psychological model called *Choice Theory* created by William Glasser. The premise is that all human behavior is chosen and that we choose our behaviors in an effort to satisfy five basic needs that are common to all humanity. They are:

- Safety & survival
- Love and belonging
- Power
- Freedom
- Fun

The theory teaches that the only person you control is yourself. You can compel another to do what you want through force or threat, but that will have minimal positive results. You can provide your MIAC with information and allow him to choose his path. But it's always up to him to decide how to respond or what actions to take.

All your problems with your MIAC result from your attempts to control his behavior in these negative ways: you criticize, blame, complain, nag, threaten, punish, and bribe. Instead, replace the negative communication with these positive suggestions. You can offer support and encouragement, listen, accept, trust, respect, and negotiate differences. By doing so, you encourage your child to feel more in control of his life. Asking him the following questions enables him to define his goals and then accept that it's his responsibility to pursue them:

- What do you want?
- What are you doing to get what you want?
- How has that worked for you?
- If you'd like to be happier and more successful, are you prepared to change your behavior in order to get what you want?

All your problems with your MIAC result from your attempts to control his behavior . . .

With severe MI, your child may know these answers but be unable to follow through to achieve positive results. In that case, it may become your responsibility to see that your MIAC is given the necessary support to achieve his highest potential. You also need to let go of your expectations for your child to change or live up to your standards. Sometimes the best you can do is wish him well and allow him to find his way, learn from his consequences, stop the constant bailouts, and hope for a different outcome. Just because it's apparent to you that he needs help doesn't mean he agrees with your assessment.

Improved parenting skills will make you feel happier and freer. New communication skills and an updated parenting philosophy make the day-to-day care of your MIAC much easier. Your interactions will be calmer, and you'll no longer need to make your child conform to rules that don't improve your relationship. You won't feel compelled to do everything possible to make your MIAC see things from your perspective. Your child's actions and words are a manifestation of his disease, and your expectations for certain behaviors from a damaged brain are your problem, not his. Forgive yourself for your poor parenting skills, and honor yourself now for your willingness to learn a better way.

> *Your child's actions and words are a manifestation of his disease, and your expectations for certain behaviors from a damaged brain are your problem, not his.*

Your expectations for your MIAC will change as you recognize what he can and can't control, but you also need to have certain rules that are set in concrete. Here is a list of my non-negotiable rules:

- I don't allow drugs or alcohol in my house.
- I won't tolerate disrespect.
- I will honor his opinion and actions as long as his ideas don't involve harming himself, someone else, or pertain to an illegal activity.
- Physical violence is never tolerated. I will take the necessary action if I feel he's a threat to himself or someone else.
- I will make sure he has what he needs. I won't buy his love.
- I won't allow him to guilt me into doing anything that goes against my values.
- I will agree to disagree without consequences.
- I will love my son just as he is.

Now that you know what to expect from your MIAC and have better tools for responding to the chaos, it's time to move ahead. Read on to learn ways to move beyond the diagnosis, beyond your apathy, and beyond your resistance to find a way back into a positive life.

Visualization Journey

Sit comfortably in a quiet place. Close your eyes.

Breathe in and out slowly to the count of three several times until you feel yourself begin to relax.

Visualize yourself in a field. In the center is a giant magnolia tree. You walk closer until you can touch the cool, smooth leaves. You breathe in the sweet scent of the flowers. Look up into the branches. You'll see a bird's nest with two newly hatched baby robins and one egg still unbroken. Momma bird chirps from a nearby branch and jumps about, worried and protective of her babies.

Climb under the low branches of this old tree and sit down. Lean against the enormous trunk. It feels rough, but warm beneath your fingers. You're in a hidden paradise, the perfect location to connect with ancient mother wisdom. All around you are dark-green leaves, tight unopened buds, and radiant, white magnolia blossoms. The aroma is comforting and familiar.

Feel the protection the overhanging branches offer, feel the sturdiness of the trunk, imagine the history this tree has seen, see the roots going deep, deep, deep into the ground to feed and nourish this magnificent magnolia.

As you lean against the trunk, imagine you can grow your own trunk; it comes down from your abdomen and digs deep down into the ground. Allow the root of your trunk to wrap three times around a shiny crystal at the center of the earth. This beautiful quartz crystal offers a golden light that radiates up and inside your body.

The spirit of an old grandmother emerges from the light. She could be your grandmother, or she could be unfamiliar. It doesn't matter. She comes with the offer of love and acceptance as she embraces you in a warm welcoming hug. She holds you tight in her arms, strokes your hair with her gnarled hands, and asks you to tell her all your fears, failures, and heartaches of being a mother. She rocks you quietly as she listens and wipes away your tears. As she continues to rock, you feel a healing energy wash over and through you.

You can feel the presence of all the grandmothers and mothers that have come before you. They're a reminder that you don't walk this path alone. As you heal your mother wounds, you also heal those who came before you and those who will come after.

Grandmother whispers softly into your ear the exact words you need to hear to feel like a worthy, powerful mom. She reaches into her pocket and pulls out a small gift just for you. It is a priceless token to remind you of her love and acceptance. You hold it in your hand as her strength and integrity fills you. You place your gift reverently in your pocket for safekeeping.

You give a deep sigh and thank Grandmother for her wisdom and her gift. You will treasure it always. It'll be a reminder of the love and acceptance she shared with you. Grandmother gives you one final embrace and releases you with these words: "Everything you need is inside of you always. Come back and visit any time you need a reminder of the love that fills you."

Slowly and steadily, you move from under the tree and walk back across the field in the direction of home. You can still feel the companionship of the other women. They will remain with you in spirit, offering you support and guidance whenever it's needed. All you need to do is call to them in your mind.

"Oh, grandmothers and mothers past and future, please send me your love in my time of great need."

Open your eyes and journal any messages you received. What words did Grandmother whisper? What gift did you receive? What fears and failures did you release?

Climbing Out of the Rabbit Hole

We are sisters
Trapped in darkness
Lost amidst the chaos
We mirror our MIAC's dysfunction
We look for better ways
We are sisters

What does "going down the rabbit hole" mean? This metaphor comes from *Alice in Wonderland* by Lewis Carroll, a story that most have heard. Going down the rabbit hole means you're entering a situation or beginning a journey that is problematic, complex, or chaotic—and becomes increasingly so as it unfolds. When your adult child is diagnosed with a severe brain disease, you enter a nightmarish wonderland. You've stumbled into a bizarre, distorted, alternate reality, much like Alice's rabbit hole. This chapter shows you how to climb out of it.

As my MIAC's symptoms became more acute, I remember saying, "I love you, but I won't go down the rabbit hole with you." While my rational brain recognized the need to keep my feet planted firmly on the ground, I unconsciously descended into my own dark hole of despair. Only through hindsight could I see that my emotions and actions had mirrored those of my ill child, not to the same degree of dysfunction, but most assuredly an echo of the changes that his illness created.

When we mirror someone, it's a subconscious imitation of their attitudes and behaviors. Why would you mirror your MIAC? As a mom, you have a strong connection and desire to help your child succeed, and when he becomes ill, you reflect his symptoms as a way to understand his experiences. Or you might do so as a way to carry some of the burden and distress for him.

> *. . . my emotions and actions had mirrored those of my ill child . . . an echo of the changes that his illness created.*

Here are some examples of how this played out in my life.

- My child had irrational beliefs—I had irrational beliefs that I could reason my child into better, more appropriate behaviors.
- My child was delusional—I had unrealistic expectations that if I tried hard enough, I could fix my child's damaged brain.
- My child was disoriented—I was confused and felt out of touch with reality. I'd been dumped into a new world without sense or rules.
- My child hallucinated—I fantasized about the day when everything would get back to normal.
- My child was anxious and afraid—I was also anxious, fearful, and uneasy about what would happen next. I walked on eggshells, in a state of perpetual high alert, always prepared for the next potential crisis.
- My child was depressed—I was despondent over the loss of my bright, healthy child and the prospect of what long-term care would look like.
- My child acted erratically—my behaviors were uncertain as I wandered in unfamiliar territory and tried to find answers.
- My child was apathetic about moving forward—I became disinterested in things that used to bring me pleasure as I remained tethered to my MIAC.

- My child was depressed about his future—I was discouraged over the lack of a future for my son.
- My child was angry at being robbed of a full life—I was furious at the obvious lack of funds and resources available to treat MI.
- My child showed intense frustration—my frustration revolved around how difficult it was to obtain care for an adult child.
- My child felt cheated by this disease—I felt cheated out of the opportunity to see my child enjoy life as a fully functional adult.
- My child felt like a victim of an unloving God—I felt like a casualty of unpredictable circumstances that would affect the rest of my life.
- My child felt he'd lost the freedom to make choices for himself—I felt like I'd lost the freedom to have a life of my own.
- My child was addicted to alcohol—I was addicted to my need to make him well.
- My child felt like a victim of an uncaring society—I was the victim in the story I told about his mental illness.
- My child was socially and emotionally isolated—I hid from the world, afraid to share what others couldn't begin to understand.

There were certain behaviors of his that I didn't mirror: aggression, violence, illicit drug or alcohol use, illegal activities, and irresponsible spending habits. I also kept my job, maintained friendships, and kept my home clean and orderly.

The Stories I Told

Once I was aware of my plunge into the rabbit hole, I couldn't let it continue. While my MIAC might be stuck on replay, that didn't need to be my future. With the necessary tools, I worked through and released my unhealthy patterns and replaced them with more positive skills to cope with the stress caused by this dark turn of events.

I started to notice that when someone asked about my children, I always gave a bright overview of my daughter's wonderful life. "She's a kindergarten teacher, married to a great guy. They have four beautiful children, and live on a farm, etc." I elaborated on how well she managed everything and how much I enjoyed our visits. Most times, that's all I'd say.

"Do you have any other children?"

My short response was, "I have a son who has a mental illness." Sometimes people would ask me to elaborate.

"He's diagnosed with schizophrenia and lives in a residential care facility about thirty minutes away."

If asked more questions, I would say, "Yes, he takes medications, and no, they don't take away his symptoms. He's not well enough to work."

One day I realized how different my emotions were behind each of these stories. There was a sense of warmth and joy when I discussed my daughter and her family, but when I told my son's story, I was restrained and somber. His was a story without color. My daughter's life wasn't always happy and perfect, but that's how I chose to see it. On the other hand, my son's life wasn't always miserable and bleak, but that's the way I chose to tell it.

I was shocked by how much this discounted my son's life. The disease has taken a lot from him, but he still has remnants of his former self. He is very compassionate toward others, loves to draw, is a formidable Scrabble player, and has remarkable intelligence.

This is my story now; it's one of empathy, connection, and kindness.

We stop to eat lunch in a busy restaurant. B gets up to refill his drink and doesn't come back. My nephew returns to the table.

"Hey, where's B?" I ask.

"Oh, he decided to help a young, disabled man fill his soda and find the right lid."

When B comes back, I say, "I hear you helped someone."

"Yeah, Mom. Everybody walked past and ignored him. He just needed a little help."

My heart fills with pride for my child, so impaired but still able to show compassion to another struggling soul.

When a child is diagnosed with a serious illness, parents—especially moms—can become stuck in the tragedy of their story. You create a story around the pain and loss, and it works to bind and hold everything together. The problems come when you don't, won't, or can't move forward. As the mom of a MIAC, you can and do hold tight to your stories as a reminder of who your child used to be and what should have been. But if you stay trapped in that experience, you lose the ability to move on and create a positive version of your current reality.

The problems come when you don't, won't, or can't move forward.

Your story is simply a narrative of your experiences. All stories contain some truth and some fabrication. You construct your story from bits of your history, current events, and possible future scenarios. Stories can tell a lot about how you choose to view what happens in your life. Like a book, your life unfolds in chapters. Some are happy, some bring disappointment, some are tragic, and some are joyous. To cling to only one page or one chapter denies you the opportunity to experience your book in its entirety. And this choice affects not only you but also everyone connected to you. In essence, you hold everyone hostage, stuck to your page of tragedy and grief. If others choose to move on, it will likely be without you.

It's hard to let go of what should have been. It's even more challenging to rewrite your story from a brighter perspective. You can choose to see your entire book as a catastrophic failure or decide that one hardship will be only a single page in your life story. It's all about attitude and gratitude. No one is promised a life without challenges, but you have the option to navigate life with grace, despite its challenges. The choice is yours. It won't change the circumstances, but it will change how the rest of your life plays out.

Change Your Mind / Change Your Story

You're the only one who can turn a page in your book. You're not the victim of your story but its author and creator. When you shift the perspective from *impotence* to *competence*, transformation begins. It's not easy to change your viewpoint, but the work comes with a wondrous reward. When you change your innermost thoughts, the world around you shifts in the most magical ways. How you decide to feel about any given situation moves you from being trapped in the event to becoming a conscious observer who has the power to define the experience.

Your world manifests from your perspective. So, how do you change the way you view the world? You start by making a decision to see things with a different attitude. You begin to rewrite the story you tell when someone asks about your child. Your words and mindset create the tone and mood of your experiences and circumstances. Consider what keeps you stuck in your story. What do you get from clinging to the old narrative of your saga? What do you want from the listener?

You're not the victim of your story but its author and creator.

If you hold tight to something horrific, you relive the experience again and again. Every time you tell your story, it cements the pain and heartache into your very DNA. In reality, the event is just a blip in your overall life story. Of course, I'm not discounting the significance of that blip or the dramatic way it changed every aspect of your life, but if you don't move on, you become lost in the pain, and that becomes the central focus of your story.

It may seem impossible to do a total rewrite of your story, but you can add an effective "but" to it.

- My child is diagnosed with MI, but he's maintained his sense of humor.
- My child is diagnosed with MI, but he loves going out to eat at his favorite restaurant.
- My child is diagnosed with MI, but he's still respectful to everyone he meets.

Focus on the good that still remains in your child. But how do you do this when your MIAC is violent, insolent, or homeless? Try this:

- My child is diagnosed with MI. He's not in my life right now, but he's always in my heart.
- My child is diagnosed with MI, and our relationship is strained, but I respect that he tries his best under the circumstances.
- My child is diagnosed with MI and is incarcerated, but I'm hopeful that this experience will be helpful to his growth.

When you add the "but," you move past the initial tragedy and create a more positive perspective.

A friend once asked me what I achieved by holding on to my sad story. Who did it benefit? What harm did it cause to keep it going? That became an *aha!* moment for me, and I took a hard look at how I described my life.

The story I'd been telling perpetuated the idea of being stuck in uncontrollable circumstances. I realized that playing the victim didn't serve my child or me. It held us captive and left us both powerless. I blamed my MIAC for my miserable life when in reality, neither of us had control over what had occurred. Telling my tragic story prevented me from offering support and advocacy to my child.

I'm not proud that I used my story to play the martyr role in an attempt to receive sympathy and compassion for a catastrophe only I understood. To repeat the same devastating story only enforced that the worst had happened, and it could never be changed.

I blamed my MIAC for my miserable life when in reality, neither of us had control over what had occurred.

Until I upgraded how I thought and talked about my situation, the outcome would remain the same. Who was the real victim here? It certainly wasn't me—it was my MIAC who'd lost the most.

When you hold on to the pain, confusion, and grief, it forces both of you to live in the past. Not only does it keep you trapped, but it limits your MIAC's ability to move forward too. Once you realize how your story denigrates your child's new reality, you can turn the page. Don't discount who your child is now. If you see your MIAC as *less than* because of his diagnosis, you're creating more trauma.

Find a healthier way to share your experiences. Make your child feel valued and worthy, even if his future looks drastically different than before. Move on, so you can give your MIAC an example to follow. Allow him to see past the diagnosis as well. Just like you mirror your child's symptoms, he mirrors the strategies you use to cope.

Before you speak, stop and think. Write down your new story. This will enable you to practice telling it until it becomes a habit. It may feel like you've dismissed the enormity of what's happened to your child and the degree to which everyone's life has been affected, but over time, you'll recognize that it's all about the weight you attach to it.

You can rewrite your story just like I did and make it about love, sorrow, pain, joy, pride, and heroes.

You can rewrite your story just like I did. My story is one of love and loss, pain and pride, fear and strength, heartache and heroism, and I wouldn't have it any other way.

Isolation

Social isolation can lead to loneliness, fear of others, and negative self-esteem. If you isolate yourself, you are in the rabbit hole, and both your mental and physical health can become damaged. With social isolation, you're less able to deal with stressful situations, you feel more depressed, and it may inhibit your ability to process information. Lack of social support makes you more vulnerable to mental health and substance abuse problems.

Emotional isolation occurs when you're unable or reluctant to share your emotions with others. Despite having a social network, you may feel isolated if you don't have someone to confide in who understands that your main focus is your MIAC's care. You may not share this pain with anyone other than your partner, which can lead to sadness and depression. Who can you turn to for support when the sky is falling?

As the mom of a MIAC, it's easy to become isolated and seek both social and emotional distance as a response to the stress and anxiety. The reasons you choose to isolate yourself are as complex as mental illness itself. Dropped into a strange world of unfamiliar behaviors, medical nightmares, and societal stigma can leave you wanting to withdraw. Isolation allows you to focus your energy on the crisis at hand without distractions. Furthermore, nobody understands the issues, the fights to get acceptable services, or the problems HIPAA laws create in this new reality. When you try to explain your challenges, many see you as an enabler who allows your child to act out. Family and friends may dismiss the severity or discount an MI diagnosis due to their lack of knowledge about the disease. Because of societal attitudes about mental health issues, it can feel unsafe to share what's happened to your child. Even the police don't see the psychosis in your MIAC's eyes when you call for help.

These are all valid reasons to separate yourself from the routines of life, but being isolated for extended periods of time keeps you ensnared in the vortex of the disease. Moms who stay isolated have more difficulty with their child's care, as well as their own. You can develop situational depression, anxiety, or both when your social and emotional needs go unmet. Mental health illnesses, such as dementia, social anxiety, and low self-esteem increase with extended isolation.

Social and emotional isolation can cause many physical problems, too, such as increased stress hormones and inflammation, high blood pressure and heart disease, and you can become more vulnerable to chronic illnesses such as Type 2 diabetes. Studies show social isolation can increase premature death by up to 30 percent. It's imperative to seek support if you feel alone, anxious, or begin to experience new physical ailments.

Isolation has a destructive effect on all your relationships. If you remain detached from others, it can lead to broken marriages, lost friendships, and fractured family dynamics. Isolation also creates issues in the workplace. If you're withdrawn and detached, it causes a ripple effect that impacts your ability to manage your responsibilities effectively.

You can't climb your way out of the rabbit hole without support from others. Isolation prevents you from being able to view your situation from a broader perspective. Your options become limited, and your ability to make positive decisions is diminished. It's impossible to make clear choices for your MIAC when you don't leave your living room or speak with anyone other than your ill child.

You can't climb your way out of the rabbit hole without support from others.

Finding Support

At first, I shared my new reality with only a few people who experienced similar circumstances. Unsolicited advice from family and strangers led me to be very protective of my child's struggles.

I felt minimized when I was blamed, judged, and ridiculed for my MIAC's behaviors and my choices for his care. It seemed that others didn't want to be more informed about MI and had no idea what an ongoing challenge it could be.

There aren't many places to turn to for open-ended support. The NAMI F2F class touched on many of these issues but offered no advice for the long haul. Support groups seemed very structured and didn't provide more than a few minutes for each member to share their story. What I hoped to find was continued guidance and examples of successful ways to navigate my MIAC's challenges while I continued to live a balanced, happy life of my own.

What a travesty to these courageous moms that society looks the other way in their time of greatest need. Millions of adults are lost to MI, but the moms and dads of these individuals also go untended. Angry, frustrated, and heartbroken, I scoured the internet in search of books that would be helpful. I didn't find any except for novels that railed against the injustices of treatment for the mentally ill, memoirs, and resources for medical professionals.

The desire to help my son pulled me out of my self-imposed solitude. I couldn't look for adequate supportive services if I didn't talk to others and share my struggles. I began to have discussions about mental illness in all kinds of situations and circumstances. I facilitated NAMI classes once or twice a year, which allowed me to talk with other moms going through similar struggles. It offered a safe space for us to discuss our emotions and fears and helped us feel understood and supported.

It soon became clear that I would need to persevere on my own. I reserved time on my calendar to work on personal growth, so I could bolster my inner strength and stability as I dealt with the daily ups and downs of my MIAC's struggles.

I won't tell you that everything changed overnight because it took hard work and determination to get where I am today. There were many times when I shared my MIAC's struggles only to hear from religious friends that more prayer would "get the devil out!" My family made sure to voice their opinions about the poor choices I'd made and to tell me that my parenting skills (or lack thereof) had caused my son's illness. Others stayed away, afraid to be around my MIAC.

Today, I don't allow the opinions of others to sway my decisions or impact my self-worth. I evaluate my goals daily and move in a direction that serves both me and my MIAC. Transition is a slow process, but one day—just like me—you'll look up and realize how far you've come.

No longer so fragile and broken, I opened up and began to share my family's story. This made me feel stronger and more secure in the world. It no longer felt necessary to stay isolated in order to maintain my personal well-being. I'd come to terms with my MIAC's diagnosis and our new normal, and I refused to stay hidden away because of shame or the fear of being misunderstood. Today I enjoy going out with friends and look forward to time spent doing activities I enjoy. I attend a monthly women's circle, take an online feminine wisdom class, work out with a personal trainer, eat out with friends, vacation yearly, participate in family time, and I don't feel bad if my son is unable to attend. Sometimes I still feel raw and exposed when I share my struggles, but those days are infrequent.

Transition is a slow process, but one day just like me, you'll look up and realize how far you've come.

You can't help yourself or your child if you hide from the world. To overcome the stigma of mental illness, you need to be front and center in this battle. When your MIAC sees you out in the world, it will hopefully propel him out of his own isolation. Only when enough of us can say that we refuse to hide in the shadows will society change the way it perceives mental illnesses and our children.

Your New Reality

When your entire world crashes down around you, when every aspect of your life is changed, when all your plans and hopes for the future are shattered, and you have a giant hole where your normal life used to be, only then do you understand what it feels like to be one of the walking wounded. Who are the walking wounded? They're moms like us who've been profoundly affected by their child's diagnosis but still manage to stumble along and try to get things done. Both mom and child are grievously impaired by the ramifications of serious MI, but only the child is treated, while the mom attempts to put her life back together with nothing but hope, courage, and a prayer.

Why isn't there anything to help these heroic moms who are desperate for support? Where are the pamphlets of information? Where are the offers of advice and encouragement? How is it that a disease that affects more people than cancer and heart disease combined doesn't address the impact it causes to the family?

You need a hand to help pull yourself out of the darkness. It's an arduous task to revive a life in the midst of daily pandemonium. Without guidance, how do you climb out of the rubble of what used to be a bright future? It can be weeks, months, and sometimes years before you're able to begin the slow process of reclaiming your own life. You can choose to begin the process today.

First, recognize where you are now. Second, understand that there's no going back to regain what's been lost. Finally, it's imperative that your new direction be based on current realities.

It can be challenging to decide how you want your life to look. Is there anything from your old life that you can salvage? You don't need to start from scratch, but be honest with yourself when you decide what stays and what needs to go. Honesty is the most important step if you're going to rebuild a life worth living, so don't bypass the significance that time and thought add to the process.

It might feel safer to hold on to memories rather than attempt to build a new life. You'd like a blueprint to follow. You want to know that the decisions you make are the right ones. Because there are no guarantees, you move in endless circles, stuck in a repeating cycle, each choice an echo of the one before—even when it's obvious they don't produce the results you hope for.

Trapped in a time warp, you hold tight to what no longer exists, unable to let go of what's gone. Why don't you want to move forward? Just because your child's stuck, does that mean you need to be as well? In order to find your way, you need to begin to live with purpose.

Don't wait for someone to give you the answers, to hold your hand, or tell you what you should do. There is no MI fairy godmother. But you do have an internal compass—your higher self—that shows you the direction to go. So, get quiet and listen to that small inner voice. If you determine where you want to end up, then before every step, ask yourself if this action will move you in that direction. If the answer is no, then it's simple: make another choice.

Get Moving

You don't need to have everything all figured out to begin. You just need to move. If you veer off course, it's easy enough to correct your path. Just take one step at a time. Start with small problems and make a decision. It doesn't matter if you make the perfect choice, as long as it's different from what you've done, because what you've been doing—which is nothing—hasn't worked. This exercise will propel you into action.

Weigh the pros and cons about the decisions you must make for your MIAC, then make a choice. If things don't work out the way you expect, then make another choice and another until you get to a place that works for both of you. Don't make decisions on a whim. Rely on your own intuition and disregard the opinions of well-intentioned family members and friends. As harsh as this may sound, this is *your* life, and you get to choose what's best for you and your child, regardless of what others think.

The ups and downs of MI are complex and can cause confusion, but you don't need to feel lost or adrift. The more decisions you make, the more comfortable you'll be as you listen to your instincts and inner conviction. Remember that your choices must be beneficial to you *and* your MIAC. Discounting your needs in favor of your child's always leads to resentment and anger. Both of you must be part of the equation when you make any decisions. Mental illness is a thought disorder, and while you can take your MIAC's opinion into account, you get the final say.

Discounting your needs in favor of your child's always leads to resentment and anger.

It's almost Christmas, and my MIAC is hospitalized again. He began hallucinating during Thanksgiving dinner.

"The pictures on the wall are moving. Listen, I taped the TV to prove to you that it's saying weird things. Here, listen. No, wait, they're messing with me. That's not what I heard!"

He's been in the lockdown unit for almost three weeks, and the staff pushes me to take him home. He's not well, but they need the bed for a sicker patient.

"It's not the hospital's job to see that he's well, just stabilized so he won't harm himself or someone else," they tell me.

"He just threatened to hurt his dad yesterday," I tell them, "so he needs to be here. He lives with his dad, who won't take B home in this condition. He needs to stay longer."

"Two more days," the nurse replies as she walks away.

I don't know what to do. He can't live with me because I work full time, and his dad won't take him back.

At my next visit, the head nurse pulls me aside and says, "He has to leave tomorrow."

"I don't know where he'll go," I tell him.

"You're his guardian. He's your responsibility, and if you refuse to take him, we'll have you arrested on endangerment charges."

"What? Did you just say you're going to have me arrested?"

"Yes," the nurse continues. "We need to release him, and you're the responsible party."

I've never even been inside a police station, let alone arrested. I feel sick. I feel so many things: anger, frustration, sadness, fear. I don't know what to do. How is this possible? I wait for hours before I'm able to talk with the doctor. I plead with him, "Do something more. My son isn't well enough to leave. I'm afraid for him."

The doctor says, "He can be enrolled in a day program through the hospital for monitoring," and with that in place, B's dad agrees to let B live with him.

He's still seriously ill, but I go along with this ridiculous plan because I don't have any other options. My MIAC isn't well enough to participate in any programs, but at least it will get him out of the house for a few hours each day.

Pivot

I understand why you feel both hopeless and helpless. Much of what happens to your adult child is out of your control.

Below are suggestions to help you pivot away from your hopeless feelings. You may experience only a few of these, or you could be feeling all of them. Be gentle with yourself and remember that you've struggled through a traumatic course of events. There's no right or wrong way to come to terms with a MIAC. It takes time and energy to change the way you look at and experience this adversity. Don't judge yourself. Your emotions are an outlet to release the pain of personal tragedy. It's normal to feel one or more of the following:

Alienated: Caring for a child with a chronic mental illness makes you feel peculiar and uncomfortable in normal social groups. When family and friends judge your parenting or criticize your choices, you feel all alone. With all-or-nothing thinking, you may assume that no one is on your side. Ask others if your emotions and thoughts are valid. It's a great way to feel more connected and realize you're not as alone as you might think. Make an effort to reach out to others who share similar circumstances; it allows you to feel less alienated.

Forsaken: Because others don't understand how mental illness manifests, many will distance themselves from you and your MIAC to avoid feeling uncomfortable. This may seem like you've been deserted when you need others most, but no situation is black and white. Have you really been abandoned, or does it just feel that way? While some people may have dropped away, it's important to recognize the people who continue to be there for you.

Doomed: Are you doomed, or does it just feel that way because things aren't going according to your plan? When you focus only on the bad, you may have the impression that your entire life is ill-fated. Create a gratitude journal to get out of this negative mindset. Agree to write down five or more things you're grateful for each day. This nudges you to think about the good that happens in your life every day.

Helpless: You feel helpless when a new problem arises, when you don't feel qualified to find a solution, or when you're overwhelmed by the lack of options. To change your perspective, reach out to others who experience similar problems. The choices available may not be the ones you hope for, but there are always choices. You're only helpless when you give up your search for answers.

Held Captive: Because of the constant care your MIAC requires, it seems like you're being held captive by his or her behaviors and irrational demands. You think that because he's your child, you must give him everything he asks for and tolerate disrespect.

The most effective way to free yourself is to create personal boundaries. Decide what behaviors are acceptable. This allows you to have a sense of control over your life. You actually have choices in how you respond to your child and what limits you enforce. When you create personal space for yourself, it doesn't mean you no longer love your MIAC; it simply means you've taken back your right to take care of yourself, too.

You're only helpless when you give up your search for answers.

Powerless: You feel powerless when you're in situations you can't control and feel unqualified to handle these unimaginable events. If you can't appreciate your capabilities, you'll discount your strength to navigate your MIAC's challenges. Make a list of your gifts. It's an excellent way to determine what skills to use when you have to make those tough choices. Family and friends can help you recognize your talents and areas of expertise if you struggle to recognize your own assets.

Oppressed: Being the mom of a newly diagnosed MIAC can be disheartening. It's a burden imposed upon you without your permission. You may want to blame someone or something for this egregious turn of events, or you might even blame yourself for your child's illness and difficulties. Whenever you feel oppressed or want to engage in self-blame, instead consider all the valid causes of negative emotions. For example, if someone tells you that you always make bad decisions, it can cause you to believe you aren't capable of good decisions, but is that actually true?

Limited: Because MI manifests as inappropriate behavior rather than a biological illness, the care available to your child is limited. That impacts your ability to find quality resources due to the lack of MI funds, available doctors, and accessible services. When resources are hard to come by, you feel that your ability to help your MIAC is limited.

Changing your attitude will allow you to move from a state of despondency into hope and optimism. You must be determined to pull yourself out of the gloom of a bleak future. You may not be sure which way will lead to a better life, but you know that if you remain stuck, it will be the end of you. So, you've got to try. You won't begin to lift yourself up until you've reached the bottom of your pit of discouragement and have a willingness to try whatever it takes to feel better.

"Hey, are you listening to me?" my friend said. "You need to get out of this depressed funk you've been wallowing in for the last few months."

I sigh. "I don't know how. My son is suffering, and I can't fix it. I don't know where to turn or what to do. It seems like any attempts will be a waste of time."

"Well, you can't stay like this," she gently reminds me.

I agreed. I'd felt grief-stricken and miserable for far too long. By nature, I'm optimistic, and looking at the dark side of life was wearing on my soul. Maybe it was time to try my hand at living a full life again. It's such a challenge to admit defeat. I realize I'm the only one who can change the outcome by changing my attitude.

Even though the good outweighs the bad, we seem to hold on to what we don't want and allow it to define us. My friend suggested that I find five things each day that make me happy. I took the exercise a step further and looked for an additional five things about my child that made me proud. Some days I'd be hard-pressed to find even one thing to add to my list, but I stuck with it, and over time, it became a habit. Even today, there are times when I need a reminder that I have a choice about the way I look at my life.

Below is my list from last week. Some of the things are quite small and simple, but they made me happy.

- The sun was shining brightly.
- It felt like fall was in the air.

- I saw a butterfly on my walk to the dumpster.
- My pets greeted me when I came home from work.
- A friend called and asked me to dinner.
- I listened to a great audiobook.
- My MIAC seems more rational and less paranoid today.
- I finalized plans for my trip to Peru next month.
- I sat on my patio and enjoyed the cool evening breeze.
- B asked to get a haircut.

When I tune in to ways that my child makes me proud, I can look past the negative symptoms of his illness. This week my son made me proud when:

- He didn't curse when I said no to a request.
- He thanked me when I bought him a few snacks.
- He was polite to others when we were at the grocery store.
- He chose to recycle bottles/cans instead of throwing them in the trash.
- My favorite was him saying, "I love you, Mom."

It takes thought and personal growth to be able to describe your days as good. You may have a bad moment or two, but overall, your life can be happy, and you can feel blessed.

Hopelessness is not a place to run and hide when you feel overwhelmed by circumstances. If you use your energy to build and create a life for yourself, you can become confident in the decisions you make for your MIAC. The more positive your attitude, the better your life becomes. The more decisions you make that support yourself, the less you focus on the bad.

> I'm at a friend's birthday party. We laugh and have a good time. It refreshes my outlook to enjoy myself. We've finished dinner and are ready to cut the cake when my phone rings.

I try to ignore it. I'm having fun and don't want to be reminded of what waits for me at home. I should've turned off my phone. I deserve to have uninterrupted time with friends, but I guilt myself and answer the phone anyway. My MIAC is talking an incoherent word salad, and I'm concerned.

"Stay a little longer," my friends urge. "He'll be fine."

But I know he won't be fine. Every time I do something for myself, I end up leaving early or canceling my plans. I reminisce about how I thought I would have time for myself after my children grew up, but instead, I'm a caregiver to an irrational adult.

Be Careful—Caregiving Takes Its Toll on You

Sometimes when you're at the bottom of the rabbit hole, you don't realize that you're sinking fast and need help. All caregivers need help, but we especially need it when we're at risk of not being able to help ourselves. Common signs and symptoms that most caregivers experience at some point include:

- Anxiety
- Depression
- Irritability
- Feeling tired or having sleep problems
- Blowups over minor issues
- Increased health problems
- Poor concentration
- Feeling resentful
- Changes in drinking, smoking, or eating habits
- Ignored responsibilities
- Avoiding leisure activities

I'm sure you can relate to many of these. I've felt all of them at some point over the last ten years.

Caregiver burnout takes those symptoms a step further. Here are some red flags that indicate you've neglected your own care:

- Decreased energy
- More colds or flu
- Constant exhaustion
- Ignoring personal needs because you're too busy or don't care anymore
- Focusing only on caregiver duties
- Inability to relax
- Impatience and irritability with your MIAC
- Feeling hopeless and helpless

If you notice these symptoms, it's time to find support for yourself, either from family, friends, clergy, or a professional therapist. Your mental health is just as important as your child's.

I drive as slow as possible and stay in the car to listen to a few additional songs and check emails, and when I run out of things to delay me, I drag myself into the house. I love my home and my child, but I'm never sure what I'll find when I return, and it fills me with dread. My sanctuary is oppressive. I detest encounters with my MIAC still in his pajamas, drunk, and incoherent. I'm so tired of the anger, frustration, and repetition of this scenario. It's a nightmare version of Groundhog Day—without the happy ending.

In some ways, it felt like everything became a nightmare overnight, but it actually took time for the changes to eat through my life. I was afraid of everything: afraid to stop, afraid of what I would see, afraid I might not be able to begin again. Afraid that I wouldn't be able to fix this terrible wrong, afraid that I hadn't done enough, afraid that my child would remain trapped in this dreadful nightmare. I wanted my life back. I wasn't trained in crisis management or as a full-time caregiver, and I didn't have the skills to run a mini-psych ward in my home.

It's easy to get overwhelmed as a caregiver to a MIAC. You need to find ways to feel more empowered. The following are some practical suggestions to make your day-to-day responsibilities easier:

- Practice acceptance.
- Embrace your choice to be a caregiver.
- Don't allow the caregiver role to become your entire life.
- Focus on things you can control.
- Find support with family members or friends.
- Share your struggles.
- Let go of what you can't change.
- Give yourself a break.
- Make time for personal relationships.
- Prioritize activities that provide enjoyment.
- Find ways to pamper yourself.
- Laugh.
- Get out of the house.

How many of these can you begin to incorporate into your life? What makes you feel healthy and happy? Make a list and start doing those things.

Here's what my list looks like:

- I need to travel. Vacations and sightseeing feed my soul.
- I need my privacy to be respected.
- I need uninterrupted time to meditate, read, watch a movie, and relax.
- I need time with friends.
- I need to trust that my belongings won't be borrowed or stolen.
- I need time away from my MIAC.
- I need to be able to use my money for things I want and need.

- I need to know my MIAC is safe when I'm not with him.
- I need a life that's separate from my MIAC's chaos.

Next, I compiled a list of what caused havoc in my life, what I wanted instead, and what stood in the way of me being successful. That way, I could see outside my circumstances and realize there's always more than one choice. Here's the list of what didn't work for me while my son lived in the condo next door:

- Constant, vigilant checks for illegal drugs and alcohol
- Daily battles over money
- Interruptions in personal time
- Disregard for my personal space
- Continual conversations about grandiose moneymaking ideas
- Doing household chores for two houses
- Caring for pets that weren't mine
- Preparing food for him only to be told it's poisoned
- Reminding him to bathe and change clothes
- Repairing damaged walls

What did I need to release in order to achieve these things? Here are some things I decided to give up:

- The idea that I can control the outcome
- The belief that my child can be fixed
- The idea that I can buy my child's happiness
- The need for my child to behave a certain way
- The desire for my MIAC to have and be more
- The assumption that I must be the one to care for my child
- The notion that I can't be happy unless my child is happy
- The conviction that I don't deserve to have a good life

The most difficult part of this process will be acknowledging what you need to change and taking steps to alter the way you look at your current beliefs. But it's time to give up your go-to responses. It isn't easy to climb out of the rabbit hole, and when you let it all go, it's scary and unnerving. But then you'll realize that the world won't end if you change the way you approach problems. In fact, life becomes more comfortable, and things start to get better. Your child's life won't look like you want it to, but you never had that much control in the first place.

When you make different choices, it might increase your MIAC's misconduct and verbal storms of profanity. Yes, you've jumped out of the pot and into the fire. Just put on your blinders and focus on your wish list when things escalate. As you hold your ground, tiny positive changes will begin to occur. Those small victories will validate your struggles. Your decisions need to be based on what's best for both of you. If a choice you're considering only benefits your child, look elsewhere for a solution. It doesn't matter if your MIAC likes your choices as long as they're in his best interest. Stop caring about whether he likes you. Your responsibility is to ensure that he's safe and cared for if at all possible. If that's not possible, then make sure you don't allow disrespect and chaos in your home or life just because your MIAC refuses help.

If a choice you're considering only benefits your child, look elsewhere for a solution.

Look at the big picture and weigh the pros and cons of each decision you need to make. Yes, you'll still need to put out fires, but you'll have a plan to follow for where you're headed. Both your lives will change, and you need to be okay with that. You can't rebuild your life and keep your MIAC's circumstances the same. No matter where your child lives, his behaviors will stay the same because his brain is affected by internal damage, not external circumstances.

These days, I visit my son once a week at the residential care facility where he lives. The staff provides meals, does laundry, helps clean, and dispenses meds. There's someone available around the clock to maintain order. He complains that he's not happy, but he's never been happy anywhere that he's lived. He says he doesn't have freedom, but he can come and go as he likes as long as he lets the staff know where he'll be. What he wants is to buy alcohol, and that's not allowed.

I'm so thankful that we've finally found a safe place for him and that I can now focus on my life without constantly worrying about him. I feel guilty sometimes, but I know this is a better fit for both of us. Is his life wonderful? Not by a long shot, but it never will be what either of us expected years ago. What I've learned is that no matter what I do, I can't make him happy, but I can certainly make myself miserable. My happiness doesn't make him feel worse, but it does enhance my ability to be positive and supportive when we're together.

As you move into the next chapter, you'll discover ways to give up that victim mentality and begin to make better choices for yourself.

Visualization Journey

Sit in a comfortable, quiet place. Close your eyes.

Breathe in and out slowly to the count of three several times until you feel yourself begin to relax.

Visualize yourself in a small, dark space. It's warm and comfortable, with an earthy smell. You feel soft fur and realize you're in a rabbit den. After a few minutes, you start to feel cramped and stiff, but you're in total darkness.

Just as you begin to feel trapped, tiny lights appear. As you look closer, you realize they're fairies, each a different iridescent color, each one holding a tiny torch.

The fairies move together and illuminate a small door. Squat down so you can crawl through it to an outside chamber. Once there, you have space to stand up and stretch. Take a few deep, cleansing breaths.

When you look back, the space you left has disappeared, and in its place is a beautiful rose bush full of unopened buds.

You follow your fairy friends as they guide you along a path. You appear to move in a tight circle, and you see the path is a spiral.

Halfway around the circle, you come to a golden bowl filled with a violet flame. The fairies tell you that this is where you leave what no longer serves you. As you walk past the bowl, you drop what you choose to let go of into the flame and watch it turn into ashes. You see the remnants of guilt, fear, outdated ideas, limiting beliefs from other travelers.

Next, you encounter a silver dish filled with tiny white scrolls tied with red ribbons. You're urged to take one, so you open and read it. The scroll contains one word as a gift in beautiful calligraphy. You might see wisdom, power, freedom, or self-confidence.

You continue your walk around the spiral. Each time around, the path gets wider, and you realize you are ascending. You notice that the rose bush has started to bloom. Each time around the circle, you drop something into the golden bowl, pick up a scroll gift, and another bud opens.

The fairies flit around you and offer support and reassurance. Continue your walk around the spiral, continue to release what's holding you back, and take the gifts until all the buds on the rose bush have opened. Take your time; there's no need to rush.

Carefully pluck one fully-opened rose from the bush, as this will be a reminder of what you have gained during your time on the path.

You've reached the outermost ring of the spiral and see a door. You bid your fairy guides farewell. Thank them for their advice and encouragement.

Open the door and step into a beautiful field. The sun is warm on your face, the breeze ruffles your hair, and all is quiet except for an occasional bird's song. You can stay in this peaceful field for as long as you like.

When ready, open your eyes and journal any messages, words, or symbols you received. What did you release into the purple flame? What scroll gifts did you receive? What color is your rose?

From Helpless Victim to Conscious Chooser

We are sisters
Helpless in our struggles
We try to find our way
We look for the best answers
Strong in our convictions
We are sisters

I'm afraid. B's behavior is crazy. He sees and hears things that aren't there. I can't reason with him. He rambles on about how people are after him.

"It's big, Mom. It'll be on the news when the police figure it out."

"Figure out what?" I ask, confused and frightened.

My stomach churns; my heart beats loud and fast. I swallow to keep down my lunch. I run to the bathroom and turn on the faucet. I'm hiding, hiding from my son. The ***shhhhhhhh*** of the running water muffles the sound as I dial 911.

I'm going to lie. It's a big lie, but I don't care. B needs help, and I don't know how else to get it. He doesn't think he's sick.

The operator answers, "911, what's your emergency?"

"My child is threatening to hurt people," I whisper. I shake, and the phone slides from my sweaty hand.

"We're sending the police," the dispatcher says. "Have him answer the door."

"How long will it be?" I stutter.

B yells, "Mom, what are you doing in the bathroom? Mom! MOM!"

Where are they? What's taking them so long? My chest feels like it's wrenching apart, and my mind shatters. I whisper a prayer, "Please hurry before I change my mind."

What if they don't believe me? What if they won't take him to the hospital? I sit on the toilet, arms wrapped around my waist as I try to keep from losing my resolve.

I can't breathe, I can't think, I sweat, I tremble. What if this doesn't work? What if the police hurt him? What if he runs away? What if they don't believe he's sick?

The doorbell rings. I take a deep, stuttering breath to calm my nerves. My head's going to explode. My heart hurts. I walk out of the bathroom, and the police are talking with B on the front lawn.

One of the officers asks me, "What did he say? Why do you feel threatened?"

Now's the time to tell my big lie. "He says he wants to kill the people who are after him."

Does he believe me? I need to convince this officer, or they may not take him. Why isn't there an easier way to get help for a MIAC? My vision dims; I feel faint; I sit down and put my head between my knees. My world spins out of control. Please let me wake up from this nightmare.

Victim Mentality

After his hospitalization, I spiraled into months of victim mentality. Why did this happen to me? I was simply trying to survive, and I held on to whatever surfaced in front of me. When I came up for air, I was trapped in the role of a martyr. A helpless victim.

What does it look like when you're a victim of your circumstances?

- You hold tight to thoughts and feelings that you're a victim but refuse to consider other perspectives or ways to cope with your problems.
- You don't take action but give up. You lack the self-confidence to make good choices.
- You let your MIAC take control of your life.
- You let negative self-beliefs sabotage your choices.
- You deplete your energy until you're desperate for support.
- You feel bitter and resentful because your life's not going the way you planned.
- You make excuses for why you give up.
- You engage in self-destructive behaviors.
- You beat yourself up for being a bad mom.
- You don't own any of the situation. It's always your MIAC's fault.

Once you're stuck, it's hard to find your way back to a healthier life. You've heard it before, but life isn't fair. We all have situations we don't think we deserve. It's easier for some people to move past unfair circumstances, while others feel they're the target of an atrocious fate.

Mental illness is profoundly unfair and quite unfathomable. Your child is normal one day, and the next, he's in the throes of a psychotic break. Being tossed into this unthinkable reality causes even the most rational person to become defensive. When everything you value in life is threatened, your natural response is to resist and deny.

You fight against what doctors tell you and cling to an irretrievable past. Each time you revisit a traumatic incident, you carve a rut of pain and heartache deeper into your spirit.

Instead of the calamity being a single experience, you feel like you've lived it a thousand times.

When everything you value in life is threatened,
your natural response is to resist and deny.

What you really want is to hold on to the child you've lost. You cling to the last moment when he was healthy—but this is also when the chaos began. You don't remember the good times but replay the wreckage of his beautiful future. You analyze it from every angle and think that there might be a way back, but that's just an illusion. The only way forward is into the deep, dark unknown. It's a frightful prospect, one that most of us are ill-equipped to handle or finesse.

Releasing what's lost is a formidable undertaking because you have to relinquish what's gone and accept something different. Of course, you want to hold on to what you recognize, what feels comfortable, what you thought your life would look like. But you're forced to let that old reality fall away.

It may feel like you've given up on and abandoned the child you remember—but you must face reality if you want to help him and yourself. You must see him as he is today. There's rarely foresight or early intervention with MI. He can't go back to his previous state of health, and he still wants and needs your support and encouragement. If you deny his diagnosis, you're denying his reality and causing him additional hardship by expecting him to live up to your memories of who he used to be.

Fear

You may be living in a constant state of fear: fear of what might happen, fear of what the future will look like. So much fear around every decision, every choice, every altercation, every doctor appointment, every fight, every hospital visit, every new symptom, every single moment of every single day. It's paralyzing.

Here are some ways that fear manifests:

- You become a perfectionist.
- You refuse to take risks.
- You procrastinate.
- You insist on being in control.
- You don't speak up.

- You distract yourself with TV, alcohol, drugs, sex, or excessive busyness.
- New physical illnesses appear.

If you recognize any of these symptoms, it's time to make different choices, even if you're afraid. Here are some ways to reduce your fearful thoughts:

- Analyze your fear. Is it valid?
- Trust your intuition. What is your inner wisdom saying?
- Release ideas that don't make sense. Does the idea hold up under scrutiny?
- Remember that you always have choices. List your options.
- Keep strong personal boundaries. Now is not the time to back down.
- Realize that everything doesn't need to be fixed. Let it work itself out.
- Let go of the small stuff. Most stuff is small stuff.
- Spend time with positive people. Get out of the house.
- Quiet your mind. Spend time without electronic devices.
- Trust your higher power. Talk with God daily.

I found it was helpful to list my fears and determine if they were valid. Certain situations created feelings of concern, anxiety, worry, and panic, so I sat and visualized how those situations made me feel. Then I wrote them down. When I had a list in front of me, I could decide if the items on that list were worthy of the time and energy it took to hold on to that fear.

As it turned out, most of the things on the list were situations I couldn't control. I had to learn to let go of them. Some of the other things meant I'd need to become more educated about MI, make different choices, and become a more vocal advocate for my son.

Here are some fears that are universal to all mothers of MIACs:

- You fear you won't be able to convince your child to seek medical help.

- You fear your MIAC won't take medication or the meds won't work.
- You fear having little or no control over your child's care.
- You fear your child may harm himself or someone else.
- You fear how others will view your MIAC.
- You fear your MIAC will become violent.
- You fear your parenting skills aren't good enough.
- You fear being blamed if your child does something inappropriate.
- You fear he'll stay ill and never have any quality of life.
- You fear you'll make the wrong decisions.
- You fear that the rest of your life will be one crisis after another.
- You fear you'll need to care for your MIAC until you die.
- You fear you won't be able to find appropriate care.
- You fear your MIAC will choose suicide.
- You fear you aren't strong enough or smart enough to deal with this.
- You fear you'll never have a life of your own.
- You fear making life-altering decisions on behalf of another adult.
- You fear your MIAC will commit a crime, get arrested, or go to prison.
- You fear your child will become an addict, become homeless, or commit a crime.

My fear stole my peace of mind. And then I read somewhere that worrying was praying for the wrong outcome, and I wondered what would happen if I dealt with the issues as they came up instead of making up problems. I'd spent so much time and energy focused on imagined problems, and when I put it in those terms, it sounded so ridiculous. What a preposterous way to live! My time and energy should be focused on what actually occurred each day and only that—nothing more.

It takes time to learn the techniques to release unfounded fear. You can't just flip the switch and stop feeling a certain way. So, you must spend time on your personal growth.

If you expand your spiritual beliefs, you'll begin to feel that something larger than you is in control and is looking out for you and your MIAC. Give your fears over to Spirit, and instead focus on what you can control. Instead of being paralyzed by fear and worry, your clarity will improve, and you'll develop a sense of direction and purpose. You'll stop floundering and will become fearless and tenacious in finding the best possible care for your MIAC. You'll become a conscious chooser.

So, when you're uncertain, afraid, or anxious, take time to figure out if what you're feeling is valid. Or have you concocted imaginary scenarios of disaster and doom? Is the sky really falling, or are you simply projecting disaster? Releasing your unrealistic fears lets you move on with your life and offers your child the opportunity to do the same.

Fear is contagious. When you become less afraid of the future, your MIAC will show more acceptance of his diagnosis and prognosis. Your apprehension is keeping you both stuck in the tragedy, but letting go offers both of you the blessing of acceptance.

> I've been trying to reach B all day. He's not answering his phone, and I'm afraid. Driving home, I contemplate all possible scenarios: he's having a psychotic episode, he's fallen and hit his head, he's overdosed on his meds, he's passed out drunk. My worry and anxiety increase as traffic slows to a crawl. My heart races, my thoughts spin, my stomach clenches, sweat trickles down my back. *What's the holdup?* I think as I grip the steering wheel tighter. I just need to get home! After fifteen agonizing minutes, the cars start moving again. The instant I pull into the driveway, I jump from the car and run to the door.
>
> I let myself into B's apartment. It's too quiet.
>
> I call out, "Where are you?"
>
> No answer.
>
> Suddenly, he stumbles from the bedroom. His words are jumbled, and he falls to the floor.

"What did you take? Did you double up on your meds?" I ask frantically.

Another tangle of incoherent words.

I'm dialing 911 when he says, "I'm drunk."

"Where did you get the money for liquor?" I ask.

"A friend loaned it to me," he slurs.

"Just this morning, we had a conversation about how bad it is to mix alcohol with your meds," I say, exasperated.

At this point, I'm no longer worried; I'm angry. No, that's not accurate. I'm LIVID. This is the second time this week I've come home to find him drunk. I'm so over his dangerous behaviors, so over his promises, so over wondering if I'm going to come home and find him dead.

I yell, "If you keep this up, you're going to die," as I throw the unfinished bottle of gin in his direction. I shout, "Finish it so we can stop playing this crazy game."

I'm too outraged to care what I say or how it sounds. My rage masks my fear, disappointment, frustration, and a bone-deep sorrow for my son. Being angry all the time doesn't feel good. It doesn't feel like me. A dark presence of pain and despair has taken over my normally optimistic personality.

Anger

I bet there's an undercurrent of fury that runs just beneath the surface of your days. Are you filled with anger at yourself, your child, God, and society? Do you feel overpowered by irritation and outrage toward everyone and everything?

This type of anger isn't usually a feeling you want to acknowledge or share with others. You want to lash out at an unfair God who allowed this to happen, at yourself for not being able to fix it, at your MIAC for not trying harder to get better, and at society itself for the discriminatory way the mentally ill are treated. Though you know it doesn't help, you can't figure out how to let go. You feel justified in your anger; you and your child are victims of this heinous disease.

Did you know that anger often masks other emotions? It's easier to be angry than to feel pain and vulnerability. In the past, I used my anger as a shield to protect me from other emotions that seemed too painful to bring into the light. Buried underneath an angry façade, I felt embarrassed, overwhelmed, helpless, fearful, depressed, exhausted, grief-stricken, guilty, anxious, stressed, ashamed, and frustrated. I wasn't sure I'd survive opening that wound and cleaning out all that festered under the surface. Those emotions seemed too big, too awful, too intense, too much to bear. I feared the tsunami of pain that would emerge if I let down my guard. So, I continued to stuff my difficult emotions until one day, my heart became full, and the dyke burst in a flood of pent-up sorrow.

When you delve deep into the reasons for your anger, you'll be able to work through what's hidden underneath and begin to understand and accept your emotions—and be more conscious of your choices. When you finally own your repressed emotions, you gain permission to state the impact your MIAC's illness has had on all aspects of your life. It feels scary to dig up what's buried, but if you stay with it and work through the feelings, they'll dissipate, and your anger will start to fade.

Below are some of the emotions that anger typically masks:

- Anger at your MIAC's inappropriate behavior masks *embarrassment* of what others may think.
- Anger that your MIAC refuses to take medication masks *fear* that he won't get well.
- Anger that you can't communicate with your MIAC masks *grief* that the healthy, rational child you knew is gone.
- Anger that you didn't recognize your MIAC was sick masks *shame* at the ways you tried to get your child to behave.
- Anger that your MIAC can't seem to follow simple instructions masks *frustration* that, as an adult, he's unable to perform basic tasks.
- Anger that your MIAC requires so much of your time masks the *overwhelm* of being a full-time caregiver.

- Anger that your MIAC will never have the life you wanted for him masks *depression* over lost dreams.
- Anger that you can't make your MIAC better masks *guilt* that your efforts to find effective treatments have failed.
- Anger that your MIAC is aggressive or violent masks *fear* that he will harm you, himself, or even a stranger.
- Anger at your MIAC for the constant chaos he creates masks the *stress* that there's no peace in your life and that you're always walking on eggshells and putting out fires.
- Anger that your MIAC has nowhere to go masks the *suffocation* you feel in a situation where there are no good answers.
- Anger that the laws make it impossible to get care for your MIAC masks *helplessness* to intervene in your child's care.
- Anger for your MIAC's safety masks *anxiety* that you can't keep your child protected.
- Anger that your MIAC is in legal trouble masks *worry* because you can't control your child's actions or keep him out of prison.
- Anger that your MIAC chooses to become an addict masks your *fear* that he will overdose and die.
- Anger that you can't spend quality time with your MIAC masks *envy* that your friends spend time doing normal activities with their adult children.

Full of repressed emotions, I finally had a meltdown in the middle of the nursing home where my mom lived. Lucky for me, her social worker happened to be coming down the hall, and he pulled me into an alcove where we could talk. More accurately, he talked while I tried to listen through my sobs. He gave me permission to take time to care for myself, and he told me to stay home and not deal with anyone else for a full week. He offered words I could use when I needed more space for my needs, and he gave me my first lesson in how to set personal boundaries.

It's remarkable what happens when you release the tight hold you have on your feelings. After my meltdown, I felt so much better and less angry. When I denied my own needs and emotions, I turned myself into a human volcano, ready to erupt. But when I acknowledged, accepted, and released my feelings, I felt like I was supporting my overall health rather than putting up a front that made it seem like I was okay.

My interactions with my MIAC and his care providers also improved. I became more patient, more considerate, and more able to maintain my calm during the continuous mayhem. I made time to care for myself, which became a daily practice. If I hadn't continually reminded myself that my needs were important, I wouldn't be where I am today.

The reason so many moms of MIACs experience anxiety and depression is because they devote all their attention and energy to their ill child and ignore themselves. As a mom, you feel an obligation to care for your ill child regardless of his age. At first, you have no problem doing whatever needs to be done to help him get well. You become involved with his medical visits, medications, therapists, hospitalizations, and other attempts to convince your child he needs help. That part is normal for most illnesses. But what's not normal is your attempts to control your MIAC, so he'll remain in treatment, monitor adherence to his medications, modify his risky behaviors, and push him to seek additional therapy when he shows signs of relapse.

> *The reason so many moms of MIACs experience anxiety and depression is because they devote all their attention and energy to their ill child and ignore themselves.*

Severe mental illness requires a full-time caregiver, and that's not something you're trained to do. You're not a therapist, case manager, doctor, addiction specialist, or nurse. As time and the disease continue, it's easy to feel burdened with the care your MIAC requires. What else could you expect? You've tried to do the job of several licensed professionals.

Even if your MIAC is aware of his illness and is med compliant, that doesn't mean he's well enough to perform daily life skills. The medications may reduce his most severe symptoms, but they do nothing for the brain damage the disease has caused. If your child refuses treatment, then you have the additional worry and stress of not knowing where he is, if he's safe, and what you can do to help. Or you could be stuck with an irrational adult that insists you need to house, feed, and finance his life. As I dove into the role of caring for my adult son, the challenges I'd faced in his childhood paled in comparison to what confronted me now.

I didn't sign up for this disaster, and neither did you. But when your child became sick, you gave up your life to live his for him. That needs to stop. He didn't ask you to do this, but as his mother, you feel it's your duty. He doesn't want the things you try to give him, but you feel like you owe them to him to make up for what he won't have. You keep trying to make him well, make him happy, make him normal, make him a productive, independent adult, but nothing will make him better. He's always on the lookout for a distraction, something to take his mind off his miserable, sad life. So, you began a cycle of giving in to all his wants. Now you're frustrated and exasperated by his incessant demands and by your paltry attempts to make his life less pathetic.

> *When your child became sick, you gave up your life to live his for him. That needs to stop.*

I began to say NO to my MIAC when he asked for things he didn't really need, and I took the brunt of his anger and frustration for that.

"You're my mom. Just this once, buy me this. I won't ask for anything else."

But a few days later, he would have another ludicrous request. This child I'd been eager to do anything for now took everything from me. Time, money, energy, my life. It seemed I'd agreed to carry my MIAC through life. What started as my desire to help him recover turned into an unhealthy and dysfunctional parasitic dance. A dance that left me hollow and lifeless. A dance that I, myself, had started and continued to perpetuate.

Perhaps it's time to get clear about what your responsibilities are. Ask yourself this question: *does what I give improve his life in any way?* It's okay to occasionally gift him an item from his wish list, but if you wait a few days, that want may turn into something else. Simply put, your child asks for things as a diversion from his illness. Consider your responsibilities through the lens of reality. Your only real responsibility is to make sure he's safe and cared for when he's unable to be so on his own, with the disclaimer that he has the right to refuse your help. When you stop trying to make things better, you'll no longer feel burdened. You can now say no to unnecessary requests and not feel guilty because you know it won't add to the quality of his life or aid in his recovery.

Resentment

I'm at work when my ex-husband calls. "B's not well. He's really sick." We've had this conversation for the last week.

"If you think he needs to be hospitalized, then call and have him transported," I say.

Dad replies, "I can't do that. He'll get mad at me. He lives with me, and I need him to like me."

I sigh. His dad makes me so angry. Why can't he handle this? Why do I always have to be the one to make the difficult decisions? He and my son share a house but don't talk to each other about what's going on. I resent the fact that I can't rely on him when things get tough.

"I handled the last episode. It's your turn," I throw back.

"I can't do it! I just can't!" he insists.

I literally see red. "Come on! Man up for once and do what needs to be done. I shouldn't have to be the one making all the difficult choices. Besides, I'm at work, and you're at home with him now." I hang up in disgust. I'm scared for my son but determined that his dad should handle the situation this time.

I talk to my coworkers about what's going on, but they don't really understand the seriousness of psychotic behavior. I take my next client. She can tell something is off and asks, "What's wrong?"

Through tears, I tell her about my conversation with my ex and complain, "He never wants to do what needs to be done. He always pushes it off on me. I'm sick of it! Just once, he needs to act like a real parent no matter how hard it is!"

She quietly asks, "Is your child sick? Do you know what needs to happen? What's really important here, who handles it or that your child receives the care that he obviously needs?"

I feel horrible. Her words cut straight into my heart. I get the message loud and clear. I tell the front desk, "Cancel all my appointments," and head for my car, calling 911 on the way to his dad's house.

I allowed my resentment of B's dad to cloud my judgment. I put my negative feelings ahead of my son's health, and there's no excuse for that. I beat myself up as I speed to his home, hoping that things wouldn't be as bad as they were during B's last psychotic break.

My son gets into the ambulance willingly, but that's just the calm before the storm. I spend six long hours alone in the emergency room with my irrational, delusional, hallucinating adult child. He has no clue where he is until they start pushing his wheelchair down the hall toward the psych unit, and then all hell breaks loose. B howls and screams, and as psychotic as he is, he knows where the attendants are taking him.

He yells, "They're going to kill me, and it'll be all your fault!"

My stomach drops as a wave of nausea washes over me. They continue pushing him down the dark, empty hallway, and I put my head in my hands and finally cry. I feel so resentful, alone at midnight in the now quiet ER. His dad wants an update, and I'm not sure I want to give him one. Maybe he should have been here if he wanted to be kept informed. I add his shortcomings to my list of the injustices mental illness has brought into my life.

Resentment is a complex, multilayered emotion. It's a mixture of disappointment, anger, fear, disgust, sadness, surprise, and envy. It's the experience of reliving past injustices, real or perceived, and the old feelings of anger connected to them. Resentments form when you become angry with a person, institution, or situation and hold on to the anger. In the end, the most harm is done to you. Constant resentment of your circumstances, your child's behavior, and others' opinions and advice is toxic. When you hold on to these feelings, they turn you into a victim, alter your perception of reality, and make it difficult to see any potential positive outcomes. The good news is that you can choose better.

Moms of MIACs are always blindsided by their child's initial diagnosis. Unable to change the outcome, you become resentful of the disease, the lack of available treatment options, the difficulties you have when you try to get help for your child, and the amount of time, money, and energy needed to handle severe MI. Your resentment is tied to your inability to make your child well. And if your family and friends don't understand or aren't supportive, the resentment grows.

In the initial stages of mental illness, hateful and hurtful behaviors occur, but you don't understand why. His attitude doesn't make sense, and no amount of discussion changes his behavior. You become his scapegoat for all the confusion, turmoil, and disordered thoughts that fill his head. You begin to resent the way your MIAC treats you and his inability to act more rationally and balanced. Surely if he loved you, he'd show you some respect and pull himself together. It feels like his actions are intentional because he takes out his angst on you.

So little is known about MI, and most people have no formal or even basic knowledge of how it manifests. That's why people offer judgments, criticisms, and unsolicited advice. It's hard *not* to be resentful toward people who have no clue what's going on but feel it's their right to berate your child and your parenting skills. Nobody would make unsolicited suggestions about the treatment of a child with cancer or kidney disease, but the same people have no problem critiquing you.

You begin to resent the way your MIAC treats you and his inability to act more rationally and balanced. . . . It feels like his actions are intentional because he takes out his angst on you.

How do you turn resentments into actions for change? Here are some suggestions:

- Decide if your resentment is fueled by anger, fear, sadness, surprise, envy, or injustice. Work through the feelings that come up.
- Recognize your role in the situation. Do your actions or words contribute to the negativity?
- Are you jealous of families with normal adult children? Do you feel that this shouldn't have happened to your family?
- Allow yourself to feel your emotions. Don't stuff them. Who can you talk with to sort out what and why you feel this way?
- What specific circumstances have contributed to your resentment?
- Stop your continual thoughts and focus on a solution. Replaying the hurt over and over reinforces the negative feelings.

Make a list of good things in your life with your MIAC. Forgive yourself and others for their insensitive actions and words. Recognize that they don't know any better. Seek a spiritual reason for this lesson. Is there something you have learned from this experience that you couldn't have learned any other way? Can you find a gift in the difficulty? Talk to a counselor. There's no shame in asking for support and guidance if you can't overcome this pain on your own.

My resentment encompassed the MI diagnosis but also included his dad's inability to make decisions, my then-current husband's unwillingness to be supportive of my needs, and my child's blatant denial that he was sick. Everyone close to me discounted my feelings, so I felt justified in my bitterness and resentment. I had to make all the decisions and then handle the ramifications they created. I remember having hateful thoughts about everyone because I was handling crisis after crisis alone. B's dad expected me to make all the decisions, my current husband didn't want any part of any of it, and I was alone in a fight with an adult child who thought I was in on a conspiracy to harm him.

Every time I thought about the injustice of it all, I became more bitter. As I continued to relive the trauma, I became the star in my very own pity party, the helpless victim in my dismal story. Looking at it from my perspective only, I'd forgotten about my child.

So, I made a conscious choice to reframe the experience. The chaos and turmoil had clouded my vision and prevented me from seeing past the struggles, past feeling I was a failure, past what my son's life should've been, past the resentment that I expected my life to be so much better. I decided to become a conscious chooser instead of a helpless victim.

It's not easy to let go of resentments, but your new choices will gradually allow you to look at your life with gratitude. That doesn't mean you'll never feel resentful, but now you can figure out why you feel that way and work through it before it grows into something bigger.

After I changed my point of view, I started asking for support. I asked B's dad to pick up the slack. He still won't make the hard decisions, but I push a lot of the smaller choices and chores his way. I divorced my second husband because my health and peace of mind were more important to me than being in an unsupportive marriage. It didn't help me to be blamed for my son's illness. My husband was unwilling to learn more about MI, which created distrust and controversy in our relationship—and more stress for me. So I let that marriage go.

Feeling Defensive

People become defensive when they're triggered by sensitive issues. When others comment about your MIAC's irrational behavior, poor hygiene habits, illicit drug use, lack of responsibility, the crowd he hangs with, his smoking and drinking, his violent words, or his refusal to go to college, you rise to his defense. Something in you snaps, and you feel the need to defend him because he isn't able to fight for himself.

Author Sharon Ellison states, "Defensiveness is an impulsive and reactive mode of responding to a situation or conversation. Rather than listening with an open heart, you respond with your metaphorical shield up and weapons drawn."

A defensive response offers self-protection from emotional pain but adds nothing to your relationships. There's no thought behind your reactions other than to protect and guard your emotionally fragile child and hold tight to your hypersensitive mother's ego. In this state, you can't listen, evaluate what you hear, or choose an appropriate response. It's always a knee-jerk reaction, spewed without thought or consideration. You're a mama bear in protective mode and will think about what you've said later when the potential threat is over. This isn't a very practical way of handling situations, but at the time, it feels like you need to safeguard your cocoon of hope and maintain your semblance of normalcy.

Any mom who deals with a MIAC experiences intense emotional pain daily. Many times, you're criticized, demoralized, and discounted as you attempt to get your child much-needed help. That puts you on high alert to defend against anyone who gets in your way. Here are some suggestions to help you lower your defenses, tear down the walls of protection, stop your need to attack others, and communicate better:

- Find ways to manage your stress.
- Listen without interruptions.

- Know yourself and know your triggers.
- When you feel defensive, acknowledge it.
- Look at the situation from different perspectives.
- Remember that what others say and do isn't personal.
- Look for common ground in difficult interactions.
- Remember that there's no right or wrong.

It takes practice to reduce your defensiveness, tear down your protective walls, and start responding rather than reacting to others' opinions. Use the opportunity to educate them about MI. When you drop your defensive stance, you can open yourself up to receiving mental and emotional support.

Blame and Judgment

> My MIAC has paranoid irrational thoughts all the time, and some days I'm just over all attempts to understand. I know it's unreasonable to think I can influence his illness and that he can't help the way he feels or thinks, but do his delusions need to impact my life?
>
> Today is one of those days. As I get ready to go out of town, I have to make sure he has what he needs before I leave. The biggest issue is his refusal to drink tap water. He insists it's poisoned. But that's not all. He'll only drink certain brands and types of bottled water, his choice of brands changes frequently, he won't drink spring water, and if the bottle caps are loose, he dumps it. Right now, he has ninety-six bottles of water that he's suddenly decided he can't drink.
>
> I purchase, deliver, and drag three cases of water up to his third-floor room. Carrying this much weight is a strain on my back. Ten minutes after I get home, the phone rings.
>
> "You bought the wrong kind of water. I can't drink this."

"Why can't you just drink tap water? You're the reason my back always hurts. You need to get over this delusional thinking. Maybe I'll stop bringing bottled water altogether."

In a handful of sentences, I blame him for my back pain, demean him for being delusional, and judge his choices. Some days it's so hard to stand back and view his world with objectivity. I know this is a trivial problem, but it never ends. Like a splinter in my finger, this irrational demand continues to irritate and infect my peace of mind.

I've thought about every scenario possible to be free of this task. I considered having water delivered, but he lives too far out in the country for that. I considered buying a reusable bottle with a replaceable filter, but he would never wash it and would likely end up with some kind of bacterial infection. I thought I'd stop buying bottled water and leave him to drink tap water, but when I tried that, he became severely dehydrated because he refused to drink anything. I considered paying his dad to deliver his water, but I can't quite stomach that. I wanted to put a faucet filter on his sink, but the sink in his bathroom wasn't deep enough.

I try to reason with him every time I see him. This makes me look like the delusional one. There's no way to reason with someone with a thought disorder.

Update: B's new roommate willingly carries the water upstairs for me. I can't begin to describe how happy this makes me. I know it's ridiculous to get worked up over this issue, but sometimes it's the small things that do me in. The joy in small victories gives me hope.

What's at the root of our blaming and judging others? We do it because we feel a loss of control, seek to avoid uncomfortable emotions, want to evade distressing experiences, or attempt to enhance our sense of being right. It's so much easier to blame and judge than to acknowledge that life's not going the way you planned. But that won't get you anywhere.

This is especially true as a mom to a MIAC. You expect a certain type of conduct from adults, especially your grown child. You know how you raised your child and are keenly aware that his choices and behaviors don't match what he's been taught.

Before you understood his mental decline, you spent most of your time trying to get him to act in more appropriate ways. And you expected him to respond to your demands to straighten up. When that didn't happen, you started to judge and blame. You critiqued his words and actions in an effort to show him how out of control he was, and when that didn't work, you begged, threatened, argued, and prayed that what you said would make a difference. As the situation escalated, you blamed your child for your stress and anxiety. You accused him of not trying, not caring, being lazy, and even acting out to get attention.

Blame and judgment cause rifts in personal communications and create distrust and anger. If you're dealing with an adult who has a thought disorder, these tactics will always make matters much worse. MIACs are confused, irrational, overwhelmed, and anxious, and to add shame and guilt to the mix is a recipe for failure. You can't humiliate and disgrace your child and expect him to change his ways—or even listen to you—because he's lost the ability to believe in your love and acceptance.

You can't humiliate and disgrace your child and expect him to change his ways—or even listen to you—because he's lost the ability to believe in your love and acceptance.

Let's look at the reasons why you turned to blame:

- Blaming others is easy.
- When you blame, you aren't held accountable for what's happened.
- When you blame, your parenting skills aren't questioned.

- When you blame, you escape vulnerability or uncomfortable feelings.
- Blame feeds your need for control, and you use it to manage a chaotic situation.

It feels good for a moment to release repressed emotional pain with blame, but it's an ineffective way to create permanent change. When you blame your MIAC, it protects your ego and portrays you as the victim in an unstable situation. But the problem with judging your child is that it reduces him down to a handful of characteristics, and due to your limited perspective, you tend to think you have him or the situation figured out. When you choose to judge your MIAC, you dismiss his feelings and experiences, and you write him off as unimportant. Criticizing blinds you to how your child perceives and relates to life. It's akin to measuring him against your own set of standards when he doesn't have the same capabilities.

There are many reasons why you judge others. They're all attempts to defend your fragile ego. None make the situation better.

- You're unable to comprehend your child's point of reality, so you speak without thinking about his perspective.
- Your MIAC makes your life difficult, and you take it as a personal assault.
- Your view of reality is threatened.
- You want to distance yourself from inappropriate behavior, make it clear you don't approve, and that you're not responsible for the situation.
- You want to make your MIAC suffer because his actions make you miserable.
- You play the blame game to protect your emotions.

Blame now becomes a distraction, a way to focus on your MIAC instead of yourself. If you make your child bad, then you don't have to look at your own emotions, and you can feel good.

The problem lies in how you define what happens as either *good* or *bad*. When life doesn't go as expected, you want to put the blame on someone or something else rather than feeling at fault yourself. It's easier to blame someone for doing something bad than to accept that sometimes good people make poor choices or do bad things. In that case, you'd have to admit that you sometimes make poor choices and also do bad things.

So, you default to rational explanations and look for reasons *why* something happened. When you rationalize an event, you're either avoiding responsibility or refusing to accept that some things in life are simply unavoidable. When you feel attacked, your first reaction is to blame, defend your position, and protect. This is how you avoid your emotions.

Blame is a form of punishment. If you don't like what your MIAC does, you point a finger, call him out, and chastise him in an effort to change his offensive behaviors. You hold your child responsible when things go wrong.

How do you get past blame and judgment and choose love and acceptance in your interactions with your child? Here are a few ways:

- Stop blaming yourself. You're wired for survival, so when you feel threatened, you lash out and blame or judge your MIAC's motives or intentions.
- Be mindful. Pause. Take some time to consider why your child did what you perceive as hurtful, harmful, or wrong. Ask for clarification.
- Look for the basic goodness in your MIAC.
- Remember that we're more alike than we are different. Whatever you feel, others are going through similar circumstances—or maybe even worse.
- Remind yourself that you look at things from a different perspective and with different abilities than your MIAC, but you both want happiness and fulfillment in life.
- Reflect on your own behavior.
- Educate yourself.

Are you expecting a behavior that your child—because of a brain disorder—isn't capable of doing? Give your MIAC the benefit of the doubt. Remember, he's doing the very best he can every single day. It may not look like *your* best, but it's always *his* best. Feel good about your choices. Brené Brown, in her book *Daring Greatly: How the Courage to Be Vulnerable Transforms the Way We Live, Love, Parent, and Lead,* says: "If I feel good about my parenting, I have no interest in judging other people's choices. . . . We're hard on each other because we're using each other as a launching pad out of our own perceived deficiency."

> *How do you get past blame and judgment and choose love and acceptance in your interactions with your child?*

How do you get past blame and judgment and choose love and acceptance in your interactions with your child? Recognize the times when you resort to blaming. Awareness comes first. If you say a lot of "you did . . . " or "you always . . . " or "you never. . . " then you're likely using blame.

While blaming others is harmful, self-blame can be positive. It's important to take ownership for something that didn't go as expected when it's your responsibility. Accept those uncomfortable experiences and learn from them.

Here are some tips to curb the blame game:

- Try to be empathetic rather than judgmental.
- Focus on understanding your MIAC and why he did what he did. Was his intention to cause harm or upheaval? Own your part of it. Everything that happens to you is at least fifty percent your responsibility.
- You choose how you feel about every situation. Did you feel triggered? How you react is one hundred percent your responsibility.
- When you react, don't let your inner beliefs overtake your emotions. Don't allow yourself to be blinded by the problem.

- Step back and evaluate before you respond. Is anyone to blame?
- Can you accept things as they are instead of how you want them to be?

It's so much easier to blame and judge your MIAC for what happens to you rather than take responsibility for your own life. But if you see every situation as an event over which you have no control, then you have zero ability to change what you don't like.

You can't make your MIAC behave in an appropriate way or have rational thoughts, but his behaviors don't need to make your life a nightmare. He's the one who needs to respect your boundaries. But you need to accept his limitations and decide what you'll tolerate and what you won't.

If you don't get a handle on blame and start making better choices, every day will be a struggle for control. You'll blame your MIAC for not trying harder and for his poor choices. You'll judge him for the bad decisions he makes and for the hell he's created for you. You'll want your MIAC's behavior to be responsible and respectful, but that seldom happens. You'll become angry and feel he has blatant disregard for your requests. You'll continue to struggle, push harder, blame more, judge his poor choices, and criticize his lack of compliance. No matter how much you try to force better behavior, nothing will change. It's time to sink or swim.

> *You can't make your MIAC behave in an appropriate way or have rational thoughts, but his behaviors don't need to make your life a nightmare.*

It's hard to accept the fact that you're the only one responsible for how your life looks. And if you're receiving support and sympathy from others by blaming your child, you may not want to give up the unhealthy victim role. Additionally, you may not want to let your MIAC off the hook.

What would happen if you didn't try to make him do better? What if he got worse—much worse? Would he feel abandoned if you didn't push him to do more? These fears keep you in that endless loop, even though blaming and judging haven't created any positive changes.

Everything is a lesson. Sometimes you just need to look deeper to find the gift. Yes, *everything,* even the most horrible event, is a gift. I can say with sincerity that I'm a better person now than I would've been if my son had stayed well. I can now see how this experience was a catalyst for my growth. When I'm able to withhold judgment, I find my interactions with my MIAC are much more pleasant. I don't blame him—or anyone else—for my feelings or what occurs in my life because I know that I choose how I feel. When I accept my own flaws and imperfections, it's easier to accept his deficiencies. To offer love feels so much better than to hold my MIAC to unattainable expectations.

Embarrassment

Sometimes I feel embarrassed by the behaviors and appearance of my MIAC, and other times I feel embarrassed *for* him because I expect a basic level of common sense and maturity that he's not capable of. On days when we have a clear, rational conversation, I forget how impaired he is until he says or does something quite delusional. Then I'm reminded that he has a profound thought disorder.

Embarrassment is a self-conscious emotion that's associated with guilt, shame, or pride. Because of the stigma around mental illness, you may feel embarrassed that your child is viewed as violent or dangerous or is incapable of self-care, and you think others blame you for his condition. A recent study revealed that family members tend to be more embarrassed by a relative's mental health challenges than they are by physical health conditions. There are ways to dissolve embarrassed feelings and discomfort around your child's disease. It's good to remember that it's just your emotional reaction to an imagined condemnation or judgment.

When you acknowledge your MIAC's inabilities, you can limit situations that could trigger inappropriate conduct. Ask your child what circumstances make him uncomfortable, so he can choose what activities he'd like to participate in. If you push your MIAC beyond his capabilities, it can cause meltdowns that will surely make you uncomfortable.

Ask your child what circumstances make him uncomfortable, so he can choose what activities he'd like to participate in.

Sometimes my MIAC wants to attend an event, and due to anxiety, overstimulation, or feelings of discomfort, he exhibits bizarre or peculiar behaviors in the form of increased anxiety, disorganized speech, delusional thoughts, or talking gibberish. When this occurs, I've learned to ignore most of it. It's simply a signal that the situation is too much for him to handle and a reminder to ask him if he needs to move to a quieter location or go home.

My natural preference is to remain on the sidelines. I'm the observer, the wallflower, and I never want to draw attention to myself. B is unkempt, wears dirty clothes and has wild curly hair, mumbles to himself, speaks irrationally, thinks people talk about him, curses when he becomes agitated, and argues the validity of what I say and who I am. And that makes us stand out. Further, he's six feet four inches tall. There's no chance of going unnoticed. At times I feel embarrassed by his lack of personal hygiene, his obvious insanity, and his inability to try to appear normal.

Part of the reason I felt so embarrassed being in public with my son wasn't about what others might think but my own reaction to his appearance and behavior. My own mom judged everyone and everything and always pointed out people who didn't look or act properly. It seems that I still had that voice in my head, whispering to me that my child didn't measure up. Because *my thoughts* caused much of my embarrassment, I've worked to release the distorted beliefs about how normal people should look and behave. What I discovered was that other people didn't pay that much attention, and if they did, it was only a brief glance in our direction.

> *Part of the reason I felt so embarrassed being in public with my son wasn't about what others might think, but my own reaction to his appearance and behavior.*

What intrigues me is that B rarely shows signs of being embarrassed by his appearance or actions. I'm not sure if it's due to his severe thought disturbance, but he doesn't seem to notice when others look his way.

Recognizing the courage that it takes for my MIAC to function in the world every day, I decided that if he could go out in public without being embarrassed, then I sure as hell better do the same. I knew I could learn to detach from others' opinions, past programming, and my own discomfort. And then, I realized that I see and feel what I expect to experience. So, if I anticipate embarrassment, then that will be my reality, but if I expect to be understood and accepted, then that's what occurs.

It's close to impossible to embarrass me today. I've seen and heard more bizarre, irrational things than I ever could have imagined. My life's been a circus sideshow of the strange and unusual. Some days I feel I've been bounced around inside a pinball machine and spit out the bottom, dazed but still alive. In spite of everything, my life's better now than before all this began.

> Tears flood my eyes, and my heart is heavy with the weight of a thousand broken dreams. I want to look away, but I can't. I watch, mesmerized by these healthy, normal young men. The comparison is extreme, the differences between them and my son. This is what normal looks like.

Each interaction is a reminder, a shard of pain that pierces my fragile heart. Tears cascade down my cheeks, my carefully constructed mask of acceptance is ripped away, and I feel exposed in the alien world of the ordinary. I feel a deep envy of these young men who look so much like my child but whose lives are filled with unlimited potential.

I'm even more envious and resentful of their parents. They have the opportunity to experience so much more than I ever will. I know it makes no sense to dream or wish, but for just a moment, I want what they have. I want to feel what they feel, experience what they experience, be free of the concern for what will happen to my son. I stand there, close my eyes, and imagine my son beside me as healthy and strong. He fits in with these young men, looks like them, acts like them. He's normal for a moment.

I'm snapped back to reality when B asks, "Why do you sound different today?"

His question is a clue that he's challenging my identity, insisting I'm not his real mom. This is my normal, this is my world, this is my child's reality. Just for a moment, I want to go back to my fantasy. Comparison is what breaks me every day, the what-ifs, the why me, the if-only-it-could-be-different, the how-did-I-end-up-here, the expectation of normal. I take a shaky breath, wipe the tears from my cheeks, visualize my heart healed and whole, and move on with my day. This is my life.

Pick Your Perspective

If your MIAC refuses medication or treatment, is violent or abusive, is homeless or in prison, or makes your life miserable, it's imperative that you choose to see things as they are without expecting them to change. I challenge you to look past the anger, past the turmoil, past the addiction, past the broken promises, past the horror of MI—and try to see the trapped, scared child behind the illness. Your MIAC does the very best he can within the limitations of his diseased brain. He didn't choose to be mentally ill, to be homeless, to become an addict, or to attack his family. Your MIAC's mind is filled with chaos and disorder. You can choose to accept what the disease has done to his thought processes and still protect yourself. It doesn't mean you condone the behavior, and it doesn't mean you allow abuse or addiction in your home. It means that you realize your child is trapped within the abyss of a damaged brain.

Your MIAC does the very best he can within the limitations of his diseased brain.

Once you start to regain some balance in your life, then you can look for remnants of your child that's buried beneath the ruins of his once healthy mind. As you pull yourself out of that dark, dismal place of regret, you begin to see glimpses of the child you remember. Be persistent as you look for the good instead of being fixated on what's gone. Create a new picture of who your child is now. List the qualities and personality traits that still emerge from time to time as a reminder to look for the glimmer of his soul behind the disease. Cultivate a deep acceptance and acknowledgment for who your child has become.

We sit in the ER again. I tremble. My heart beats wild and loud as I run to the nearest restroom to vomit. I hate this place. It's a reminder that I have failed yet again to help B get better. As I sit under the glaring, harsh waiting room lights, misery washes over me. So much time, energy, and money wasted on yet another attempt to get him help. As he watches the nurse's computer to make sure it's not recording him, I relive the last few months.

We've exhausted all medication options, so I turned to a functional medicine doctor as a last resort.

Doctor visits, herbal remedies, blood and nutrition tests have cost hundreds of dollars each month. It takes hours to purchase healthy foods, monitor his meals, and make sure he remembers to take all his supplements. Over the last six months, I've seen small improvements. I'm cautiously optimistic. B even says he feels well enough to go back to work part time. He lasts less than one week at that job. He quits because he's sure everyone is plotting against him.

My stomach churns, my head's ready to split, my shoulders droop as I realize he's no better than when we began this long journey. Head down to hide my tears, I admit defeat to the MI monster that has taken my intelligent, beautiful son.

Over the last ten years, I've poured endless time, money, and resources into attempts to fix my MIAC. Are things different? Yes and no. Is he better? Yes and no. Did the things I struggled to do for him make a difference? I don't have an honest answer to that.

My MIAC is slightly better, but he's not well, and he's definitely not healed. Did the multiple strategies, doctors, or therapies I tried help, or is it the passing of time that's shifted his disease? I don't have the answer and, unfortunately, neither does the medical community. What I do know is that I wanted to do everything within my power to make my child's life better.

I'd wager that your MIAC's mental health has become your new project. You've read every book and article about MI you can find, poured countless hours into researching brain disease, worked to find quality health care providers, talked until you're blue in the face trying to convince him he's sick, and investigated every holistic treatment option available. You feel it's your duty, your obligation as his mother, to keep going until you find an answer. Would you have put so much effort into it if you'd been told there were no answers? Would you have made different choices if you'd known that normal would remain only a memory?

> *Would you have put so much effort into it*
> *if you'd been told there are no answers?*

Guilty and heartbroken over what my son will miss, I'm easily persuaded to buy the things he asks for. One day it was an outlandish business idea, and he just needed five hundred dollars. Another day he wanted to create a card game and needed a computer program. Every day it's two dollars to buy soda or snacks at the gas station. It's something every day—an herbal supplement he wants to try, expensive food that will make him feel better, just a few bucks for cigarettes. It never ends, and the more I give him, the more he wants. It's a distraction from his life to spend money on things he believes will help him feel better.

I mistakenly think I'll make his life more bearable if I give in to his constant demands for money when in reality, I've created a money monster. By never saying no, I've sent the message that money can fix his problems and that I have an unlimited supply of funds. I don't.

And yet, it's so much easier to give him what he asks for than to deal with him when he yells, begs, or becomes hostile when I refuse. The constant barrage of verbal coercion exhausts me. *Maybe if I give him what he wants, he'll go do something instead of hovering around me trying to persuade me to give in to his demands. I just want him to stop pestering me, to stop making me feel guilty, to stop acting irrationally, to stop behaving like a ten-year-old.* Reality hits home when I calculate the amount of money I've given him each month.

The real eye-opener was that his quality of life is no better, his mental health is no better, his thought disorder is no better. I've exhausted every avenue, and all I have to show for it is my own ruined life. All of his purchases were poor choices, and none of them could make him better.

The more money you give your child, the worse he may actually become. Like an addict who waits for his next fix, he doesn't have the space to learn any skills to cope. You need to stop. Stop giving away all your time, stop using up all your energy, stop handing out all your money—you just need to stop. All this spending is your own distraction from the fact that your MIAC has an incurable disease.

The facade of recovery and a return to normal has to be obliterated in order for you to begin to take your life back. Then the hard work starts as you step back from micromanaging your MIAC, work to rebuild your life, and allow situations to unfold naturally. It starts when you say no more often, spend time doing things you enjoy, and stop trying to fix the unfixable. You'll get so much pushback at first that you'll want to give up and go back to what feels comfortable, but in your heart, you know that you need to create change to protect your own sanity.

> *The facade of recovery and a return to normal has to be obliterated in order for you to begin to take your life back.*

So, how do you do that? Stop and question each decision you make about your child's care. Here are some questions you can ask:

- Will your time, energy, or money spent on *(fill in the blank)* enhance the quality of your child's life?
- If you don't do *(fill in the blank)*, will your child's health or mental stability be damaged?
- How will doing or not doing *(fill in the blank)* impact you, your health, your finances, and your happiness?
- In the long run, will this decision make a difference?

These are basic questions, and you may come up with different ones, but it's important to consider all the consequences of the choices you make for your MIAC.

As you become healthier and stick to your convictions, your interactions will become more positive. You won't give away more than you have, and while your child will still expect and demand certain things, you'll be able to say no and feel okay with that decision. He'll always do more taking and less giving due to his brain disorder, but you'll be the one who decides what to give him. No more trying to make up for a dismal life, no more feeling guilty, no more giving in to unreasonable demands, no more buckling under all the begging. It'll become your habit to run every choice past your qualifier questions.

With time, your MIAC will realize that he can no longer manipulate you with guilt or wear you down with his continual requests. Life becomes calmer, and you'll feel more in control.

Now that you've got a handle on healthy choices for yourself, it's time to modify your expectations for your child, yourself, and others.

Visualization Journey

Sit in a comfortable, quiet place. Close your eyes.

Breathe in and out slowly to the count of three several times until you feel yourself begin to relax.

Visualize yourself on the side of a beautiful river that glistens in the sunlight. You take the path along the river's edge and enjoy the sound of the gurgling water as it washes over small rocks. The air smells fresh and clean, and you watch as an occasional bird swoops down to catch a fish.

In the distance, you see a boat dock. You continue to walk in that direction, curious.

At the dock, you find a small rowboat bobbing gently up and down with the current. Look closer, and you see that your grandmother is sitting inside. She beckons you to climb in with her. You take the seat in the back of the boat near the oars. You've never rowed a boat before, but Grandmother assures you that she'll help you navigate.

You set out and enjoy the scenery. You feel the small boat gently rock with the current as you head down the river. Grandmother hums a gentle tune. You feel peaceful.

Up ahead, you see a fork in the river, and you need to decide which way to go. You're not sure which is best, but Grandmother reminds you to listen to your heart and your gut. You choose a direction and continue on.

You keep rowing. Each time you come to a fork, you look inside yourself and choose as Grandmother encourages you. You feel safe and serene.

Up ahead, you see dark clouds beginning to form. Should you turn back? You aren't sure you can handle the boat in a storm. You are uncomfortable and a little fearful. What will happen if you keep going? Grandmother sits quietly and waits for you to make a decision. She will be with you whatever choice you make.

You decide to turn back and begin to turn the small boat around.

Now you are rowing against the current. You have to pull hard on the oars. Every time you think you've made progress, the strong water pushes you back.

Unsure what to do, you stop. The current grabs the boat, and you're now traveling down the river backward, unable to see where you're going. Grandmother encourages you to turn the boat around, so you can see what's ahead. In a soft voice, she reminds you that it isn't possible to go backward on the river or in life. You must live in the present, and you need to face forward to handle what the future may bring.

Now you have only one option. Life is like that—sometimes you have choices, and sometimes you don't. You row into the storm as you think longingly of the peaceful waters behind you.

But the storm requires all your attention. All your focus is on what's ahead. You hold tight to the oars, aware that if you lose one, your chances of staying on course are reduced.

You're vigilant, and you keep rowing, moving forward until the storm is finally behind you. When you stop to catch your breath, you see the beautiful placid river as it stretches around the bend in front of you.

You row toward the river's edge. Grandmother turns around to share a few words of wisdom with you.

"Your life is like the boat. If you go with the flow, you handle things as they occur. You may hit a few storms now and then, but you know there is clear water on the other side. No storm lasts forever. Just hold strong to your intuition, and you can weather any disturbance.

"On the other hand, if you try to turn around, that's when you run into trouble. It isn't possible to row against the current, and you can't relive the past. If you don't use your intuition, you turn in circles without going anywhere. So, remember, child, you don't have to go fast, but you must continue to move forward. You can and must choose which fork to take and pull over to rest when you grow tired. But never try to go back. You get stuck when you can't make a choice, when you're at a fork in the river, or when you want to turn around. Even if you can't see what's around the next bend in the river, it's always best to move forward."

Grandmother helps you out of the boat and onto the riverbank. She gives you a long, loving hug and wishes you well. You stop and take a few deep breaths. You can hear the river gurgling, smell the moist earth, and hear the sounds of the forest close by. Spanning the river, you see a beautiful, iridescent rainbow.

When you're ready, open your eyes and journal any messages, words, or symbols you received. What did you learn while rowing your boat? What messages did the river give you? What did Grandmother smell like? Did she leave any gifts?

Expectations are Planned Resentments

We are sisters
Bound by expectations
We hold on to lost dreams
We come to terms with what can't be changed
We learn to live in a new reality
We are sisters

B asks, "Can I clean my own condo? I don't need your help. Let me take care of it myself." He wants to show me that he's capable. I'm hesitant but want to see for myself what he can handle on his own. My expectations are high as he outlines his detailed cleaning plan.

I offer a couple suggestions and ask, "Would it help if I give you reminders?"

"No, Mom. I can do this without your help."

Yippee! I'm so tired of cleaning his place, tired of bribing him to help me clean, tired of micromanaging his life.

A month later, I take in the fiasco around me. I can't believe what's happened in a few short weeks. Gagging from the smell, I cover my mouth and nose with my sleeve as I survey the wreckage of his once clean home. My eyes jump to the kitchen and scan the disaster. The trash is pungent with rotted food, the sink and countertop stacked with moldy dishes, and the stove is covered in a thick layer of grease and dirty skillets.

I shudder and move toward the noxious smell that wafts from the spare bedroom. This can't all be from the litter box, can it? The box overflows with feces. I cringe and take a step closer to check out the bed. The comforter is saturated with cat pee, the mattress ruined. The smell makes my eyes water. A shiver of nausea snakes through my belly.

Do I even dare check the bathroom? I steel myself and head for his bedroom first. Foul, sweaty body odor assaults me at the door. The sheets have an oily impression of where he lies, and in the corner is an enormous pile of rancid clothes. There's a crusty bath towel on the floor and what looks like a pool of dried blood. What happened there? This looks like a crime scene.

I muster the nerve and head to the bathroom. It's worse than a gas station restroom. I don't even want to step through the door. The toilet looks like something exploded in it, stiff washcloths stick to the side of the tub, and the bottom of the shower curtain is black. How did this happen? Where did his plan go wrong? How is it possible to accumulate this much filth in such a short time? I walk out of the condo and close the door behind me.

Alone in the hallway, tears prick my eyes as I give up all expectations I've had for B to live independently.

Expectations create many problems. Most of your struggles are caused because you expect that something will happen a certain way, and if it doesn't, you're miserable. You've created a fantasy world of what your future will look like, what your child's future will look like, what's appropriate behavior for others, and how you think society should act and treat its citizens. Expectations are nothing more than wishes, dreams, hopes, and assumptions that your life will unfold in accordance with your internal plan. "The primary cause of unhappiness is never the situation, but your thoughts about it,"

shares Eckhart Tolle from his book *A New Earth: Awakening to Your Life's Purpose.*

Expectations are nothing more than wishes, dreams, hopes, and assumptions that your life will unfold in accordance with your internal plan.

Your Expectations

When life follows your expectations, you're usually happy. But when things fall apart, you feel the need to argue, push, and struggle to move them back into alignment with your plan for a good life. You get resentful. You're under the false notion that you can control how life unfolds and that you can put it back on track when it goes terribly wrong.

What would happen if you let go of your expectations for yourself and others? What if you put more energy into accepting what occurs rather than trying to change it? The goal is to live in *acceptance* rather than *expectation*. While most expectations are easy to identify, unspoken expectations can cause the most harm. Coupled with their unrealistic nature, you've created the perfect recipe for relationship failure.

Think about it; you live most of your life in a state of expectation. You have expectations about traffic, the weather, how work will flow, how your family and friends should act, how busy the grocery store will be, how quickly the waitress will serve you, how good the food will be, how your child should behave, and what his life will look like when he's grown. Your life is a constant state of expectations—which only sets you up to feel miserable, angry, and resentful.

Where do expectations originate? Are they learned from family or society? Are expectations right or wrong? How do you change or upgrade your expectations? How do you let go of what doesn't serve you? Below are some expectations we all have:

- You want others to think like you do.
- You expect others to adhere to your moral and ethical code.
- You expect others to treat you a certain way.
- You want others to do things the same way you do.
- You expect others to reciprocate kind deeds.
- You want others to like you.

Unspoken expectations are tricky because they may be hidden from others and sometimes even yourself. These are tied to childhood wounds, family dynamics, or religious beliefs. They may only make sense to you, and they aren't always rational. For example, if I do this, then you need to do that. Because we're in a relationship, you need to treat me a certain way. Certain types of people or behaviors are bad. You expect your child to think and behave like you. Children should do or be *(fill in the blank)*. To be a good mom, you must do *(fill in the blank)*. Good people do or don't do *(fill in the blank)*.

Unrealistic expectations can be hurtful and harmful. For example:

- The belief that certain behaviors, when not performed, are deal-breakers in relationships
- The belief that your child and your family can live up to your demands
- The expectation that life should be fair
- The belief everyone needs to agree with you for you to feel good about yourself
- The desire for others to know and do what you want without the need to ask
- The idea that you can change your MIAC

When family and friends don't agree with your unrealistic expectations, it creates drama and turmoil in relationships—and resentment on both sides. If you can't recognize the truth about a situation; if you wait for solutions to show up rather than create them; if you feel doomed to failure or need to have certain things or people in your life to be happy, then you need to reconsider your expectations and determine their validity.

We all frequently get triggered by our expectations. One of my triggers is when others don't respect my time. In my mind, they should have the courtesy to be on time and let me know if they'll be late or can't make it at all. It used to make me angry if someone didn't treat me according to my expectations. I felt disrespected, used, and unworthy. Being on time might be a societal expectation, but it's unrealistic to think that everyone will always be on time. I now realize that being prompt is an expectation I have for myself, but it's not something I expect others to follow. Their reasons for being late have nothing to do with me.

Unspoken expectations hide in the back of your subconscious and patiently wait to jump out when others don't measure up. Until you dig a little deeper, you may not even be aware of them. Maybe you feel that others should reciprocate a kindness, but your expectation is never voiced. Or you expect that if you give your MIAC money, he has to do what you say and follow your rules. Eventually, you feel that others are taking advantage of you when they don't adhere to your hidden agenda, and then you become angry and retaliate out of resentment.

The word *expectation* could actually be replaced with *hopes and dreams*. From the moment your child is born, you imagined and hoped for only good to happen in his life. You couldn't comprehend anything cruel or malicious destroying this beautiful new person, and you'd do everything possible to prevent that. You had so many expectations for your child because you wanted him to have what you consider a wonderful life. You expected his life to unfold and follow traditional norms. Further, you assumed that if it didn't, then you'd both be miserable. There are no guarantees, but you envisioned how you wanted his life to be. And when that didn't happen, you grew angry, bitter, and resentful.

Of course, your real life reminds you that you don't have complete authority over your child. Plus, your MIAC has his own ideas of what his life will look like, and his view may be different from yours. Even when you know they're no longer valid, why do you continue to hold so tight to your expectations? The answer is very simple: things that are familiar and comfortable make you feel safe, and those that go against your internal compass makes you feel unprotected and vulnerable.

When your expectations are challenged by new information, and you still cling to them, it's time to evaluate why you're resistant to redefining your beliefs. What's going on in your subconscious that keeps you stuck in old thoughts and behaviors?

There are several reasons why you might get stuck in your beliefs and continue to struggle, suffer, and make yourself sick. These can cause you to fail, refuse to change, and impede progress toward what you want. There are always hidden payoffs when you stay stuck. Which of these resonate with you?

- What are you avoiding when you hold on to expectations for your MIAC? Are you afraid of change, responsibility, love, success, failure, visibility, or vulnerability? What do you need to give up to let go of your expectations—hopes, dreams, what you thought things would look like?
- Who do you punish and/or love when you hold on to outdated beliefs? Do you choose to fail or refuse to be happy just to prove that your MIAC's behavior and life are awful? Is this your way of punishing your child, yourself, God, your spouse, family, parents, and everyone else? Does it prove that they don't love you enough when they don't abide by your rules and beliefs? Maybe you hang on until everyone lives up to your expectations and apologizes for making you miserable. This, after all, proves that you're right. Or maybe, out of love for them, you refuse to change and do better. Do you have a hidden belief that if you really love them, you'll continue to suffer and struggle beside them?
- Are your emotions *righteous* or *valid*? Do you feel guilty, angry, hurt, depressed, or (*fill in the blank*)? Do you refuse to express the emotion honestly and let it go and, instead, complain to everyone but your MIAC, who's the cause of the unpleasant feelings? Do you deal with the situation indirectly as a way to sidestep feeling vulnerable? Is what you're feeling someone else's fault, or do you need to own the emotions?

- What are you holding out for—a promise that your MIAC will make changes that improve his actions and behaviors?
- Do you manipulate to gain pity? Do you play the victim? Do you want an audience to feel sorry for you? Are you a martyr or noble sufferer? Do you suffer in silence yet expect everyone to know what you're going through and then punish them because you suffer? Do you secretly want everyone, especially God, to follow *your* plan and expectations?
- Do you feel entitled because you feel better than or less than others and expect special treatment? Does being the mom of a MIAC put you in a special class of sufferers?
- What are you afraid to lose if you make changes concerning your MIAC? Will you lose friends, attention, excuses, invisibility, your child's love, the opportunity to control everything—or the chance to stay miserable?

After years of ever-expanding diagnoses (ADHD, Tourette's Syndrome, Asperger's, PTSD, strange behaviors, poor impulse control, an unstable job history, an eating disorder, and addictions), I thought that when B was finally diagnosed with a mental illness, life would get back on track. Hospitalization, therapy, and medication should put him on the path of a normal, healthy young adult, right? That expectation was an unrealistic pipe dream. With no prior knowledge of the prognosis and recovery curve for severe mental illness, I quickly learned how faulty my assumption was.

> B looks okay. He's out of the hospital, on medications, and knows he's sick, so he should be able to do something. All he does is sit on the couch and say he doesn't feel well enough to do anything else. Maybe he needs to get out of the house, volunteer, or find a part-time job. He pushes back so hard when forced to do anything.
>
> Why can he recite what he should do but is unable to complete basic tasks? Why can't he follow suggestions to

reduce his anxiety? Why does he freak out every time we get in the car to go anywhere? Why doesn't he bathe or change his clothes? What's with the strange dietary choices? On and on it goes.

Every expectation I had for my MIAC ended up being unrealistic and impossible for him to follow. Let me repeat that: *every single expectation was unrealistic.*

Was he lazy, manipulative, or just being defiant? I was convinced that my child wasn't even trying. I reasoned, pleaded, begged, coerced, and bribed him, but none of it worked. My thick brain refused to accept that he wasn't capable of the most basic life skills. We struggled daily—me expecting him to be healthy and well while he was trying to make me understand that he wasn't capable of meeting those expectations.

> *Every expectation I had for my MIAC ended up unrealistic and impossible for him to follow. Let me repeat that:* every single expectation was unrealistic.

All my suggestions fell on a disordered brain. He wanted, but wasn't able, to initiate any changes or improvements, and I droned on and on about what he should do. *You need to take a shower. You need to change your clothes. It's time to clean your room, wash the sheets, and dust. Let's go to the grocery store. How about you volunteer one afternoon a week? I'll go with you. Let's play a game, go for a walk, or watch a movie. You need to find a hobby. Why don't you read a book? Let's go visit your sister. How about going out to lunch? Are you ready to look for a part-time job? Do something, anything!* Instead, he just laid in bed all day.

Nothing ever changed. Day in and day out, we continued to argue and struggle, push and pull at each other, as I tried to force him to live up to my expectations. My MIAC tried, but he wasn't well enough to verbalize that this wasn't possible. Our lives were an endless circle of trying and failing. I expected to see incremental improvements over weeks, months, and years. He expected to see progress, too. I became so tired of pushing him to do something that resembled progress or growth, and we both grew weary of the game I perpetuated. There were no winners, only losers.

When I made him go out to run errands with me, he'd be in bed for the next two days. Doctors told me that if he only sat on the couch and watched TV two years after a psychotic break, that was progress. How was that possible? Why hadn't doctors, in the beginning, given me more realistic expectations of what recovery looked like in severe MI? Wouldn't it have been beneficial for everyone involved in this tragedy to be honest about the probable prognosis?

Over a period of five years, very little had changed. He talked about how he wanted things to be different. I talked about how I wanted better things for him, but nothing changed. I started to recognize that my expectations were mine alone. His expectations were very small and revolved around internal changes, and they weren't about his life going back to normal but about feeling better. So, I backed off and let my son do what he wanted. If he said he didn't feel well enough to do something, I didn't push.

B wanted to stop the voices, stop the hallucinations, stop the anxiety, make a few friends, have a pet, and live a somewhat independent life. My expectations were quite different. I expected his life to be better and for him to be independent. I wanted him to take care of his personal hygiene, maintain his home, have a part-time job, learn how to follow strategies to relieve anxiety, be responsible with his money, reduce his angry outbursts, and find constructive ways to fill his free time. We were both trapped in an endless loop of unrealistic expectations.

"We're in a cycle of pain that repeats with no progress," I told his case manager as we sat in our annual review.

"Until he can master the basic life-care skills," she said, "he's incapable of moving to the next level of recovery."

I was stunned. All this talk about recovery had been nothing but wishful thinking and false hope. Instead of using the word *recovery*, which implies a return to a former level of performance, the professionals should talk about a new *limited level of ability*.

It had been cruel to suggest that my MIAC could regain what was lost. It misled his family and B, perpetuating a cycle of hope followed by shattered dreams. Wouldn't it have been better for everyone to understand the truth of the disease up front?

You won't be able to immediately curb your expectations for your MIAC, and there will still be days when you want to remind your MIAC about what you think he needs to do. You'll bite your tongue in an effort to stop forcing your wants on your child.

But when you look at the big picture, do any of the things you want actually matter? While some things do, the majority don't. Being dirty never killed anyone, a clean room doesn't make him better, having a job won't add to his worth, and staying busy can't fix a damaged brain. Let go of the illusion that anything can make him different. None of the things you want for your child are possible without a healthy brain, and none of your expectations will make his brain better.

The only expectations you should have relate to good manners. You should expect your MIAC to be polite and respectful to you and others. If he starts to badmouth you, walk away.

Don't argue or try to persuade him to think or act the way you want him to. Don't reprimand or punish; instead, gently encourage. Pick your battles. Stop the continual arguments about what he should be doing. This truce will benefit both of you. Your MIAC can relax and be who he is, and you can enjoy simply spending time with your child without excessive concern about every detail. If your child is verbally or physically abusive and lives with you, you need to decide where to draw the line and what you'll enforce for your own safety.

In hindsight, you'll see how your expectations caused harm. They created a no-win situation for both of you and invited tension and anxiety into your relationship. You made your child's life much more difficult because he couldn't conform to your wishes.

When you give up your expectations, you give up your hope that one day, he'll go back to his former abilities—and that allows you to accept and love who he is now. Notice that I didn't say you have to *like* who he is now. Nor do you have to put up with unacceptable behavior, but you'll realize that he can't control his actions. Remember, his lack of control isn't a free pass for him to do as he pleases. You can and should hold on to certain behavioral expectations if he's living in your house.

I call and call, but my son doesn't answer. I drive home, thinking he's hurt or dead. Knots of fear and anger sit heavy in my stomach. What has he done now? Maybe he fell and hit his head, maybe he's drunk and unconscious, maybe he overdosed? My hands shake, my throat is tight, sweat runs down the back of my neck. Just answer the phone. Please, just answer the phone!

A friend heads to my house to pick up a package I have for her.

"Let yourself in," I say. "I'm a few minutes away. I'm worried about B. He won't answer his phone."

"He's probably okay," she assures me, but has no clue what a severe MIAC looks like.

I try not to speed, but pictures of my dead son fill my mind. Is this how it's going to end? Home at last, I jump out of the car. My heart pounds in my ears as I run for the door. I find my friend in a chair, my son pacing the room. He walks in circles, babbling nonsense, and then I see he's wearing only boxers.

"Where are your pants?" I ask him and get more gibberish.

My friend asks, "What's wrong with him?"

"This is what severe mental illness looks like. This is the ugly face of insanity," I say.

"He's drunk again," I continue, "after he promised this morning that he'd stop—not a silly little drunk, but an alcohol poisoning drunk. On top of his six psych medications, this could kill him."

Suddenly, the fear and anxiety I feel morph into a flash of red-hot anger. Gone are my expectations of being a perfect mom, of understanding that he's sick, of showing any compassion for what he deals with every day, and in its place is an uncontrollable fury fueled by panic, despair, frustration, and responsibility.

"I've had enough of this!" I shout. "If you want to die, then just do it, so we can stop playing this game of chicken. One day you'll drink too much, and it'll kill you, and at this point, it would be a relief to have this daily nightmare over with."

My friend looks on in shock. But she hasn't walked in my shoes for the past eight years.

I feel a deep sense of shame for what I said. Abject failure fills my heart. I facilitate a class on how to handle situations like this, and yet I've fallen short of my expectations for myself. I'm sure my friend thinks I'm a horrible mother for wishing my son dead. My one saving grace is that he's so far gone, he won't remember what I said—but I will. As hard as I try to do the right things by him and for him, some days I'm not even capable of basic decency. I won't need to ask his forgiveness, but forgiving myself will take time.

As for my friend, she was thrown into the fire, had a front-row seat to witness what caring for a MIAC looks like on a bad day, and lucky for me, she offered me compassion and forgiveness.

This is a reminder that trying to be perfect doesn't work. By stuffing all my emotions, they eventually burst forth like an overstuffed suitcase.

When do you decide that enough is enough? How do you come to terms with your inability to make your child healthy? You have so many unrealistic expectations for yourself, such as:

- You need to be perfect.
- You need to be a supermom.
- You need to give 100 percent all the time.
- You need to see positive results to feel like a good mom.
- You need to be in control of everything.
- You need to fix your MIAC.
- You need to give your child whatever he wants because he can't achieve it on his own.
- You need to tolerate his bad behavior because he's sick.
- You need to make him happy.
- You need to teach him how to take care of himself.

One day, you'll wake up and realize you're in the same place you started. If you continue to tread water, you'll surely drown. No amount of energy or discussion on your part will make your child think or behave rationally. Your attempts to live up to your expectations of what a perfect mom should be will do you in. If you don't revise your expectations for yourself, you'll become a casualty in this fight.

No amount of energy or discussion on your part will make your child think or behave rationally.

It's time to adopt more realistic expectations for what your role should be as the mother of a MIAC. You must accept the fact that you cannot change your child's prognosis. As you struggle with your shoulds, woulds, and coulds, remind yourself to let go of all the harmful, unrealistic expectations.

- Recognize your expectations as insanity on your part.

- Evaluate the standards to which you hold yourself. Do any of them seem attainable?
- State your expectations out loud. Are they realistic? Would you hold your friends to those standards?
- Call a time-out for yourself. Tell yourself to stop being ridiculous! Take a break from it all and breathe deeply.
- Find the humor in your expectations.
- Forgive yourself for not being perfect. Forgive your child, too.
- Let it all go. Write your expectations on a piece of paper, and then burn the list. Create a new list of attainable goals.
- Offer yourself the same grace you offer others when they make mistakes.
- Challenge yourself to get comfortable with being imperfect. Then you can accept imperfection in others.

Once you ease up on your expectations for yourself, everything feels easier. It no longer seems like you're rowing against the current but that you're allowing circumstances to have an uncomplicated flow.

It's not a one-and-done thing. You'll still have expectations, even after years of work to let them go. Every time you think you've hit the bottom of your expectations bucket, a few stragglers will float to the surface, ready to be plucked up, inspected, and released. It's a lifelong process. It's a difficult habit to break, this need for everyone to behave according to your ideals. You'll still find yourself asking your MIAC to do things normal adults do without being told. When that happens, laugh at yourself and say, "Let it go, Mama. Let it go."

My revised expectations for myself as the mom of a MIAC are now:

- To *love him* no matter who he is or what he's capable of, even on the days I don't like him.
- To *excuse his behavior* when I know it's a symptom of his brain disease. It doesn't mean I condone his behavior, but I understand it's his illness and not him.
- To remind him of *his value and worth* regardless of his recovery.

- To acknowledge and remind him of *his courage* in the face of ongoing suffering and struggle.
- To *encourage his attempts* to meet his goals for growth, even when he's not successful.
- To *apologize* when I get angry because I allowed him to push my buttons.
- To always be an *advocate* for him and his care.
- To allow him to be who he is and *stop trying to fix* him.
- To treat him with *respect* and *compassion*.
- To *allow* him to refuse treatment or help.

Marital Expectations

B's in the lockdown psych unit for the second time in a year, and the prospect of his long-term prognosis has me free-floating in a sea of despair. I can't think, my heart aches, and I want to curl up in the fetal position and cry myself to sleep. Today everything feels too heavy to carry alone, and I just want to sit next to my husband (B's stepdad) and feel his arms around me.

"Hey D, I'm really struggling today. Do you have time to talk with me for a while?"

He looks up from the computer. "It's my fantasy football draft night. The pick is in five minutes. Can you give me half an hour, and I'll come find you? Don't bother me until then."

"Okay," I say. I distract myself with mindless TV while I think about how his hobby seems more important than me.

The longer I sit and wait, the more upset and resentful I become. Is it unreasonable to expect him to drop everything and be there for me? Am I selfish for expecting him to put me first? My brain spins a web of stories about how he must not love me, how I don't deserve his time and attention, how I shouldn't have asked for help. I feel sick, sad, and so terribly alone.

I keep an eye on the clock as time slowly ticks by. Every minute feels like an hour. I start to cry. It's now been an hour, then two, then three, and I have to acknowledge that he decided that my problem isn't worth his time.

What's wrong with him? He saw how upset I was and promised to be available. What kind of husband does this to his wife during a crisis? I can't believe this is happening in the midst of everything else.

So began the end of my relationship with my second husband. I was willing to compromise on a lot of issues, but I had certain expectations for my spouse that were deal-breakers. I expect to be supported in a crisis, I expect him to keep his word, and I expect him to be emotionally available. What's the point of marriage if your husband doesn't have your back, is unreliable, and trivializes your needs? That was one of the hardest days of my life. I felt like everything had come apart in the span of two short weeks.

Going through this life-altering event with my son changed me as a person. I was no longer willing to put up with things I'd overlooked in the past. I cut ties with family members who weren't supportive and made the difficult decision to get divorced. Being alone with my grief felt better than living with someone who chose to be emotionally absent. It was hard enough to deal with what was on my plate. I didn't need to be blamed for my son's illness or criticized for the choices I had to make. I wanted to think that, as a couple, we would be there for each other if something terrible happened. My husband was adamant that my son would never live with us, which made my decision to divorce easy.

Being alone with my grief felt better than living with someone who chose to be emotionally absent.

I also had unfulfilled expectations for my son's biological dad. I wanted him to be a partner in the legal responsibility for our son. When we were married, he'd never been willing or able to make the hard decisions, and that didn't change when B became ill. Even though my son lived with his dad, every time he needed to be hospitalized, I had to handle it. So when the hospital recommended that we seek legal guardianship, I was responsible for finding and paying for an attorney, going to court, and becoming my son's legal guardian. The court even questioned why his dad didn't want to be a guardian too. It seems he wanted to have his opinion and wanted to be in charge, but he didn't want the responsibility of making decisions that affected our son's life.

Expectations of Family and Friends

My expectations extended beyond just my spouses. Mental illness scares people. People don't understand it, it can appear out of nowhere, and recovery is often limited. Others want to blame the odd behaviors on bad parents, laziness, or a lack of self-control. Or they simply act like your child no longer exists.

I believe that family and friends do this to distance themselves from the randomness of MI. Why? Because it terrifies them. If it can happen to a family member or the child of a close friend, then it could also happen to their child. It's easier to put on blinders than to acknowledge and have contact with the mom of a MIAC.

At a time when the support of family and friends is needed most, they fade into the woodwork of their own lives and distance themselves from the MIAC as if he's contagious. They also distance themselves from you. When family and friends don't know what to say or don't agree with the MIAC's inability to control his behavior, they move on without you. Most don't want to become more educated. While you're completely wrapped up in the care of your MIAC, family and friends only want to know the bare minimum.

Ironically, the closer the family member, the more the diagnosis impacts your relationship. Not only do they remove themselves from your child's life, but they may blame you for his illness. *There must be a reason for this*, they think. It can't be random chance. You see, the world becomes an incredibly frightful place if bad things happen for no apparent reason. Distancing themselves has nothing to do with how much these people care but because they're uninformed.

If the stigma against MI is going to stop, it will come through a collective understanding of how it manifests—and the more people who understand, the better. Everyone's life is touched by mental illness in some way; it just looks different in different families. MI can be expressed through anxiety, depression, addiction, failure to launch, anger management issues, mood dysregulation, aggression, OCD, addiction, violence, homelessness, or incarceration.

Your child's diagnosis and long-term prognosis is an all-encompassing event for you, but for others close to you, it barely registers as something to think about. At a time when you really need someone to be there for you, many choose to be unavailable. You need someone to talk to, share your grief with, and help you navigate this new reality. But your expectations for family and friends could be altogether unrealistic. As a consequence, you feel terribly alone when you desperately need support and empathy. Their reluctance to support you feels like a slap in the face, but it's not personal.

Mental illness is a zebra in a herd of horses. It's the only disease where the sick person is blamed for the symptoms of their illness and their inability to control the outcome. Nobody brings you a covered dish or asks what they can do to help when your child becomes irrational, psychotic, and delusional. In their minds, a hospital stay and chronic disease diagnosis is a one-time event. Most illnesses can be managed with medication and/or therapy and rarely involve ongoing hospital stays. Everybody understands physical illnesses, but mental illness is riddled with false assumptions, misunderstandings, and stigma.

It's the only disease where the sick person is blamed for the symptoms of their illness and their inability to control the outcome.

Family and friends ask me how often I visit my son, but they don't understand what a visit with him is like. I drive half an hour to stare at him and listen to his irrational chatter for fifteen minutes and then drive home. He's not well enough to watch a movie, read a book, play cards, listen to music, take a walk, or have a normal conversation. Other visits consist of me delivering cigarettes, bottled water, and snacks. Some days he goes to the store with me, and some days he insists I'm an imposter, and I turn around and go home.

No matter how many times I explain how things are to others, it never seems to sink in. Friends and family assume he's going to get better and can't comprehend how difficult our visits are. I expected that, over time, they'd begin to grasp the complexity of my son's illness, but that didn't happen. Again, it's not personal.

When your world shatters, every aspect of it is affected. You literally close the book on your old life and need to write another. Anything that doesn't serve you, that doesn't add value, that doesn't make you feel good, that doesn't move you in a positive direction, needs to go—and you need to move on. This might seem drastic, but if you're going to survive this nightmare, anything that doesn't help you needs to be removed.

You had no clue what mental illness looked like until it came into your life. And your family and friends have no frame of reference either. They just don't know. You can either be angry and resentful that they don't want to understand, or you can choose to educate them. Somebody has to start the conversations about this tragedy that affects so many families. Make it your mission to talk to people about your child, his struggles, and your struggles in hopes that the information you share will start to change the way people view MI.

When I began to share my story, people I barely knew seemed eager to learn more, and many shared their own stories of struggle within their families or with close friends. They welcomed the information I offered. In these instances, it helps me feel like I'm making a difference. I can't help my son, but I can help guide other moms as they navigate life with a MIAC.

The hard truth is that relatives won't live up to your expectations. Every assumption you have for everyone close to you changes the instant your child becomes mentally ill. The biggest lesson is that when you have expectations, you set yourself up for disappointment. Just because you'd do something for others doesn't mean they will do the same for you.

The biggest lesson is that when you have expectations, you set yourself up for disappointment.

Expectations for Care

I received a call from the psych hospital, and the same nurse that refused to acknowledge that my son was a patient yesterday says, "B will be released in the next twenty-four hours."

"What are you talking about?" I ask. "He's not well enough to be released. He's only been there five days. He's still hearing voices, is delusional, and extremely paranoid."

How can they think he should be released? I try to wrap my head around this news. I'm anxious and afraid for him.

I ask, "Why? Why? It took six months, the police, and a signed affidavit to get him into the hospital."

"He says he's no longer a threat to himself or others, so by law, we have to release him if he doesn't want to stay."

"But didn't we just determine that he's psychotic and unable to make decisions in his own best interest? So now he's had five days of meds, and all of a sudden, he's able to think for himself?" I can't believe this is happening.

What kind of healthcare system allows an obviously delusional person with a diagnosed thought disorder to decide when he's ready to leave treatment? He's not even living in this reality. He thinks people are trying to kill him, thinks all food and water is poisoned, sees people who aren't there, and thinks everyone is in on an elaborate plan to hurt him. I worked so hard to get him into the hospital and expected they would keep him until he was at least close to well.

I tell the nurse, "B has no money, no phone, no car, no friends, and no place to live."

She doesn't seem to care and reiterates, "He will be released by eight tomorrow morning."

I feel sick, frustrated, and disgusted with the way our mental healthcare system operates.

B is released with no call to me or his dad to come pick him up. He shows up at his dad's house in the afternoon. He walked three hours to get there. He's dehydrated, delusional, and seems no better than when I committed him five days ago.

I want to scream and cry and howl at the maltreatment of the mentally ill. How does someone go from a lockdown psych ward for the most severely ill to being released on his own recognizance after a few days? Why must I fight a battle just to get my MIAC the care he so desperately needs and deserves?

I expected him to get better. I expected the law to be on my side. I expected the hospital to offer advice and support. I expected this to begin recovery for my child. I am both disappointed and devastated.

We live in one of the wealthiest industrialized countries, and I expected mental healthcare to be comparable to the care offered for any other disease, but that isn't the case. How is it possible that an illness that affects more people than cancer and heart disease combined receives so little funding? Why aren't there enough doctors, enough hospital beds, or enough insurance coverage for those who suffer from serious mental illness? Where are the treatment programs, day centers, and suitable safe housing? Not only aren't these necessities available, but society doesn't see the need to provide adequate services that benefit the mentally ill.

The services and care offered for MI have never been equivalent to the quality and care for other chronic diseases or illnesses. I expected more. I expected better. What I expected wasn't attainable. What I found was that there are too few outpatient resources, too few inpatient treatment options, and a shortage of specialists. Psychiatric boarding, which entails keeping patients in emergency departments because appropriate mental healthcare is unavailable, has become the norm. Jails and prisons are among the largest venues for mental health services when the medical system fails. Because hospitals deny treatment when your MIAC refuses care, many with MI are released as soon as they're no longer a threat to themselves or others, rather than when they're well. This leads to many other social ills, such as increased homelessness, addiction, and incarceration.

And it's hard to access the doctors. For most doctors, you'd make an appointment and receive treatment on your first visit. But with behavioral health, you have to make an appointment for your child, persuade him to come to the appointment with you, and then try to get him—in his highly unreasonable state—to sit and answer questions about his mental health during an extensive evaluation. It's more than obvious that he needs help.

Your expectation is that he'll be seen by a psychiatrist as soon as the evaluation is complete. Then you learn that you need to make another appointment for him to see a doctor at a later date. All this is moot if you can't get your MIAC to acknowledge that he's sick and needs treatment, can't get the police to facilitate, or can't get the hospital to admit him.

Today I learn that the earliest available appointment for B is in two weeks.

I look incredulously at the nurse and ask, "What am I supposed to do until then?"

"If he becomes a threat to himself or you, take him to the emergency room or call 911."

Really? This is all the help he gets? It took me fifteen phone calls and three months to find this treatment facility, as well as two more months to get my son to agree to come with me—and all they offer is an appointment weeks away. He needs help now, right this very minute, but even the hospital won't take him.

I wanted to scream at the injustice of this flawed system. I didn't understand until that day why people become addicts and live on the street. Now I know, and that knowledge leaves me heartsick and broken. It's apparent that I'll have to fight for every service and treatment my MIAC will receive. I feel a deep sense of failure.

My son has seen four doctors in eight years, and that doesn't count the doctors assigned to him during his inpatient hospital stays. After three years, his first doctor passed him on to someone else because B was no better. After two years, the second doctor asked B what medications B thought he should be on because he was at a loss for what might help him. Doctor number three made us wait four hours for an evaluation, and then B was hospitalized before his first actual visit, and doctor number four just looked at B and asked if he wanted to change his cocktail of meds in any way. How in this day and age, with all the technology we have, is it still nearly impossible to find adequate professional treatment options? I expected so many more opportunities for recovery and ongoing treatment. I expected . . .

Finding safe, supportive housing that's affordable is almost impossible. Housing is available for Down's syndrome, autism, physical disabilities, and seniors but is difficult to find for mental illness. A social worker during B's last hospitalization was able to locate a potential residential care facility. He still needed to be interviewed and vetted to live there. B's insistence that he would run away almost disqualified him. I begged the supervisor to give him a chance.

Because my son became sick in his early twenties, his SSI disability payments are under $800 a month, which limits his housing options. The home he stays in is very old and in need of repairs. Every room houses up to four individuals. They each have a small locker/closet, and they share a bathroom. Staff is supposed to help with cleaning and laundry, but that doesn't happen often. Three meals a day and snacks are provided, but they're laden with fat and sodium and include almost no fruits or vegetables. Of course, the residents probably wouldn't eat healthier options.

The upside is that the staff cares about the residents and are very compassionate. There are a few nicer facilities, but that would require me to supplement B's income by $1,000 or more each month. I expected these facilities to meet certain health and cleanliness standards, but that bar sits low. Nobody reports code violations because then where would our children go?

Time to Stop

While I will continue to be frustrated by the lack of support and services available for MI, I need to stop bemoaning the injustice of it all and accept the system for what it is: inadequate, understaffed, underpaid, and hopelessly behind on research. My energy is better spent on finding available services instead of complaining about what isn't available. My dissatisfaction with the way things work won't create change. At some point, I'll become a more outspoken advocate for better mental healthcare, but for now, I need to concentrate on the care and stabilization of my son.

> *My energy is better spent on finding available services instead of complaining about what isn't available.*

My desire to argue and complain to the professionals who treated my son didn't generate better care or create more choices for medications or therapies. So, I made the decision to look at the things I could be grateful for. To acknowledge that the system is broken and I can't fix it made me feel like a failure. When I let go of that, it freed me to be more positive. It's not easy to turn your thinking around and start to see the world from a place of abundance instead of lack—especially when your child struggles and suffers. When you choose to be angry and bitter at what services aren't available, at medications and therapies that don't work, or at the lack of affordable quality housing, it makes you miserable and doesn't offer any additional hope to your child. And that's exactly what you both need: to feel a little hope.

Instead of entertaining negative thoughts, I now think and say this:

- The medications that are available don't work well, but I'm grateful the meds allow my son to be somewhat rational and reduce his psychosis.
- The doctors don't know how to treat him, but I'm thankful there are doctors who choose to dedicate their lives to help patients with severe MI, even when they can't always find an effective solution.
- There are no places for the mentally ill to socialize, but even though my son talks about his desire to hang out with friends, I know that he never will because it causes him too much anxiety and stress.
- The hospitals are so short on beds that critically ill patients are released before they should be, but I'm grateful that I live in a country where the option to have my son hospitalized is available. Because of the laws about what constitutes a need to be hospitalized, the doctors and staff can't keep the patients they know need long-term care. It's a triage method of care. All they can do is stop the worst symptoms and move on to the next crisis.
- The HIPAA laws make it almost impossible to advocate for my MIAC, but I'm thankful that many doctors and nurses will bend the rules when they feel it's in B's best interest. I've become creative and have found ways around the privacy

laws. I understand how frustrated the medical professionals must feel to be bound by laws that cause more harm than good.
- Fights with the government for assistance are difficult, and it took several years with specialty attorneys to attain what my child rightly qualifies for. But I'm grateful to have found a compassionate attorney and judge who saw how incapacitated my MIAC is and granted disability benefits. That money isn't much, but it eases my financial burden and allows my MIAC access to doctor visits and daily medications at no cost to either of us.
- I shouldn't need to become my son's legal guardian to have the right to be involved in his care, and I shouldn't have to pay an attorney to have that right, but I'm thankful that, as my son's guardian, I'm a better advocate for his care and safety. I can be involved in his treatment plans and am able to handle his finances for him.
- Even though my son's residential care facility is in a rundown house, I'm thankful he has a place to live where he has the opportunity to socialize with others and is fed, safe, and has a roof over his head. To be honest, none of them notice the scuffed paint, stained linoleum floors, or grime accumulated in every corner.

I still feel my expectations for better mental healthcare are valid, but I also see how advocating in various ways serves me better than annoyance and malice. I volunteer once a year as a NAMI F2F facilitator, which offers guidance, information, and community support. I speak up when asked and explain my son's condition. I have NAMI cards on my desk at my business to elicit conversations about mental health. I have and continue to become the mentor that I looked for in desperation when my son first became ill and amidst his many hospitalizations.

Advocacy is the only way we can change how MI is addressed. The more of us who speak up about our experiences as we deal with and care for a MIAC, the more we can stop the stigma attached to serious brain illnesses. Educating everyone we can is the first step in helping mental illness be better understood and accepted. When we as a society can accept that mental illness and addiction are not choices, then strategies can be enacted to help those who struggle with these horrific illnesses.

Each day, you can make the conscious choice to view what happens with your MIAC from a place of thankfulness and gratitude. It's not always easy. Some days the only thing you may be thankful for is that he doesn't live under a bridge, but it will make you feel better to have a positive attitude. Be hopeful that, in the future, society will stop blaming the mentally ill for their disease and create a cohesive system of integrative care for these unfortunate individuals.

When you're more grateful, it also has a positive impact on your MIAC. If you wonder how this is even possible, the next chapter offers strategies for creating boundaries, personal freedom, and opportunities for finding happiness.

Visualization Journey

Sit in a comfortable, quiet place. Close your eyes.

Breathe in and out slowly to the count of three several times until you feel yourself begin to relax.

Visualize yourself walking through a forest of evergreens. The air is moist with the scent of pine, the ground underfoot is soft with needles and moss, and you hear crickets chirping and an owl hooting softly nearby. You wear a heavy backpack.

Follow the path as it winds amongst the trees. Feel yourself relax as you go deeper into the woods.

Up ahead, you see the ground begin to slant upward. You follow the path as it leads up and around the side of a mountain. The path takes you around and up. You go higher and higher with each rotation.

The climb becomes more difficult because of the heavy backpack you carry, so you stop to rest. You need to keep the backpack with you, but you need to make it lighter.

Look in the backpack. You see that it's filled with rocks of different sizes. Each rock symbolizes an expectation you have for yourself, your child, your family and friends, or the medical community. Now is the time to decide which rocks you want to keep and which you're willing to leave behind.

You see a beautifully wrapped gift box in the brush. In order to take the gift, you must make room in the pack. What expectation will you release in order to have room for the gift? Leave as many rocks behind as you want, and gently place the gift in your backpack. Notice how much lighter it feels already.

Continue on the path up and around the mountain. Every few minutes, you find another gift box; each is as beautiful as the one before. Continue to sort through your rocks and determine which ones you must leave behind in order to make room for the gift boxes. Repeat this process until you fill the backpack with gifts.

Now that your pack is lighter, you can climb easier, and you see the top of the mountain ahead. Stop at the summit and look out over the world below. From this vantage point, you can see the many piles of rocks you left behind. Make a list of the feelings you let go of—anger, disappointment, resentment, misunderstanding, stress, conflict, and anything else you'd like to release.

Take a deep breath of the fresh, crisp air and notice how much lighter and unburdened you feel.

Sit on the ledge and look out over the forest below. Pull out the gifts you acquired along the way. You didn't realize you'd picked up so many, did you? Begin to unwrap them and hold them to your heart as you absorb what they offer. Each one holds an irreplaceable treasure—relaxation, happiness, gratitude, contentment, open-mindedness, being present, joy, freedom, playfulness, love, acceptance. Add any other gifts you received.

Stay on top of the mountain as long as you like. When ready, begin the walk back down. Notice how much easier it is, how much lighter your heart and steps feel. Before you realize it, you've reached the bottom.

Now open your eyes and journal any messages, words, or symbols you received. What rocks did you leave behind? What gifts did you receive? In what ways do you feel different?

Is It Yours to Carry?

We are sisters
Bound by codependency
We refuse to let go
Tied to our suffering children
We reclaim our personal sovereignty
We are sisters

This is the most important chapter in this book; I considered its placement carefully. I thought about putting it at the beginning of the book, but the progression up to this point is crucial. Here's the message you need to hear: your relationship with your MIAC has become one of codependency, and until that changes, you can't move ahead with your own life.

Codependency is defined as any relationship in which two people are so invested in each other that they can no longer function as independent individuals. It could also be called *relationship addiction* or an *enmeshed relationship*. Whatever you call it, the boundaries are blurred.

Here's the message you need to hear: your relationship with your MIAC has become one of codependency, and until that changes, you can't move ahead with your own life.

Codependent moms blame their children for their own problems and misery and are unable to take responsibility for creating their own happiness. Brené Brown, in *Daring Greatly: How the Courage to Be Vulnerable Transforms the Way We Live, Love, Parent, and Lead*, says, "What often passes as love in common human understanding is primarily attachment, dependency, and possessiveness."

I grew up, like many of you, in a dysfunctional family. My dad was an alcoholic with undiagnosed anxiety and depression, and my mom had anxiety that she attempted to manage with perfectionist behaviors. I learned to be codependent early in life as a way to keep myself safe in my home environment. My mom called me her "assertive self," and from a very young age, she leaned on me to handle every situation that made her feel uncomfortable. That behavior continued until her death. When I didn't do as she wanted, she withheld love and acceptance. It didn't occur to me that things could or should be different. I didn't know what I hadn't been taught about personal boundaries. Maybe you had a similar experience.

When my son became sick, I subconsciously adopted those same strategies to cope. It made complete sense that I would give him what I thought would make him happy. But being in the caregiver role for everyone in my family made me miserable. In 2015, everything fell apart. My dad moved into a nursing home, and my mom's rare Parkinson's disorder became worse, and she required in-home care. It fell on me to handle all the details. Two months later, Dad died. That summer, my daughter received a kidney cancer diagnosis, and three months later, my MIAC was diagnosed with colon cancer. By Christmas, my mom needed skilled nursing care, and I was ready for a white jacket in a padded room.

I was the financial and medical power of attorney for my mom, the guardian for my son, and I was also trying to run my own small business. It was a nightmare. My brothers and I discussed the decisions we needed to make, but they left the paperwork and meetings about our mom's care to me. My son's father refused to make any decisions regarding B's care because he didn't want the responsibility. I didn't have any boundaries at this point, and I struggled to find the tiniest shred of good in my life. My days revolved around taking care of everyone else. Nobody ever asked if I was okay.

If you look and act strong, people let you handle the things they don't want to. And they'll continue to impinge upon your personal space until you finally collapse or erect walls of protection. But you're only responsible for the following things: your words, behaviors, actions, efforts, mistakes, ideas, fears, and the consequences of them. You are *not* responsible for your child's words, behaviors, actions, efforts, mistakes, ideas, fears, or the consequences of his actions.

Read that paragraph as many times as you need. Let it sink in. This truth will never change. You are only responsible for yourself and can never be responsible for or control your MIAC's choices, words, or behaviors.

I couldn't find much information about a link between moms of MIACs and codependency, but it seems to be a huge problem. As children mature, parents allow them to make more of their own choices, which helps them learn necessary life skills. But what happens when, due to a mental illness, your adult child regresses and is unable to make wise choices or even meet his basic needs? As the mom, you jump back in and begin the parenting cycle over again, only this time your child doesn't achieve a level of maturity that leads to responsibility and independence. Instead, you cling to your child with attempts to drag him into responsible adulthood, and both your lives become fused into one dysfunctional wreck.

> *You are only responsible for yourself and can never be responsible for or control your MIAC's choices, words, or behaviors.*

You feel it's not only your duty but also your obligation to care for your child until he regains his normal abilities. But what if that doesn't happen? What if your MIAC doesn't learn from his mistakes? What if there's no hope for independence? What if he refuses all your attempts of help and support? How do you learn to back off and allow your child to face consequences that could lead to better understanding and growth?

> Jittery and anxious, I'm always on edge as I watch my MIAC for signs of relapse. I can't relax or let down my vigilance, not for a moment. I'm exhausted. I'm not even with him, and I'm focused on what he is or isn't doing, his health, his irrational behaviors, his medications. I know I spend too much time worrying about what might happen, but my mind won't stop looking for solutions. I feel physically sick. My head hurts, my stomach twists, I can't sleep, I feel myself sink into the quagmire of codependency. Does this sound familiar?
>
> I feel physically tied to my son's well-being, unable to let go and go back to my own life while he remains sick. This has become my obsession, my need to get help for him. How did I end up so far down this rabbit hole? One minute he was diagnosed with a chronic, severe mental illness; now, three years later, I'm so enmeshed in his life that I've lost myself. How did I go from supporting his recovery to making it my sole purpose? I know I have to stop this, but I'm not sure how to untangle myself from him. I know it's not good for either of us, but what would happen if I stopped? What if everything falls apart?

How did I go from supporting his recovery to making it my sole purpose?

Your personal boundaries are so overlapped with your child's that you can't see yourself as an individual anymore, which feels scary, ridiculous, and sad. If you don't figure out how to pull away, this horrible disease will claim both your lives.

You don't know where you stop and your child begins. The edges of your being have overlapped with those of your ill child. You're now one big blur of emotional pain. Your desires and emotions have become so enmeshed that you don't know the difference between what's yours and what belongs to him. In an effort to help your MIAC regain some aspects of his former life, you've breached your physical and emotional boundaries, and he let down his boundaries to feel a sense of safety and protection. You both look for control as you move through this new and frightful diagnosis. It was natural to bind yourselves to each other and sail into this storm together. But now, you're likely to pull each other under and drown.

> *In an effort to help your MIAC regain some aspects of his former life, you've breached your physical and emotional boundaries, and he let down his boundaries to feel a sense of safety and protection.*

How much of what weighs you down isn't yours to carry? Dr. Margaret Paul, the author of several books on love addiction, offers these signs and symptoms of enmeshed parenting:

- Your child's good or difficult behavior, success, or failure define your worth.
- Your child is the center of your life, your sole purpose in life.
- Your entire focus is the care of your MIAC, and you forget about your own care.
- Your happiness or pain is determined by your child.
- You're invasive in your need to know everything that your child thinks or does.

Let's look at the signs of unhealthy boundaries. How many of these apply to your behavior with your MIAC?

- Are you overwhelmed or preoccupied with your child's life?

- Do you allow your child to take as much as he can from you—time, energy, money, personal peace, feelings of safety and enjoyment—without consequences?
- Do you let your MIAC direct how you live your life?
- Are you strong only in order to take care of your child's every need and want?
- Does your happiness depend on your child's quality of life?
- Do you often feel taken advantage of but don't speak up?
- Is it hard for you to say no because you fear ramifications?
- Do you feel like you're the only person who can do certain things the right way for your MIAC?
- Do you stuff your emotions when you're treated poorly?
- Do you give all your time to your MIAC?
- Do you feel guilty if you enjoy yourself?
- Do you make sacrifices for your child that have a detrimental impact on your life?
- Do you always feel like a victim with no control over events?
- Are you out of touch with your own needs?

I answered yes to every single one of these questions. I wasn't sure how to create boundaries that supported my well-being and growth or what it looked like to be sovereign over myself. I love Brené Brown's statement, "Daring to set boundaries is about having the courage to love ourselves even when we risk disappointing others."

There are many benefits to creating strong personal boundaries:

- You'll say no without feeling guilty.
- You'll have more mental, emotional, and physical stamina.
- You'll be able to speak your mind with ease and convey a clear message.
- You'll feel more appreciated and valued.
- You'll be more in touch with your needs and wants.
- You'll have more emotional balance and happiness.
- You'll have more freedom and courage to be yourself.
- You'll experience increased self-esteem and self-worth.
- You'll take responsibility for your happiness.

Furthermore, there are several myths about personal boundaries that many consider to be true. But abiding by them creates relationship issues. Consider these:

- *It's selfish to have personal boundaries with your child.* This is flat-out wrong. When you have boundaries, it creates a better atmosphere of mental and emotional health for you both.
- *Your relationship with your MIAC will suffer if you establish personal boundaries.* When you break codependent patterns, it can cause initial upheaval, but all relationships will grow stronger when boundaries are enforced.
- *Your MIAC won't like you if you have personal boundaries.* Clear boundaries may anger the ones who benefitted from your codependent ways, but so what? Others who care about you will respect you for setting boundaries for yourself.
- *Personal boundaries will make you unhappy.* When you create boundaries, at first it will feel uncomfortable, but they'll lead you to be more empowered and in control of your life. Personal boundaries will result in greater contentment and less drama with your child.
- *Personal boundaries sound too rigid.* They aren't. Boundaries are flexible and can be modified to fit your MIAC's unstable circumstances.

Because my own parents weren't there for me when I needed help, I naturally focused on giving my child the support I didn't receive. The more my MIAC failed, the more I thought it was my responsibility to fix his life. Because he wasn't capable of living on his own, I made it my mission to teach him to be independent. I tried to enable him, and that's exactly what I did; I enabled my son. And when you enable someone, regardless of their diagnosis or ability, it creates a sinkhole of misery.

Because B wasn't rational enough to plan for his future, I made those types of decisions for him. I thought what I did was in his best interest, but I overstepped his boundaries and caused both of us so much heartache. All attempts to help my son recover failed.

The more I pushed him to behave a certain way, the more drama and struggle I created. Our lines became blurred, and I took on all responsibility for his life. The more I grasped the decisions that should have been his, the more he blamed me for everything that was wrong in his life. He saw everything that happened to him as my fault.

The more I grasped the decisions that should've been his, the more he blamed me for everything that was wrong in his life.

At some point, all moms of MIACs fall into the pit of codependency. You're so desperate for your child to have a good life that you're prepared to give up part or all of yourself to make that happen. And until you're knee-deep in the tumult of MI, you can't see that your MIAC can't receive what you're so eager to offer. You don't add anything to his toolbox of skills; you simply deplete your own ability to function and have an independent life.

Codependency can be triggered by trauma—and that's exactly what life with a MIAC is: drama and trauma. Codependents don't know how to ask for what they need, and they give *even when it harms them*. Even though you have the best intentions, you're in over your head.

Things will continue to spiral out of control unless you change how you interact with your MIAC. The hole you're digging has no end. The choices you've made have turned him into a clingy, manipulative adult, and you are angry, frustrated, and disappointed. Obviously, your child isn't going to change because it benefits him to be dependent on you. When you enable him, you encourage him to expect and demand more and more. Best-selling author Evelyn Roberts Brooks says it best: "When we try to manage the lives of others, we do both them and ourselves a disservice."

> *When you enable him, you encourage him*
> *to expect and demand more and more.*

Every time something important regarding my MIAC's disease fell through the cracks, I was determined to control that aspect of his care. Before I knew it, I was doing it all and didn't ask what he thought about my choices. Like a juggler, I knew that if I didn't keep all the chainsaws in the air, he might get hurt. When he fooled around with how many meds he took, I made it my job to dispense them. Because he lived next door, I checked daily to make sure his cats were fed and the litter box cleaned. If he didn't eat, I cooked meals for him. When he didn't bathe, I withheld his cigarettes until he did. Even when his dad took him to visit his psychiatrist, I thought I needed to go too. I didn't trust that my son or his dad would relay the proper information to the doctor.

If I gave up control, I thought my son's illness would become even worse than it already was. It was uncomfortable for me to let things slide, to give him the opportunity to fail and face the consequences, or to let his dad help. The more paranoid and delusional he became, the more I clung to the belief that I could change what happened by handling his life. I, too, became delusional.

Did this work? Not at all! The more tightly I controlled B's every move, the more he felt smothered. He always said he wanted the freedom to make his own choices. But how could I let him make the terrible choices I knew he would? I'd have to clean up the mess. Stressed and exhausted with my attempts to stay on top of things, I was in a no-win situation. I was resentful and angry all the time. Something needed to change, but I wasn't sure what to give up and what to continue. I struggled with our boundaries—or lack of them.

I wasn't just codependent; I was a codependent caretaker, which is a horrible combination. Can you relate to the following?

- Are you exhausted, anxious, frustrated, and irritated?
- Do you feel like you always have to put your MIAC first?

- Do you think you're the only one who knows what's best for your child?
- Are you judgmental, or do you feel annoyed when your advice is ignored?
- Do you seem compelled to help, give with strings attached, and discourage independent thinking from your MIAC?
- Do you see self-sacrifice as a virtue?
- Do you think you're always right?

I'm sure you don't like that you answered yes to many of these. Every single item describes how most of us deal with our sick children. I always felt like an effective problem solver, but this knowledge put me in my place. We were both stuck in an ugly, debilitating cycle of enabled codependency.

The first step out is to recognize what doesn't work and then learn better ways to communicate. It seemed like so much work to change the way I interacted with my son, but I knew things would only get worse if I didn't change. Here's a fair warning: the moment you decide to make a different choice, get ready to feel uncomfortable.

I worked hard to create clear boundaries between myself and my son. I know what's mine to handle and what isn't, and when I'm unsure, I take time to question whose it is to carry. I won't lie to you. One of the most difficult things I've had to do is let go of my need to fix my son, but it's also offered the most rewards. I struggle daily to put myself first.

Below are some of the healthy relationship guidelines I try to follow. How would you answer these?

- Can you say yes or no and be okay with what your MIAC thinks?
- Are you okay when your child doesn't listen to or follow your advice?
- Can you keep a strong sense of your own identity while you care for your child?
- Do you respect yourself even if your MIAC doesn't?

- Can you determine whether the problem is yours or your MIAC's?
- Do you allow abuse or disrespect from your child?
- Can you voice your own wants, needs, and feelings?
- Are you solely responsible for your own happiness and fulfillment? Can you allow your child to be responsible for his?
- Can you stick to your opinion without deferring to your MIAC?
- Do you know your physical, emotional, and mental limits?
- Do you allow your child to push you beyond your limits?
- Do you allow your MIAC to compromise your values or integrity?

I go back to these questions when I struggle to stay in my own lane. Our boundaries have overlapped for so long that it's still difficult to stay untangled. I store these reminders in my phone and pull them up whenever I wonder if my intentions are serving us both. They are a helpful point of reference for navigating our interactions.

"Can I have two dollars?" B asks. "I promise to spend it on soda or a snack from the gas station."

I'm frustrated. I hate this daily money game. He starts asking for money five minutes after I wake up. He worries that I'll forget. Every day it's a different story, why he needs a dollar or two more.

"I want to buy my friend a soda," he says. Or "I'm going to save it so I can buy a video game."

Every day I say, "No more," and then I give in and give him extra. I feel guilty that he can't work and doesn't have his own money. It makes him happy to spend a few dollars. At this rate, I'll go broke before he learns how to budget the little that I give him. I'm not even out the door, and he asks for more.

Yesterday he came home with lottery tickets.

I stomped my foot and shouted, "I'm not giving you another penny, not ever." At least not today, I think.

I used to give him his allowance on the first of the month. It would be gone in two or three days. Then I gave it to him once a week, and he'd go through it in one day. So here I am, doling out two dollars every day, and he still wants more. Apparently, I've taught him that I won't stick to my word if he begs and pleads. I stopped wondering why my MIAC keeps doing it and started asking myself why I keep allowing it. I realize I've created my very own money monster.

It's so hard to say no when I know his life is miserable. But enough is enough. It's up to me to decide what I will and won't do and then stick to it no matter what my MIAC says. This will be the first step to creating a healthy financial boundary with my son.

The first few days are rough. He screams, pleads, begs, slams doors, and calls me names, but I stick to my word. When I leave for work, I feel incredibly guilty and sad. I second-guess myself throughout the day. He has everything he needs, and money doesn't make his life better. It's a distraction for him to spend, but he needs to find another diversion. If he asks for something and I feel it will add value to his life or it's an item he needs, I'll buy it for him, but only if it fits into my budget.

It's an ongoing struggle for both of us. He always tries to guilt me back in.

I learned at a very young age that I needed to please my parents to receive the love and acceptance that I needed and wanted. Raised to meet their emotional needs instead of my own, I observed their moods and behaviors and attempted to diffuse their tension, anxiety, and anger. My needs got met if—and only if—their needs were first met. My parents never learned how to set healthy boundaries, so we were all dysfunctional. You most likely had a similar upbringing.

Ignored boundaries can manifest in the following ways:

- If you deviate from acceptable family norms, you're considered bad, and this creates problems within your relationships.
- You disassociate from your MIAC's problems by toughing it out or denying your true feelings about the situation.
- Sometimes, as a distraction from what's really happening in the family, you subconsciously create artificial problems unrelated to the true crisis.
- You may choose to play the complaining martyr or defensive victim role when your MIAC violates your boundaries.
- You might be angry because your emotional needs are ignored.
- Feeling smothered by your MIAC's demands is a sure sign that your personal boundaries are being breached.

Dysfunctional boundaries cause emotional pain, depression, anxiety, and even stress-induced physical illness. Balance is the key. Unhealthy boundaries allow anyone and everyone into your personal space, while rigid boundaries prevent others from being in your life and make you feel isolated. Without boundaries, you can't separate your emotions from your child's, you spend all of your time trying to please your MIAC, you blame your child for your problems, and you refuse to take responsibility for meeting your own needs. It's imperative that you set personal boundaries.

If you're not accustomed to setting boundaries, you might feel guilty or selfish when you begin, but boundaries are necessary for your health and happiness. Boundaries are guidelines—or rules—that you create to state what you consider reasonable, safe, and permissible ways for your child to behave around you. They also define how you'll respond if your MIAC oversteps those limits. You get to decide what your boundaries are and how you'll respond when your MIAC violates your personal space.

It's imperative that you set personal boundaries.

I learned the concept of *relationship containers* in a women's empowerment workshop. It helps me to view boundaries as physical containers instead of something intangible. I visualize that my boundaries keep out what can potentially harm me, like a net or filter that catches people who ask me to give more than I should. I also created a gatekeeper to monitor my space. On days when I struggle to maintain my boundaries, I call on my gatekeeper, Archangel Gabriel, and ask her to stand watch over my personal space. I ask that she give me strength, support, and wisdom to make the best choices for myself.

When I created my personal boundary container, I filled it with these guidelines of how I wanted others to treat me. Your container might look different, as we all have a unique spin on what's important for our well-being.

- I need a clear division between myself and my MIAC, so I can discern which are his feelings and which are mine.
- My beliefs, my feelings, my money, and my time need to be respected.
- I require honesty in our interactions.
- I will give what I can freely give as long as it doesn't harm me in any way.

The following tips will help you set healthy boundaries:

- Be clear, calm, firm, and respectful as you create and share your boundaries with your MIAC.
- It's not necessary to justify, become angry, or apologize for your boundaries.
- Your MIAC's reactions are not your responsibility. Be prepared for your new boundaries to be tested. Don't vacillate.
- Apologizing to your child will send a mixed message and weaken your resolve.
- Expect this to take practice, determination, and time. You're learning a new skill.

- It's helpful to have support from people who respect your healthy boundaries and to cut ties with those who are toxic and accustomed to taking advantage of you. This may apply to your MIAC if he's unable to respect your personal boundaries.

I recognize that my MIAC has stepped into my container when I feel pressured, discounted, or am asked to disregard my feelings. When my child lies or withholds information, I know he's trying to disregard my boundaries. My MIAC pushes into my space when he doesn't follow through on an agreement, demands that I do something for him, or makes me feel guilty to get his way.

Most of my interactions with my MIAC involve me overstepping his boundaries because I want to keep him safe and help him lead a more productive life. I allow him to breach my boundaries because I can't make him well.

Your MIAC's constant demands can lead to many angry altercations. How do you create boundaries when you don't even know what healthy boundaries look and feel like? How do you create boundaries with a severely ill child without feeling guilty? How do you create boundaries that benefit you but still allow for your MIAC's safety?

You may construct a boundary only to remove it when the pushback becomes too much. Setting boundaries takes practice and determination, so start with small issues and work up to setting bigger boundaries. This approach allows you to get comfortable with this new skill.

One day I couldn't do it anymore. The burden seemed too big, and I felt ready to snap. I felt empty and had nothing more to give. Absolutely used up, I remember saying out loud, "This has to stop. It's going to kill me."

Each day with my MIAC was a continual battle of wills. It felt like dealing with an insolent teen instead of an adult. It didn't matter how many times we discussed something, how many reminders I gave him, how many notes I taped to his fridge; nothing ever changed. If

I gave in and did what I said I wouldn't do, it opened the door for bigger demands and more manipulation.

Brené Brown's quote from *Daring Greatly* described my dilemma perfectly: "I've always looked for better ways to manage my exhaustion and anxiety. I wanted help 'living like this,' not suggestions on how to 'stop living like this'. . . For women, boundaries are difficult because the shame gremlins are quick to weigh in…"

Exhaustion laid me flat, and I was ready to call it quits on everything, change my name, and move to a deserted island. When I began to change the habit of putting others before me, it was slow going. I put up a boundary and then let it collapse. This happened again and again until I became stronger in my determination and convictions. It helped to create boundaries with people who weren't close to me and those I wasn't already entwined with. Then I worked on boundaries with my child. It felt like a gigantic weight lifted off my chest, and I could finally take a full breath again.

Prentis Hemphill eloquently states, "Boundaries are the distance at which I can love you and me simultaneously." It's wonderful to be in control of your own life and not feel resentful and angry about doing more for others than you want to.

Initially, your MIAC will have trouble accepting your boundaries because it will force him to deal with his own issues and feelings. He's used to being able to plead with or heap guilt upon you until you give in, so now's not the time to waffle. Your MIAC will still push you, but the more you tighten your hold on your boundaries, the less guilt you'll feel.

And you must stay outside his boundaries and stop trying to fix his problems. Allow your MIAC to figure things out—or not. That's his choice. The bottom line is that you stay in your lane, and he stays in his. Anything else creates a collision of wills.

Be clear about what you'll allow and what you'll do for others, as well as what you won't allow others to do to you. Brené Brown says, "One of our greatest barriers to compassion is the fear of setting boundaries and holding people accountable. The heart of compassion is really acceptance."

Some days you may need to work a little harder to maintain those lines, but in the end, healthy boundaries are the best way for you to offer compassion and empathy to your MIAC. The only time I step into my child's circle is when I feel his choices will have a negative impact on his mental health or cause him harm. He doesn't like that intrusion, but it's my duty as his mom to be there in those situations.

I'm visiting B. As I walk into his room, I immediately start to clean up, throw trash away, empty water bottles, and wipe up spills. I pick up a pillow and blanket and put them in the closet, and B loses it.

"Stop moving my stuff! That closet isn't clean. Now I have to wash my blanket again."

I start to argue, then stop myself. He has so little control over his life, I think. Does it matter if these sit out? I notice his feet and cringe. They are black and crusted with dirt and dried skin. Yuck!

Quietly I ask, "Do you think it's time to soak and scrub your feet? Your nails look like dog claws. Would you like me to cut them?"

"Mom," he says, "I'll take a shower later and wash my feet."

"Okay," I say. I've heard this for the last three weeks.

I take a deep breath and drop the conversation about his feet. I want him to be able to make a few choices for himself and have some say in what happens.

I've brought a Scrabble game with me and ask if he'd like to play. We head to the dining area, and for the next hour, we play. He seems almost normal, and we both have fun and laugh. He even comments, "Mom, it's starting to snow. Maybe you should leave before the roads get bad."

"No," I say. "I want to finish the game." We have so few normal moments, and I don't want to cut this one short.

I will hold this memory close to my heart. This is a rare occurrence. I focus on the game and the simple everyday conversation we have as we play. I force myself not to think about the last time he showered, about his long, dirty hair, about the food he doesn't want to eat because it's contaminated, or about the rash he thinks is caused by poisoned water. That's his reality, and I decide to let him choose what he wants to believe instead of trying to reason him out of his delusions.

We have a great visit, and that's what I'll remember. He even wins the game, but I'm not surprised; he's a formidable player. I hope that's what he remembers also, the time we shared over a game, instead of my attempts to refute his reality or make him do things he doesn't want to do.

We've discussed codependency and your inability to detach from your MIAC's life, but it's also necessary to add the idea of *personal sovereignty* into the conversation. You may not be familiar with the word sovereignty. Polly Young-Eisendrath describes personal sovereignty as, "You get to choose from what is available in order to be intentional with your life. When you feel in control of your life, you know yourself to be the author of your actions and know that you always have choices." From a spiritual perspective, it's your divine right to choose what you say, how you act, and what you believe, as long as it doesn't violate another. Nobody has the authority to take that away from you.

Instead of breaching your MIAC's boundaries, you can learn how to hold space for him. To hold space means that you're prepared to walk alongside your child on whatever journey he's on without judging him, without making him feel inadequate, and without attempts to fix him or influence the outcome. When you hold space for your MIAC, you open your heart, offer unconditional support, and let go of judgment and control. Holding space for your child is an act of liberation vs. violation of his personal sovereignty. Even if your child isn't in your life, you can hold space by accepting the choices he makes.

This is where the slope gets slippery. How do you offer your MIAC personal sovereignty when he has a severe mental illness? How do you allow him to maintain his personal boundaries and still keep him safe? How do you allow him to feel heard and seen when you need to make life decisions on his behalf? Can you accept that his path is not what you'd choose but still let it play out? These answers will be different based on the severity of the MI, how eager you are to relinquish your control, and how willing your child is to accept your help.

> *This is where the slope gets slippery. How do you offer your MIAC personal sovereignty when he has a severe mental illness?*

Is it possible for you to see your MIAC's journey, no matter how terrible, as something that serves his soul's purpose? I believe it's not only possible but also essential for you to honor the life he's been given to live. What if he's homeless, or what if he can't provide for himself? Do you help him by providing those things if he's unappreciative and violent toward you? Should you drop your own personal boundaries to see that his needs are met if he constantly disregards you and your feelings, steals from you, or is physically aggressive toward you?

I challenge you to honor your MIAC's journey, whatever it may look like. If you can have a connection, great. If not, love him from a distance. Your love for him won't last if you continue to let him treat you with disrespect. You'll end up despising and even hating your child. Don't allow this to happen. Create stronger personal boundaries, accept his right to make his own choices, and hold your love for him in your heart. You may be surprised at what changes occur when you don't try to fix or control your MIAC and allow him to make whatever poor choices he will. You can figuratively walk beside him and hold space for his journey without doing anything to help other than accepting that his journey is his.

There are many ways to hold space for someone, including yourself:

- Practice being fully present and mindful.
- Listen to understand, not to respond. When you actively listen, your child feels heard.
- Validate and name the emotions being shared. You might need to dig to uncover the feelings, repeat them, and thank him for sharing with you.
- Avoid trying to fix or minimize what you say. Speak truthfully.
- Acknowledge how your MIAC is feeling, even if you don't agree.
- Offer acceptance and understand that what's being shared is his reality.
- Create a safe container for your child to share all aspects of his life. Accept the good and the bad of who he is.
- Support your MIAC's intuition, knowledge, and wisdom. Allow him to have input into his own life.
- Trust that he can take care of his needs, even if it's only one thing that he does for himself.
- Realize that the things you think are important may not be important to your child.
- Be aware of your own responses, defenses, and story. You view everything through your lens, not your child's perspective.
- Respond with compassion and understand where he's coming from.
- Listen from your heart, not your head, and respond with love.

When you're afraid for your MIAC, you try even harder to control what he does. It's a no-win situation. The tighter you hold, the more he pulls and resists. It's a continual battle of wills. You want him to be safe and have a decent life, but the constant struggle is exhausting and fruitless. How do you handle an adult who doesn't believe he's sick and who wants and feels it's his right to make his own choices but makes poor decisions that impact his well-being? Where do you draw the line and decide to become his legal guardian? Or do you choose to leave him to his disastrous choices and hope he'll learn to accept his limitations and seek the help he so desperately needs? There are no easy answers, but in the end, you need to decide what you will and won't do for your peace of mind.

> *There are no easy answers, but in the end, you need to decide what you will and won't do for your peace of mind.*

I want my son to be as independent as he's capable of being, but at the same time, I want to keep him alive. When he moved into the condo next door to mine, it seemed like a good compromise. He would have some personal space, and I would be able to keep an eye on him. It sounds good even as I write this, but that's not how it turned out.

My MIAC became very clingy whenever he felt anxious, which was all the time. I respected his space and knocked and waited for him to let me in, but he couldn't grasp that I expected that same respect regarding my home. He came into my condo at all times of the day and night. He would come to borrow/steal food, money, and medication while I was at work.

I let him decide what and when he wanted to eat, but he would only eat one meal a day of chips and salsa. I really wanted him to learn to take care of himself and his needs. I didn't care if he did it the way I did it, as long as he was doing well. He didn't eat regular meals, didn't shower, slept on filthy sheets, and walked the complex all night. This wasn't what I'd visualized. He wanted to decide when and what he should do.

This went on for a while, and then I would step in and make him shower, etc. I spent my time at work worrying about what he was or wasn't doing. None of my efforts created positive changes in his life or had any effect. I was chasing an elusive normal. The only way for him to learn to do things differently, if he was even capable, was to let him learn from consequences. It became apparent that tough love would be the answer. MIACs learn the same way addicts do—by suffering the consequences of their actions and not being bailed out by well-intentioned parents.

I close my eyes to take a short nap. I'm so tired. I just need a few minutes to rest.

My phone starts to ring. I don't answer.

"B, I'll be unavailable for an hour," I'd said five short minutes ago.

Maybe it's a spam call. It rings again, and again, and again. Okay, it's not somebody selling something. I get up and turn the ringer off, take a deep breath, close my eyes again, and try to relax. My neck hurts, my eyes burn, and I'm so tired.

I hear my condo door open. Really! He's thirty-one years old, and I just told him not to bother me. I get out of bed and storm into the living room.

"What are you doing in here?" I yell. "I told you less than ten minutes ago to leave me alone. What's your problem? Why can't you listen, for once? Unless the house is on fire or your arm is hanging by a thread, get out now!"

"But I have a question," he says.

"Nope, no questions," I say. "Get out! I mean it! Boundaries, you have no personal boundaries, and I'm over it!"

He leaves, angry. I don't care. I'm so tired of it all. I'm done, and now I'm stressed and angry. My heart beats too fast, and I'm unable to even rest.

I replay what just happened. How could I have handled it differently? Why do I feel so angry? Why does he always find a reason to bother me? Then I get it. Although I said I'd be unavailable for an hour, I didn't cut off his access to me. I created this game by not sticking to my word, and he knows it.

Lesson learned. From now on, the phone goes on silent, and I put the chain on the door. I'm not sure if that will work. He might just keep knocking. Better yet, I'll make a sign to hang outside my door that says, "Do not disturb." This seems like a lot of work, but an uninterrupted hour would be worth it. From now on, when I say I'm not available, I will not be reachable until I decide to be.

It sinks in—again—that I'm not dealing with normal.

A year after B moved next door to me, he made a few friends in the community. They were all similar to him. They also had mental health issues, but they weren't criminals and seemed nice enough. He became very close with one particular young man because they were the same age and had similar interests.

R became a loyal friend but was a terrible influence on B. They decided to start a business helping the older neighbors with chores. They made a few dollars each day, which they spent on beer from the corner gas station. I tried to put a stop to this, tried to explain to my son how this could interfere with his meds and prevent them from working. He always assured me that he wouldn't buy beer, but most days when I got home, he was drunk.

At work all day, I was unable to monitor my son's activities, and asking the neighbors not to give him money was useless. Some days B would seem okay when I got home, and other days, he couldn't stand up without falling over. I was at my wit's end. I begged, pleaded, and threatened. Nothing worked. He wanted to make his own choices about how to live his life.

One day I had a rational conversation with him before I left for work, and two hours later, his dad called to tell me he was lying on the kitchen floor, unresponsive. What had happened? Of course, his dad didn't call an ambulance. I got home at five, and B was still out of it. Stumbling and slurring, not making sense, and obviously still drunk—or maybe drunk again.

This was the last straw for me. It was obvious that when left to his own choices, things didn't end well. I forced him into the car and drove him to a hospital that specializes in mental illness and addiction. Extremely unpleasant on the drive, he tried hard to bait me into an argument, but I was determined to go through with this. Why did it take five hours to evaluate an obviously irrational individual? He was dirty, had an open cut on his head that he didn't know how he got, had scabs on both knees and one elbow, insisted that I wasn't his real mother and that I was the one who was mentally ill.

I think, *How much more information does the hospital need? How long do I need to sit here and absorb his taunts and accusations? As his legal guardian, I need to stay until they're sure they're going to keep him.* Eventually, they decided to admit him to the locked unit—his fourth hospitalization in seven years.

At last, I head home, and all I can think is how relieved I am that someone else is responsible for him for a few days. No guilt, just relief. The independent living experiment is over. I can't delude myself anymore. It's an obvious and profound failure.

My son spent almost four months in the lockdown psych unit. He needed ECT (electro-convulsive therapy) in order to break out of his catatonic delusional reality. It required a court order, and of course, his dad let me know that my choices were going to fry his brain and kill him, but I made the best decision in a difficult situation.

While he was hospitalized, I let the social worker know that B couldn't come home or live with any other family members and that she needed to find a place for him to stay. Independent living wasn't an option. He wasn't capable of even the most basic self-care, and he needed constant supervision to stay alcohol free.

He's been in a residential care facility for over a year now and still hasn't regained the level of functioning he had before his alcohol binge. Do I blame myself? No. I couldn't constantly watch him, and we both needed to learn that he wasn't able to care for himself.

Today my son's journey through this life is his and only his. I wanted a higher level of independence for B, but he can't manage that, so I've changed my goal to healthy dependence. The only time I step in is if he makes decisions that are dangerous to himself or others.

His residential care facility provides meals, dispenses meds, and checks for contraband. Staff remind and encourage him to shower, keep his room clean, and do laundry. I let him decide how to decorate his room, where he wants to store his belongings, when and if he eats, and what we do when I visit. He can decide to eat the meals they provide or make something for himself.

It's hard to see him there, hard to refrain from suggesting that he shower and change clothes, and hard to stop myself from cleaning up the accumulated trash. I work hard to allow him to make a few decisions for himself. He can walk to nearby restaurants or stores and even come home for a visit, but most days, those things are too much for him. Many of the choices he makes have a negative impact on his physical health. If they shorten his life but add to the quality of his days, I'll accept those choices.

When you handle your child's many ongoing issues, it causes stress and anxiety if you don't have or adhere to healthy boundaries. Your MIAC's thought disorder makes it impossible for him to create and maintain reasonable boundaries for himself or to recognize yours, so it's imperative that you do the work to create a structure of boundaries for both of you.

Boundaries are proactive, responsive, and grounded in self-responsibility and self-care. Ultimatums are reactive and cause you to blame your child for your own lack of boundaries. Boundaries create harmony; ultimatums foster discord. Here are some tips on how to set boundaries in a healthy manner:

- Set your limits and decide what's acceptable to you in a peaceful time before you're involved in a tense situation.
- Be as specific as possible, or you might be coerced into giving too much.
- Your limits are individual and are determined by your personal values.
- Know what's most important to you, then hold strong to protect it.
- Tune in to how you feel. Try to understand what your emotions are telling you. Do you feel taken advantage of or used? Discomfort, resentment, and anger are signs that your boundaries have been breached.

- If you always give in to your MIAC's demands, ask yourself if your child shows you as much respect as you show him.
- If your boundaries are too loose, it might be due to your misguided attempts to maintain love, acceptance, or keep the peace.
- Your interactions shouldn't be about winning but should consider what's fair to everyone.
- Know when it's time to set a boundary, and don't be afraid.
- Compromise only if you can maintain your own boundaries.
- Say no without apology or ambiguity.

Your MIAC's thought disorder makes it impossible for him to create and maintain reasonable boundaries for himself or to recognize yours, so it's imperative that you do the work to create a structure of boundaries for both of you.

What are some ways to say no? Which of these resonate with you?

- This doesn't work for me.
- I can't do that for you.
- I need to draw the line at _____.
- I'm not comfortable with your behavior. You need to leave.
- This isn't acceptable to me. Please don't do that, or I'll need to _____.
- I'm not available at this time.
- I've decided not to do _____.
- I don't want to do that.

What other statements can you come up with that don't blame, judge, or sound derogatory but still uphold your boundaries? Remember, there's no need to explain your position. Always voice a statement rather than a question to be debated.

When you take a stand to uphold your personal boundaries, it's important to:

- Voice your requests with confidence. Talk in a calm, quiet tone.
- Look your MIAC in the eye as you state your position. Your MIAC will receive your message better if you're firm and respectful.
- Refrain from yelling or criticizing.
- Plan what you want to say and the exact words you'll use before discussing a touchy subject. Practice will make you more comfortable when sharing your viewpoint.
- Compromise isn't required, but give and take may make your MIAC more receptive.
- Listen and consider your child's opinion, even if you don't agree. Feeling heard creates acceptance.
- Write down your boundaries and allow him to read them in private if your MIAC can't focus or listen respectfully.
- Don't expect your child to agree. This isn't about his approval. It's about creating boundaries for your well-being.

When you aren't comfortable enough or assertive enough to voice what you need, your MIAC will walk all over you. Issues with self-worth can make it difficult for you to state your wants and needs effectively. You may not recognize your needs after disregarding them for so many years. If you've always put your MIAC first, it'll be difficult to believe you have rights or that your needs, feelings, and opinions have value. Building strong boundaries will be uncomfortable if you fear your child's rage or retaliation. It can be incredibly scary to open up and express your true feelings because you fear your child will stop loving you if you don't give in to his demands.

> *When you aren't comfortable enough or assertive enough to voice what you need, your MIAC will walk all over you.*

Communications between you and your MIAC are likely dysfunctional due to your child's distorted thought processes. Often, your talks will degrade him, and you'll nag, beg, blame, and shout, which causes your MIAC to tune you out or become defensive. If your child doesn't seem to hear your message, it may be because you're too passive. Create consequences for breaching your boundaries and then stick to them. Your MIAC looks for loopholes to escape through, so if you back down, use impractical punishments, or show pity, your child will gain the upper hand. It's your response that needs to change, not your MIAC's behavior.

Here are some things you may be doing that don't support you:

- You tell your MIAC not to come over without calling first and then allow him into your home uninvited.
- You tell your MIAC you don't want to talk with him and then text him.
- You ask your MIAC not to call until morning but answer the phone in the middle of the night.
- You tell your MIAC you won't give him money, and then you do.
- You give attention that reinforces negative behavior, such as when you nag, complain, or answer the phone and say, "I told you not to call." This doesn't change the unwanted behavior; it reinforces it.
- You subconsciously sabotage your efforts.
- You allow him to disrespect you.
- You say no to drugs in your house and then allow him to stay when you know he's using.

Every time you loosen your boundaries, you'll regret it. Your frustration will be with yourself. You're the one who's supposed to think rationally, but apparently, you're not. Emily Maroutain says it best in *The Book of Relief*, "You're not stuck. You're just committed to certain patterns of behavior because they helped you in the past. Now those behaviors have become more harmful than helpful. The reason why you can't move forward is because you keep applying an old formula to a new level in your life. Change the formula to get different results."

Some days I checked out and just let things unfold. Funny that those days weren't any different from the days I tried to orchestrate my son's behaviors and thoughts. Did it serve me to always be anxious and stressed? Did it allow me to have the life I wanted or make better choices for my MIAC? Of course not. It was time to let go of trying to micromanage my son and to let the chips fall where they may. If I asked him to do something and he didn't do it, or if I didn't ask him, the result was the same. Maybe I needed my head examined for creating these stressful situations when deep down, I already knew the outcome wouldn't be the one I wanted. At some point, you realize that you've done too much for your child, and the only choice is to stop and leave your MIAC alone. Walk away. You're not giving up. You need to draw the line between determination and desperation. What's meant to be will eventually happen, and what isn't, no matter how hard you try, never will be.

When I decided to draw my boundaries, set limits, and allow my son to have his say in some things, I thought everything would fall apart. Some situations became much worse at first, but over time, things became much better for me, and my son's health stayed the same. Our individual worlds didn't come to an end, and my MIAC didn't hate me. This brighter way to experience life didn't stop stressful things from happening, but now I don't have to claim them as my own. By knowing what's important to me, clearly maintaining my boundaries, and exercising lots of self-care, I've significantly reduced my stress level. Is my son well? No, and he likely never will be, but by living my life instead of trying to help him live his, I'm in a balanced, happy place. Does he hate me for putting up boundaries? No, of course not, because at the same time, I allow him to have his boundaries and limits. If it seems impossible to adopt this mindset, the next chapter will help you get there.

Visualization Journey

Sit in a comfortable, quiet place. Close your eyes.

Breathe in and out slowly to the count of three several times until you feel yourself begin to relax.

Visualize yourself lying on the grass. Look up at a beautiful starry sky. Hear the crickets chirp and the leaves rustle in the wind. Each time you take a deep breath, imagine your lungs filled with peace, and when you exhale, release all your anxiety and stress.

Spend a few minutes inhaling and exhaling until your body feels calm and light.

Look up at the stars and find one that shines brighter than the others. Imagine it comes down to Earth and enfolds you in a soft violet light three feet in every direction. It feels warm, comfortable, and inviting. It feels like home.

You notice fireflies around you. They flit and bob through the night sky, circling around you in lazy arcs.

Catch one of the fireflies in your cupped hands and assign a personal boundary to this beautiful little bug. Place the bug into your star circle. Do this again and again; catch more and more fireflies until you have one for each boundary that's important for your well-being.

Notice that the fireflies can't escape the glow of your star cocoon. These are your fireflies, nobody else's. They'll stay with you and protect you just as your star circle protects you.

If you find it difficult to have boundaries with a particular person, visualize them in the grass near you.

Look up and find a star for them, pull it down, and place it gently around this person. Notice that their starlight glows yellow. You don't need to add anything else to their circle as that's for them to do.

Notice when you move closer together, your star circles overlap. The areas that are combined make an ugly brown color. This is a reminder that everyone's star circle needs to stay separate.

As you get up to leave, thank your starlight for the protection it will continue to give you. Any time you need support, visualize it surrounding you in all directions. This is your sovereign space, and nobody is allowed to enter or tamper with what's inside.

When ready, open your eyes, and journal any messages, words, symbols you received. What boundaries did you put into your star circle? Who else did you create a star circle for? Do you feel different? Remember, your violet star circle is with you always, whenever you feel overwhelmed or need protection with your personal boundaries. The other person also has their protective yellow circle, and it's your responsibility to keep them separate.

Inner Peace Begins When You Let Go

We are sisters
We hold on for dear life
Lost in delusional thoughts
We seek normal
We find our inner strength
We are sisters

In the car, eyes closed, I want a moment of normalcy before going inside to find out what my MIAC has or hasn't done today. The burden of his constant care has suffocated me. I try hard to help him be the best he can be, but it never works out the way I intend. I'm desperate to have a life of my own, have time to relax after work, and for him to live his life independent of me. But when I open my eyes, he's there, staring into the car window. I take a deep breath and hope this will be a good conversation—not another mess I have to handle.

I get out slowly and gather my things.

"What do you need?" I ask.

"I need five dollars to pay R back. I borrowed it from him today to buy cigarettes," B says. He's forgotten that I gave him money this morning. If I give him five dollars, will he leave me alone for a few minutes? Sadly, I consider giving it to him just to buy myself a few minutes of peace.

Before I go inside my own home, I enter his condo, start his laundry, wash the sink full of dirty dishes, scrub the greasy stovetop, and empty the overflowing litter box—all things I asked him to do before I left for work. I posted his chore list on the fridge.

"Why didn't you do what I asked you to do?" I say. "You know it's important to keep your place clean. What did you do all day?"

B doesn't have an answer; he never does. Why can't I ignore the mess? Why do I think it's my responsibility to clean it up? Will he ever learn how to take care of himself, or will I be stuck doing everything for him until I'm old and dead? I take a few deep breaths and try to relax my shoulders. I'm so tired that I want to cry. I need to figure out how to let go of controlling his life before it kills me. I feel guilty and sad for him when I don't help, but something has to give, or I'm going to lose myself inside the chaos of his illness.

Why do we feel the need to control? Psychotherapist Victoria Lorient-Faibish explains it this way: "Parents of adult children often have a hard time letting go. Their expectations are dashed, and they feel the need to get in there and either save their adult child or control the choices they make."

When your child is mentally ill, the transition is even more difficult. As you watch his life unravel, your natural inclination is to step in and offer support and guidance. But is it your place to decide what's best for him? If your child continues to screw up, is it your responsibility to forcibly control his actions and choices? Where do you draw the line when your child has a severe thought disorder? Kahlil Gibran, author and philosopher, says it best: "Our anxiety doesn't come from thinking about the future, but from wanting to control it."

Control

Many problems are caused by control issues, especially when you have a MIAC. Maybe you want to control your child's experiences because of things that happened during your own childhood. Past trauma and abuse make you want to hold tight and steer all your interactions to reach the desired outcome. When you lack trust, have anxiety, feel the fear of abandonment, have low self-esteem, or are afraid that you'll fail, you want to control things. Being a perfectionist and the fear of experiencing painful emotions are also factors. When you tighten your hold over your MIAC, it leads to escalating problems and perpetuates a cycle of control, rebellion, control, and resistance. The more you try to control an issue, the more it controls you.

Wanting to control your MIAC's choices and behaviors stems from your subconscious fears, unexpressed emotions, anxiety about what might happen, or your lack of coping skills. It's an unconscious, self-protective mechanism. You think you're helping your child, but instead, you're using control to manage your anxiety. Of course, a severe MI diagnosis causes an incredible amount of stress and fear, and most parents don't have the skills to cope with it. It's human nature to hold tight as your child's life deteriorates. It seems imperative that you do all you can to get him back on track for a happy future.

The more you try to control an issue, the more it controls you.

Letting Go Is the Answer

"When you believe you're losing control, you grab tight. When your greatest fear comes upon you, you clench your fists and teeth, close your eyes, and hold on. You must learn how to let go. When the time comes for growth and change, you must have the courage and faith to let go," says inspirational speaker, author, and life coach, Iyanla Vanzant.

Why do some people find it easier to let go, and others find it almost impossible to release their grip? Perhaps you wanted more control even before your child became sick and then ramped it up when you received his diagnosis.

Letting go of the past is not the problem. It's letting go of the possibility that things could be different that haunts you. That's the struggle. To let go of the past, you must let go of *your version* of the future and start living in the present.

The present is where you live, and now's the time to start letting go of control of your adult child. You can begin the process by qualifying the choices you make for him or her, which allows you to see if making those choices for them is warranted. The answers to these questions can offer valuable insight:

- Can you afford to do (*fill in the blank*)?
- Will it aid your MIAC on his path to recovery?
- Will he responsibly use what you give him?
- Is there something different you could do to help instead?
- Will this help with your child's future independence?
- Is your behavior a choice or a dysfunctional pattern?
- Will your MIAC continue to ask for (*fill in the blank*) if he gets it?
- Will any of the things you're doing make your child well?

I not only wanted but also needed to feel in control of every situation in my MIAC's life. It gave me security, alleviated anxiety, and lessened my ever-constant fear. But my need to control everything was a total waste of time. The more I held on, the bigger the disaster became. I started micromanaging my son's life when he was a small child and showed signs of ADD, Asperger's, and Tourette's syndrome. Losing control felt like ripping off a limb. I wanted him to grow up to be an independent, successful adult who was able to handle his needs, interact with others, and manage his own life. When B was diagnosed with severe paranoid schizophrenia, it seemed even more critical that I stay on top of his needs since he wasn't capable.

The more paranoid and delusional he became, the more I thought I could change the outcome by controlling his life. Did this work for him? No, not at all. The more I controlled his every move, the more smothered he felt. He wanted the freedom to make his own choices, but how could I let him do that when he made terrible choices? I'd be the one left to clean up the mess. It was a no-win situation, and I was resentful and angry all the time. Something needed to change, but I wasn't sure what to give up and what to continue to do for him. I was concerned for his future and safety—although he never seemed to be.

Once I stopped micromanaging, I could see that I had other choices. I saw my need for control and the problems it created—not only for me but also for those around me. I began to notice that when I was too tired to do anything for my son, things didn't fall apart, and if they did, I didn't try to fix it for him. Some days I simply didn't care what he did or how he did it. He went for weeks without a shower, ate only once a day, and sneaked beer. Talking to him about these choices didn't do any good; it was like asking the cats to clean their own litter box. Things started to decline in every area of his life, but it was evident that my control hadn't changed his behaviors, so I decided to let it *all* go to see where we'd end up. I went from keeping a tight rein on him to simply doling out his meds each day. I let him make poor choices, though I knew at some point, we'd face a day of reckoning.

That's what happened six months into my "letting go experiment." I'd let him make poor choices, lie to me, and quit caring for himself and his cats. Our come-to-Jesus moment actually lasted several months. One evening, he continued to drink too much, and it became apparent that he'd been hiding it for longer than I realized. For safety's sake, it was time to take back some control. I asked him point-blank, "Do you want to die?" and he said, "No, Mom, definitely not." So, I had to step in and get him to the hospital. That stay lasted almost four months, and a year later, the decline in his reasoning is still noticeable. The months he spent in treatment gave me time to evaluate what would be best for him, what would be best for me, and how to make the necessary changes.

Initially, I felt extreme guilt for how his mental and physical health had declined, but my attempts to control his life had never been successful. It took both of us to experience physical, mental, and emotional declines before realizing that control or not, my MIAC was incapable of being independent. Did my hard work put him in a better place? Did my control over every aspect of his care have any significant impact on his abilities? Was he capable of more now than when first diagnosed? While there were incremental improvements, the answer was an unequivocal **NO!**

Furthermore, we were both miserable. Is B happy now? No, but he hasn't been happy since he became sick. If he's going to be miserable wherever he lives, then he might as well be in a care facility where professionals can keep watch.

When you let go of controlling your MIAC's life, it can feel like you've given up. Will it be your fault if his poor choices cause a relapse? First, you need to differentiate between what's your responsibility and what to leave to him. The goal is to stop controlling your child and his journey with MI and to offer support and/or step in only when it's absolutely necessary. To do this, you must see the bigger picture.

Learn to Discern

You have to discern between what's dangerous and what's simply inappropriate. For example, not bathing isn't harmful unless it goes on for so long that your child develops skin infections. The same applies to dental care. How long can your MIAC stay healthy without brushing his teeth? Should an eating disorder be considered a problem? Do you allow him to smoke because it makes him feel better but can potentially shorten his life? Is living on the street ever a good choice?

Look at the immediate impact an issue has on your child's overall mental and physical health. Using alcohol and illegal drugs is a hard no, while poor food choices and inadequate personal hygiene aren't going to kill him. Some MIACs choose to be homeless for reasons we can't understand, preferring the freedom to do as they choose over living in a safe, dry home.

I can't begin to describe the relief that washed over me when I realized I didn't need to control every aspect of my MIAC's life anymore. It's a relief for him to make some of his own choices rather than have every decision made for him. When you realize that your control didn't change anything or help your child, it becomes easier to let things flow.

Here's something I ran across that I hope will bring you peace as you apply it to your MIAC:

LETTING GO doesn't mean you stop caring; it means you can't do it for your MIAC.

LETTING GO isn't to cut yourself off; it's the realization that you can't control your child.

LETTING GO doesn't enable but allows learning from natural consequences.

LETTING GO is admitting you're powerless; it means the outcome isn't in your hands.

LETTING GO isn't to try to change or blame your MIAC; it's to make the most of yourself.

LETTING GO isn't about caring *for* your child; it's about caring *about* your child.

LETTING GO isn't meant to fix him but to support him.

LETTING GO isn't to judge but to allow your MIAC to be a human being.

LETTING GO isn't about arranging all the outcomes but allowing your child to impact his own destiny.

LETTING GO isn't meant to be protective; it allows your MIAC to face reality.

LETTING GO isn't to nag, scold, or argue but, instead, to search out your own shortcomings and correct them.

LETTING GO isn't about denial but acceptance.

LETTING GO isn't about you adjusting everything to your desires, but for taking each day as it comes and cherishing yourself in it.

LETTING GO doesn't mean you criticize and regulate your MIAC. It means you try to become what you dream *you* can be.

LETTING GO isn't to regret the past but grow and live for the future.

LETTING GO is to fear less and to love more.

~Author Unknown/references to MIAC or child added

Logical Consequences

To think you can control an adult is insanity. Unless he tries to harm you, once your child is grown, what he does or doesn't do is his business. As your child matures, you're responsible for giving him space to learn without your interference. It's vital for his development, your relationship, and your mental health and satisfaction. Mind your own business unless he asks for advice or an opinion.

When you refuse to allow your child to experience the consequences of his actions, you rob him of valuable growth and maturity lessons. Mistakes are opportunities to learn. If he never has the chance to own his problems, he loses the ability to overcome challenges and remains emotionally immature.

> *When you refuse to allow your child to experience the consequences of his actions, you rob him of valuable growth and maturity lessons.*

If you're unwilling or unable to allow your child space to grow, then the following could occur:

- Your child may remain stuck with an adolescent mindset, unable to develop critical thinking skills.
- You enable your MIAC to continue destructive behaviors and to make poor choices.
- Your child will become resentful of your interference, and your relationship will suffer.
- You can lose your own identity, become enmeshed with your child, and devalue your own life.

You must focus on yourself and not get lost in your child's drama. Let go and see what happens. You might be surprised by what your MIAC can do when he doesn't have you to rescue him. Even if he fails, he'll have learned a valuable lesson, and you'll know more about his capabilities. It's your responsibility to step in and find accommodations and resources to keep him safe only if you find that your MIAC can't take care of his basic needs—and that only applies if he wants your help and is willing to accept it. If not, you need to let go.

Detached with Love

Of course, you don't stop loving your MIAC. You just do it from a distance. Author, teacher, and spiritual guide, Harold Klemp describes detached love as allowing others to exist without forcing your will upon them. *Detached with love* is the concept of letting go of your child's problems so that you can concentrate on your health and well-being.

So, how can you detach with love and handle crises without telling your MIAC what to do and how to do it? Try some of these suggested ways to share feelings, rules, and consequences with your out-of-control MIAC:

- I feel _____ when you do _____.

- In my house, these are the rules. You don't have to follow them, but if you don't, you can't stay.
- These behaviors are not okay in this house. You can do as you please somewhere else. I will do what's necessary to have you removed.
- I love you but will no longer bail you out from your poor choices. If you threaten me, I will do what's necessary to keep myself safe, even if that means calling the police and filing charges.
- Unfortunately, I don't have money to give you. I hope you figure out your problem. I'm here if you'd like my advice.
- I wish I could let you live here, but last time things didn't go well for either of us.
- If you continue to call, text, or harass me, I will block your number for my peace of mind.
- I know you don't like me being your legal guardian, but it's my responsibility to keep you safe. If, in the future, you show that you're capable, then I'll gladly give you the option of caring for yourself.
- I know you don't like that I control your money, but you won't have enough for living expenses if I don't.
- I understand that your disease is causing you to behave this way, but I won't allow you to treat me like this. I will take the necessary steps to keep myself safe.
- I realize you would like another chance, but I need to see the following improvements _____ before I give you that chance.

All your interactions will probably end in a struggle of wills, and that collision of wills always results in some sort of damage. When he refuses to comply with basic house rules, disregards your personal boundaries, or threatens your safety, then it's time to move past the drama. Agree to disagree and move your MIAC out of your house. You can choose to pay for other accommodations, hook him up with social services, or decide that he needs to figure it out for himself. Do what's best for you, and don't be swayed by your MIAC's unreasonable demands.

When you let go, something magical happens: you give God room to work.

As you become more aware of your boundaries, you begin to see how damaging it is to violate your child's boundaries. He needs to believe he has some control over his life, words, and choices. If you decide everything for him and he has little control over his disease, it's critical to leave some things within his power. Your child needs to feel heard and have his feelings acknowledged, and he needs to feel worthy of love and acceptance. You have to let go—for both of you. You have to allow him to make choices and experience the consequences. You have to make space for both of you to heal and come to terms with this scary new reality. If not for him, then for yourself.

> *You have to let go—for both of you.*

Some days it'll be hard to let your child have his opinion, especially if he's irrational. It'll take practice and patience to let your child speak his mind without disagreeing. Just listen. If you disagree, your MIAC may think you don't honor his opinion. He's desperate to convince you that what he experiences is real. Allow him his point of view.

When you give your MIAC a voice in his life, it creates a calmer environment for both of you. You'll feel more respect and love for each other when your individual opinions are acknowledged. If he's unable to accept your position, it may be time for him to be on his own and make his own choices.

Letting go of my death grip over my son's life was the best thing I've done since his diagnosis. Every day I'm grateful that B's not violent and that he's not homeless. He could have chosen to be aggressive and refused to stay in residential care. He could still decide to leave and go back to drugs and alcohol. He could choose to leave the home he's in and live on the streets. Because of what I've been through with him, I'd allow him to make that choice. I wouldn't like it, but I would let him see if that works better for him.

My MIAC knows that no matter what choices he makes, I love and respect him, and because of that, our relationship is closer than ever. I would love for him to make good choices for himself, but I know he isn't capable at this time. And because I let go of trying to control him, B let go of resisting my help. We don't always agree, but life is so much easier now than I ever imagined it could be.

I also realize that just because we've reached a truce, there's no guarantee it will always be this way. His disease could progress to the point that he becomes completely unhinged and aggressive. Whatever happens, I will still love him, even if he's not in my life.

Today, I see my options. I know the limits of my power. The only thing I can do is make sure we're both safe, whatever that takes.

Your MIAC needs to put forth as much effort toward getting better as you put toward his recovery. You can't drag or carry him into a happy, successful life. He has to want to be in a better place for himself. Maybe the issue isn't that he doesn't want to be better but that he's not capable of more. But carrying him as he resists and protests won't get him there either.

Doing His Best

I thought back to the start of my son's illness and made a mental list of the things he'd done without help since his diagnosis. I compared it to what I'm capable of doing when I feel terrible. Interestingly, our lists were very similar. On days when I'm sick, I accomplish only the basics—nothing more. I don't bathe, change clothes, brush my teeth, or even get up to fix a healthy meal. I eat whatever I can find and lay in bed all day. What if that's the answer: my MIAC is doing his best every day because it's the best his sick brain can do?

Once I acknowledged that B was doing the best he could every day, based on his debilitating disease, I understood how hard it was for him to live up to my expectations. My assumption that he could relearn specific skills, paired with his expectations of a normal life for himself, created stress and anxiety, and it caused my son to shut down even more.

Nobody wakes up and thinks, *Today, I'll be the worst possible version of myself.* No. If you slack off, it may be that you don't feel well, are tired, or feel overwhelmed. Everyone is doing the very best they can, given their circumstances. What your MIAC does may not look like my best or your best, but it's his best.

When you start to let go, you'll learn to remove your emotions when circumstances escalate. This doesn't mean you won't feel emotional during an event or a crisis, but you'll choose to put your feelings aside while you calmly deal with the matter. You can't make reasonable decisions if you're emotionally overwhelmed. Visualize taking off your mom hat and putting on your caretaker cap, so you can do what needs to be done, rather than trying to control or guilt your MIAC into doing what you think is best. Look at each situation as if it's your job to find a solution for a young man (or woman) who's struggling to do right. This approach can remove the frustration and defuse the event. By letting go and accepting where he is, you allow him to come to terms with his limitations too.

---

*What your MIAC does may not look like my best or your best, but it's **his** best.*

Do You Have to Be Right?

There are several ways to let go and stop feeling you have to be right. The following questions and advice can help you discern how to handle situations involving your MIAC.

- Is it more critical for you to be right or happy?
- Are your reprimands justifiable, and will they create the change you want?
- What do you want to prove?

- Do your actions help or change the situation?
- Is it possible for both you and your MIAC to be right?
- Can you accept that nobody is right or wrong?
- When you make your MIAC wrong, it will never make either of you happy.
- Change your focus, and it creates neutrality.
- Life is better when you look at everything through love-tinted glasses.

When you let go of being right, you also let go of the outcome. Letting go of your attachment to a particular result takes courage, vulnerability, and you have to admit you don't have all the answers. There is peace in letting go.

Could you remove the labels of *right* or *wrong* and consider what happens as an educational experience rather than a game of win or lose? If you must be right, you're likely to judge your MIAC when he doesn't agree with you or do things your way, which humiliates him and makes him feel like a failure.

---

*If you need to be right all the time,
it makes you focus on other people's flaws.*

I've spent too much time in arguments with my son when he was delusional. I thought that with enough talk and reasoning, I could convince him that his thoughts weren't rational. I made a point to show him how unreasonable he behaved. I knew I was right, and I wanted my son to see things my way. We would have angry shouting matches as we each tried to convince the other that our way was the right way. It never led to anything productive, but it did create many hurt feelings.

"A shower will give you a better outlook. Clean clothes will make you feel less depressed. A walk or some exercise will reduce your anxiety. Stop pacing. It only makes you more nervous. No more coffee. It makes you manic. Get up—lying in a dark room just makes you more tired. Try to listen to your iPod to stop the voices. If you ate regular meals, you probably wouldn't have a headache. When you drink beer, it keeps your meds from working. I'm your mom, I know I'm right, I know what I'm talking about. Please just do something I suggest."

He would try to do what I asked on rare occasions, but it never seemed to produce the desired outcome.

> I'm so tired of parenting an adult as if he's a small child. An adult who doesn't do anything I ask of him. I'm slumped on the couch, reading an article about school-age children who can't listen or do what's expected. The article explains that most children don't comply with parental demands because they're asked to do something they aren't mature enough to handle.
>
> The article got my attention. What if my son isn't capable of doing the things I ask? How long will I continue to beat my head against a wall of mental illness? What if this isn't about being right or wrong but about a damaged brain?

Remember, you're dealing with someone who's irrational and delusional, not clear-headed and mature. The truth is that you're the one who needs to change. It's time to let go of your need to be right. *Right* doesn't fix anything. *Right* doesn't make your child better. *Right* doesn't move you forward. *Right* doesn't work with mental illness.

You don't drown when you fall in the river; you drown by staying there. It's clear that your *right* way of thinking isn't working, but can you give up your attachment to the outcome of your MIAC's disease? Will you be able to let his actions dictate what you need to do? What if things don't turn out the way you want? Can you accept that's how it will be? How will you adjust when your child's behavior decides the outcome instead of you?

You can't change your MIAC's thoughts or behavior or expect him to realize things need to change. So you need to start the process of saving you both. Letting go feels like you're not smart enough to figure out how to win this battle, like you've given up hope, like you've walked away because things got too hard. "Sometimes letting things go is an act of far greater power than defending or hanging on," says the brilliant author Eckhart Tolle.

If I'd known years ago that letting go would save me, maybe I would have loosened my grip sooner. Releasing my need to be right was my life vest in the storm, and letting go of my need to know the outcome is what pulled me out of the water. Letting go saved me from going under with my MIAC. It was scary to let go, but treading water was no longer an option.

It was a gradual process. Each time I was successful, it made it easier to take another step, until one day, I was okay with not being in control, not having all the answers, not knowing the outcome. I was okay to just live for that day.

Has my MIAC changed his choices or behaviors? No. He's the same, but I'm entirely different in the way I handle my son and his disease. Letting go was never about changing my child; it was always about making changes in how I see and react to him and his MI. It took almost drowning in a sea of chaos to recognize that I'd always been wearing a life vest and had the power within to weather life's storms.

With mental illness, there are ongoing crises that inhibit healing and lower the chances of recovery. Letting go means adjusting to a lower performance level, not returning to normal. After years of pushing and pulling, fighting and screaming, hoping and praying, you're frustrated and exhausted. It's time to let go.

Let Go of the Illusion of Control

Unfortunately, your MIAC may never take your advice or receive the help needed to live a healthy, productive life. Your child's disease may prevent him from accepting any assistance, which can be challenging to accept—that there's nothing you can do until he wants help.

Sometimes when you step away, it forces your MIAC to see that he has a problem and needs help, and at other times, it will have no effect. Either way, you need to accept the reality that you don't control what happens in your child's life unless you seek guardianship or he allows you to have a say. Regardless, you still can't change his prognosis.

You may cling to the fantasy that when you give your MIAC money, allow him to live with you, condone his drug or alcohol use, bail him out of jail, or let him abuse you, that you're in control. In reality, the opposite is true—you've allowed your MIAC to control you. If your child controls what happens in your house, how you spend your money, where you go, whether you feel safe, and what you do in your free time, then you're not in control of your own life.

Is it your MIAC's fault that things have gotten so out of hand? The answer is, "No, it's the disease's fault." Your child wants desperately to be better, but giving him money, letting him live with you, or exercising control over every aspect of his life can't fix a broken brain. Spiritual leader Sri Chinmoy says, "Surrender is a journey from the outer turmoil to the inner peace." It's a journey we all must take. The sooner you start, the sooner you'll get there.

I'm going to propose a very controversial idea, one that might be tough to consider. No matter where your MIAC is, what his living conditions are, whether he lacks money or housing, or he's incarcerated, his brain still functions the same. His behaviors and choices don't change based on external circumstances. Yes, if he has better living conditions, he'll have the opportunity to eat healthier food and have access to medical attention—but only if he's willing to accept that support. Many MIACs refuse all help because of their paranoia, delusions, and inability to recognize their illness. At some point, you have to acknowledge that you've done everything within your power to help your child, and there's nothing more you can offer. You need to stop your efforts to control his life and focus on rebuilding your own. You won't stop loving your child, but you'll only continue to offer support if it doesn't harm you. You don't need to lose your life to his mental illness.

You need to stop your efforts to control his life and focus on rebuilding your own.

The Money Trap

"What are you doing? This money needs to last you all month. When it's gone, don't ask me for any more."

I can't comprehend how fast B spends it. I feel sick to my stomach. I've always been frugal and thoughtful about what I purchase, but my son blows through money like it'll evaporate if he doesn't spend it immediately. What should I do? It's his money, but as his guardian, shouldn't I decide how he spends it? Or do I let him do what he wants?

I confront him. "B, what do you think you're doing? This is ridiculous! You have to stop and think about what you're buying. This can't go on. You have to stop!"

B laughs at me. "Mom, it's my money. You can't tell me how to spend it. I'm an adult, so I get to choose how I spend my money. It's mine!"

The guilt settles in. B has so little control over anything in his life. Maybe I think I should let him have this.

Two months later, he's violently vomiting every day.

"What's wrong with you?" I ask.

I check his purchase history and see that he's bought various herbs and is mixing crazy concoctions and drinking them. He's ingesting way more than the recommended amount, and I've had enough.

I change his monthly deposit to weekly. Hopefully, this will change his spending patterns. Any time B's given the opportunity, he buys some sort of herb or supplement. He always looks for a way to get high.

Next, I stop the credit card and dole out cash as he needs it, hoping that this will curtail the choices he makes. Why can't my son handle money? Does he even hear what I say? I feel like he makes stupid choices on purpose just to thumb his nose at me. Will I have to monitor his spending for the rest of my life?

Our dysfunctional financial dance went on for far too long because I refused to see the obvious. Even when I curtailed B's access to money, he still managed to get neighbors and friends to give him cash to buy beer and CBD gummies. In the end, his clandestine drinking caused a severe psychotic break, and he landed back in the hospital. I finally saw that I couldn't control his behaviors and hold down a job. At the same time, I finally let go of my belief that he could ever handle his finances.

We'd played this game for far too long, and I did us both a huge disservice when I repeated the same scenario and expected a different outcome—not only with money but also with all his other life choices. So much time wasted, so many arguments, so much energy spent on meaningless talks, so much heartache. My mantra now is that actions speak louder than words. I give B a couple of chances to handle his affairs and then evaluate if that's a skill he can perform. If not, I take over or make arrangements to have it handled for him.

Today I don't give my son many chances to show me if he's capable of more. If he asks to be responsible for a life skill, I give him a couple of tries without any guidance, and if he's not able, I let him try again with support. If he still can't handle it, he doesn't get any more chances unless I see significant improvement in other areas. There are no arguments. I watch his actions, not his words. It's difficult to accept that he's lost most of his abilities, but it hurts us both if I act like that's not true. When I ignore the truth, it puts my son in the awkward position of trying to do something he can't just to please me.

You've made it through this challenging chapter. I'm so proud of how far you've come on this journey to reclaim your life. Now that you've let go of so much, you'll have time to add self-care into your schedule. We'll explore ways to care better for yourself next.

Visualization Journey

Sit in a comfortable, quiet place. Close your eyes.

Breathe in and out slowly to the count of three several times until you feel yourself begin to relax.

Visualize yourself walking along a path. You enter a field, and in the center is a hot air balloon. It's a beautiful multicolored balloon. You can't wait to climb in. You've always wanted to ride in a balloon.

You climb in and sit on the bench. At your feet, you notice stones of all different sizes. You realize that you'll need to get rid of the weight before the balloon will rise off the ground.

Reach down and pick up a stone close to you. You see that it has a message etched on its side. It reads, "Let go of what you can't control." You hold the stone close to your heart, take a deep breath, and toss it over the side. The balloon has lost a little weight, but you still need to get rid of more.

One at a time, select the stones you're ready to release. Some of them will be small and easy to toss over the side, and others will require both hands and considerable effort to throw them out of the basket. As you go through this process, make a mental or physical list of the things you're releasing. Examples might be letting go of your codependency with your child, letting go of knowing the outcome of your child's disease, letting go of bailing your MIAC out, letting go of the need to be right, letting go of the idea that your child will recover. There are no right or wrong answers; just listen to what comes to mind or sits heavy in your heart.

Notice that as you throw more stones over the side, the balloon starts to lift off the ground and rises higher and higher.

The more the balloon rises, the more you can see. The landscape below you takes your breath away. Take in the beauty all around you. Breathe in the fresh air and listen. Just listen to how quiet and still the world seems. Stay here as long as you want, enjoying the beauty.

If you want to go higher, let go of more stones. You can do that now or save some for your next balloon ride. You can come back to this field and ride anytime you want.

If you've finished your journey for today, imagine that the balloon slowly descends until it gently lands back where you started.

When you're ready, open your eyes and journal any messages, words, or symbols you received. What stones did you toss over the side? What did the scenery look like as you gazed over the side of the balloon? How did the air smell? Did you see any birds? Do you feel lighter? Is there a calmness you didn't have before? Is your head quiet and your heart peaceful?

Self-care Isn't Selfish: It's Survival

We are sisters
We care for our MIACs
We've forgotten about ourselves
We feel guilty
We shift our focus to healthy choices
We are sisters

Stress is a physical, mental, or emotional reaction to any change that evokes a response or requires adjustment. It happens when an event or thought makes you feel frustrated, angry, overwhelmed, or nervous. Long-term stress can have harmful, permanent effects on your overall health. Stress can manifest as depression, anxiety, irritability, memory or concentration problems, compulsive behaviors, mood swings, fatigue, headaches, digestive issues, chronic pain, changes in appetite, difficulty sleeping, skin problems, lowered libido, muscle aches, reduced productivity, and lack of motivation. It's important to have skills to cope with stress and ways to manage it before it turns into something more serious.

We all experience stress every day. Some stress is positive, like starting a new job or having a baby. At other times, it's negative, such as making a big mistake at work or caring for an ill parent.

When your child becomes mentally ill and requires continual support, that causes a different type of stress. It's never-ending and out of your control. If you don't learn to adapt your responses to the chaos of MI, your anxiety can negatively impact every aspect of your life. The most powerful weapon against stress is your ability to choose one thought over another. You can train your mind to see the good in every situation and every experience, which will make every day a good day, perhaps with only a few bad moments.

> *The most powerful weapon against stress is your ability to choose one thought over another.*

You can choose to judge every experience as good or bad, or you can choose to see everything from a place of neutrality. You've been taught to see life in black and white when it's actually comprised of many shades of grey. Duality forces you to choose one side over the other, but neutrality allows you to see things as they are without attaching a label to them. Remaining indifferent or uninvolved doesn't mean that you don't care what happens. It simply means that you're emotionally detached from the event or outcome.

If you can learn to view things as an observer by stepping outside of the situation, then you won't be as stressed by what occurs. As difficult as this sounds, there are ways to mentally separate yourself from situations, but it requires that you find a quiet place inside yourself.

Accumulated psychological trauma produces negativity. Having an uncertain future can create fear, uneasiness, anxiety, tension, stress, and worry. And when you choose to live in the past, it causes guilt, regret, resentment, sadness, and bitterness. The idea is to live in the present, in the *now*, and only think about what's happening at this moment. I try to follow the RAIN method created by Tara Brach for a more balanced perspective.

R — Recognize what's going on
A — Allow the experience to be just what it is
I — Investigate with kindness
N — Natural awareness (not emotional attachment) so you don't identify with the experience

Problems are inevitable. Some can be anticipated, while others seem to drop from the sky. The good news is that every problem has a solution. It may not be immediately obvious, it may not be the solution you hope for, and you may have to wait for the answer to appear, but a solution can be found. Sometimes it involves letting go. Sometimes the problem is yours to solve, and sometimes it belongs to your child.

Whenever you refuse to change the way you approach a problem, you're choosing to stay stuck. Read that again and really let the words sink in. Are you choosing to be miserable?

How do you create inner calm in spite of circumstances? One step, one day, one change at a time. It isn't easy to decide to see things through a different lens, but the end result is a happier life.

Irrational Interactions

Almost every interaction with my MIAC has the potential to cause stress, which then turns into anxiety. My son is delusional, highly paranoid, and has daily hallucinations. All these symptoms create fertile ground for unbridled stress to occur. It's difficult to deal with my child, even when he has a reasonably good day. I have to watch every word I say, or his calm mood can escalate into a game of "he said, she said." Many times, he hears something different from what I've actually said, and this leads to accusations, threats, and anger. Never knowing how our visits will go adds to my tension. There's no normal in our visits, just altered-reality confusion.

Last month we started to play a game, and ten minutes in, he told me he was bored and wanted to quit. He insisted that he couldn't breathe properly and needed to go to bed. The following week, we played an entire game of Scrabble and had a great visit. The next week, he thanked me, his sister, and her family for coming to see him for the holidays.

He said, "I feel you really care for me because you showed up."

That day he sounded rational and normal until he began to explain why washing your hair makes it fall out. The next time I saw him, he was unable to do anything but sit on his bed and mumble, and today he called me to demand that I get ahold of his doctor because he needs vitamins. During our call, he insisted that there was someone else talking on the phone with me. He became angry when I assured him that I was alone.

Each visit is like being dropped into a pinball machine, bouncing from irrational thoughts to paranoid theories, then spit back into reality, stressed and anxious.

Friends and family don't understand what it's like to deal with a MIAC day after day and never reach a level of normalcy. Each day is different and brings new challenges, or sometimes just familiar chaos. My plans can change on a dime based on what I need to handle that day. Most of us deal better with life when there's a sense of routine and normality. How do you become comfortable not knowing what each day will look like? How do you adjust your thinking to always expect mayhem? How do you learn to let it all go and accept whatever each moment brings?

I drive home with thoughts of the party I'll attend tonight. I'm excited to spend time with friends and have looked forward to it all week. As I pull into the driveway, I see my son's dad and girlfriend waiting by my door. My heart beats faster. This can't possibly be good news.

I jump out. "What's going on? Are you here visiting B?"

He says, "We've been waiting for over an hour. We made plans earlier to come visit with B, but he won't answer the door or his phone."

In a flash, my day has changed. I'm fairly certain I know where B is, and I call his friend. He doesn't answer. I jump back into my car and drive around the block to his friend's house. The whole time my brain races. What's happened? Is he hurt? Is he drunk? Is he dead?

I run to the front door and knock loudly. Someone better answer, or I'm calling the police. B's friend finally comes to the door and lets me in, and there's my MIAC passed out on the couch, unresponsive.

"He wanted some beer," his friend says to me as I try to get B to open his eyes or answer me.

My son tries to stand and falls flat on his face. He's too big for any of us to pick up, and I ask his dad to call for an ambulance.

Of course, my ex says, "You need to call because you're B's legal guardian."

I respond with, "I didn't ask you to be responsible. Just make a call."

My ex's girlfriend tries to reason with my incoherent son and his friend. Unbelievable! I run back to my car to grab my cell phone and call 911. I can already see how my night will end, and I'm angry and stressed that my plans have fallen through once again.

B's dad heads home. I follow the ambulance to the emergency room because I have to sign him in for treatment. His blood-alcohol level is off the charts, and yet he now tries to convince the officers that he only drank one beer. We're all amazed that he can talk and that he's not dead from alcohol poisoning.

This is the third ER visit this month for intoxication. I'm furious! I'm afraid for my son, and the stress makes my head pound. I give my son the tongue lashing he deserves for ruining my plans. Then the nurse comes in.

"You need to calm down," she says.

She has no clue what I deal with on a daily basis. No clue at all! But I take a deep breath and realize that my MIAC won't remember a word of what I've said, nor will he remember being drunk or riding in the ambulance.

Will this ever get easier? Is this what the rest of my life will look like? If his drinking doesn't kill him, it might just kill me.

Some days I think that I can't do this anymore. The stress and anxiety suck the life out of me. I think that next time, I won't let it get to me. And yet, each time, I feel the adrenaline rush in, and I'm in fight-or-flight mode again. By the time I calm myself down, I'm in the middle of another incident. I don't want to become accustomed to the chaos because it might make me callous and unfeeling. I don't want to be desensitized to the discord so that it begins to feel normal.

I don't know how to distance myself from what happens and still deal with my son.

At times like this, you can't change the event, but you can change your response—which could change the outcome. Your response won't always change the outcome, but you always have control over your response or whether you choose to respond at all. Does everything require a response? Do you need to be emotionally tied to the outcome? You get to choose how to react or feel about every encounter. You choose whether to view it emotionally or to be objective.

Hermann Hess, in *Siddhartha,* says, "Within you, there is a stillness and a sanctuary to which you can retreat at any time and be yourself."

Self-Care

You're almost always stronger and more capable than you believe yourself to be. When you focus on self-care, you can reduce or eliminate anxiety naturally. Multitasking or interruptions by your MIAC should be avoided during self-care. This time is just for you, so you can replenish your spirit and feed your soul. Below are some self-care ideas. Doing only one a week can start to make a difference in your attitude and how you feel about yourself and your child. Don't try to do them all. Just take small positive steps.

Shower Meditation

When you take a shower, visualize washing away your stress and anxiety. Pay attention to how the water feels, what the soap smells like, and how the sound drowns out all other noises. Visualize all your negative thoughts and feelings washed away. Feel the sadness, regret, anger, and depression leave your body. Notice how much lighter you feel as you watch the water swirl down the drain. Your heart will feel lighter, and your day will seem brighter.

Morning Rituals

Perform these slowly and with intention. Take time to feel the relaxation seep into your body and mind. Rushing defeats the purpose. Clear your mind of everything else but what you're doing.

- Cleanse and revive: wash your face and drink a cup of tea or coffee.
- Attract abundance: make a list of three things you're grateful for.
- Breathe in peace: slowly inhale and exhale to the count of four (six times).
- Ignite relaxation: light a candle, burn incense, or diffuse oils.
- Connect with Spirit: meditate or pray for ten minutes daily.
- Move to change: stretch your body with ten minutes of yoga.
- Manifest joy: write out your goals or intentions for the day.
- Nurture with nature: walk outside, pay attention to the beauty.

Boost Your Physical Well-Being

- Take a long, leisurely bath
- Book and enjoy a massage
- Drink a smoothie full of healthy, fresh ingredients
- Bake your favorite cake
- Dance to upbeat music
- Walk the dog
- Drink more water
- Make time to get eight hours of restful sleep
- Add in fifteen minutes of exercise
- Have a spa day and paint your nails a fun, new color

Boost Your Mental Wellness

- Read a book by your favorite author

- Play a board game you enjoyed as a child
- Try a new activity
- Write a list of goals
- Find a tutorial and create origami animals
- Declutter a drawer or closet
- Reminisce over old photos
- Work a jigsaw puzzle
- Start a new hobby
- Play a word game
- Create a scrapbook of your favorite photos

Improve Your Emotional Health

- Phone a friend
- Write in a daily journal
- Take an afternoon nap
- Listen to soothing music
- Get or give a twenty-second hug
- Ask a friend or family member for help
- Take a few minutes to have a good, cleansing cry
- Fiddle with a stress ball or yoyo
- Sing to the radio
- Make a point to smile throughout the day
- Find things that make you laugh

Spiritual Practices

Your spiritual health is the foundation that underlies your well-being in all other areas. Expand your spiritual practice with these activities:

- Meditate for five minutes twice a day
- Create ambiance with scented candles
- Try a restorative yoga class
- Work in your garden
- Take a breath-work class
- Be kind and show gratitude to everyone you encounter

- Paint or draw
- Pray or chant
- Offer to help a neighbor or friend

As you work to create more self-care, remember that you're allowed to have days where you struggle; you're allowed to put your needs first; you're allowed to take a break; you're allowed to ask for help or support; and you're allowed to have reactions and feelings about your MIAC that are less than loving.

When you take care of your needs, your stress will be reduced, and your days will feel more positive. Initially, it will be hard to make time for yourself without feeling guilty, but the more you practice, the easier it gets. Your anxiety will decrease significantly.

If you become nervous or frustrated, stop and do something just for yourself before your emotions take over and lead to anger and resentment. Practicing self-care will improve your relationship with your child. It may seem like you don't have time to do anything for yourself, but you can't make wise choices about your child if you don't put yourself first.

Ongoing Stress

Stress hormones send your body into fight-or-flight mode. Those signals are meant to protect you, but if you experience a continued stress response, you put your health at risk. Chronic stress causes many health conditions. The list is long and includes every organ and body system. Your central nervous system is in charge of cortisol and adrenaline and sends you into high alert. If your body never has a chance to return to normal, then your health is compromised.

After dealing with a MIAC for years and years, you can become numb to your ongoing stress. Your new normal is to be anxious and nervous all the time, but that doesn't mean your body gets used to the onslaught of stress hormones. Every day that you hold on to the stress makes you increasingly unhealthy.

The truth is that you're the only one who can decide when you've had enough and start to take steps to live a healthier life. Your ill child doesn't want his MI to impact your health and well-being. Watching you make yourself sick is another guilt added to your already overburdened MIAC. The best gift you can give your child is to model appropriate self-care and wellness routines. It gives your MIAC an example to follow.

Before B moved into the condo next door, he lived with dad, and that didn't work well for either of them. Living in the condo was a new experiment to see if B is capable of semi-independence. He's excited, and I'm optimistic that he'll be able to have a somewhat normal life. His dad and I haven't given him many opportunities to grow or show us what he's capable of, so this is a big step for everyone.

Initially, B seems overwhelmed, but that's understandable because this is a big change for him. I didn't realize what a big change it would be for me as well.

By the third week, I begin to see how dependent and incompetent B really is. Because Dad didn't allow him to do much or let him make any decisions, we didn't know what B was capable of. He needs a huge amount of handholding and support to start and finish the most basic household or person hygiene tasks. In the fourth week, I woke up in the middle of the night in excruciating pain. My thumb was throbbing so badly that I couldn't sleep. By morning I was miserable and called around to find a doctor I could see that day.

Listen to Your Body

I struggled just to make it through each day and couldn't wait to get home and crash on the couch. In the years before my son's first psychotic break, I was diagnosed with fibromyalgia. I'm sure it was caused by all the stress I felt from dealing with my MIAC's erratic behaviors, drug and alcohol use, and the inability to figure out exactly what was going on with him. Whenever I did too much, I paid for it with increased pain and fatigue. I didn't realize that my health issues were related to the stress and anxiety I felt about my son's mental illness and his uncertain future.

When B moved next door, it was the beginning of a terrible year for me. I hurt most of the time but only took pain meds when I couldn't stand it anymore. I struggled in every area of my life. At work, I'd hired a new employee and couldn't even train her. My mom was in hospice, and I was trying to teach my son to live independently. Nothing seemed to work out.

During my time off, I read a lot of books. *You Can Heal Your Life* by Louise Hay shed some light on my hand issue. Louise said, "Illness, however mild or severe, is an indicator of your emotional state, caused by your thoughts and focus."

Hmmm . . . an interesting idea, so I looked up what emotions cause hand issues.

Hay described how hands involve holding and handling, clutching and gripping, grasping and letting go, all ways we deal with experiences. The issues I was troubled by—my son's neediness, my mom's illness, growing my business—were all part of the cause for my hand problem. I also learned that the right hand represents the practical things we deal with, whereas the left hand represents our relationships. My right hand was the one giving me problems.

Everything I was trying to handle had overwhelmed me, so my stress manifested as a hand issue. This all made so much sense, and once I realized why this happened, I was able to address the situations that caused my stress and heal my hand. My hand is now pain free and has been for several years without surgery.

When I learned how good our bodies are at giving us information, I began to question any physical symptoms I experienced. They always correlated to what was going on with me emotionally and were a sign that I needed to spend time with my feelings and focus on better self-care. I now have a regular self-care routine that I stick to religiously. I walk daily, work with a personal trainer, meditate, eat healthy (most of the time), have alone time, make time for fun and friends, and get a monthly massage. Because my son noticed my interest in meditation, he tried it too. My MIAC might not be able to stick to a routine, but at least he tries on occasion to manage his stress.

Buddha wisely taught, "Stress is the gap between our expectations and reality. The bigger the gap, the more stress. So, expect nothing and accept everything."

Lowered Expectations

My expectations now are very low for my son. At first, it seemed like I'd let go of any hope and opportunity for him to recover. But my lowered expectations have stopped my son from trying to do more than he's able to, which helps prevent relapses. Yes, I said that by lowering my expectations for my MIAC, it helps prevent relapses. I'm not suggesting that all his relapses are caused by overzealous expectations, but they can contribute to overall mental deterioration. As I've lowered my expectations, my own stress and anxiety are less than they've been in a long time. I accept his behavior as it is—a manifestation of his disease.

> *. . . by lowering my expectations for my MIAC, it helps prevent relapses.*

Some days my son is more functional than others. And I do have certain expectations that are non-negotiable. For example, I don't tolerate threatening or aggressive behaviors, drug or alcohol use, or disrespect.

The more attention I paid to my health, the better I've been able to cope with my son's disease. As I wrote this book, I had some new physical symptoms crop up because my normal downtime was filled with writing, and it took a toll on my well-being. When I recognized what was happening, I changed my schedule to allow for more self-care each day. Within a few weeks, I felt better.

Our bodies remind us when they're being neglected. You only get this one body. The better you care for it, the better it will support and serve you. Your body houses your soul. Treat it as the sacred vessel it is.

Acquired PTSD

"There is no timestamp on trauma. There isn't a formula that you can insert yourself into to get from horror to healed. Be patient. Take up space. Let your journey be your balm," states relationship coach Dawn Serra.

PTSD (post-traumatic stress disorder) can develop from emotional, mental, or physical abuse or other emotion-based experiences. It can also evolve from caring for a severely ill child. Dealing with an irrational, aggressive, or violent MIAC is an extraordinarily stressful event. Any situation that threatens your life or safety is considered traumatic. Feeling frightened and helpless can also leave you traumatized. These can be one-time events or can be ongoing and cause relentless stress. If you're unable to work through your painful emotions and process what's happened, or if you become stuck reliving the experience, then it can manifest as PTSD.

Symptoms of emotional and psychological trauma are difficult to diagnose because they can look like many other issues. If you feel any of the following, you may consider a visit with a professional to determine if you suffer from PTSD:

- Do you feel disconnected or numb?
- Do you feel sad or hopeless?
- Do fear or anxiety cause you to withdraw from others?
- Do you notice confusion or difficulty concentrating?
- Do you feel guilt, shame, or self-blame?
- Do you feel anger, irritability, or have mood swings?

Caring for a severe MIAC can cause shock, denial, and disbelief. Not addressing your emotional needs can lead to further impairment and suffering. When you read over this list, you can see that at some time or another, you've experienced all of these symptoms.

In my research, I couldn't find any information on the incidence of PTSD in parents caring for a MIAC. It seems that an entire group of people has been oddly omitted from this illness. A psychotic MIAC can unintentionally inflict trauma on others, especially his or her parents. Caring for a severely MI child is similar to being on the frontlines of a war. If your MIAC has exhibited any of the following behaviors, it could be that you're struggling with symptoms of PTSD:

- Does your MIAC rage, have angry, explosive outbursts, or temper tantrums? Do reasonable demands make him blow up? Does asking about a job interview cause him to scream obscenities at you? Does your suggestion that alcohol inflames his symptoms cause him to throw things?
- Does your MIAC exhibit chronic aggression and violence? Does he punch holes in the walls when distressed or when someone doesn't agree with his thought processes? Does he get into shoving matches with family members over trivial matters? Does your child become a bully to get his way? Does he destroy your personal property? Are you physically or verbally threatened?
- Has your MIAC harmed or threatened to harm people or animals? Have you been physically assaulted, punched, kicked, strangled, or had things thrown at you? Have you been pinched, poked, shoved, had your hair pulled, or been threatened with a knife, gun, or other item used as a weapon?
- Has your MIAC threatened or attempted suicide? Has he repeatedly threatened suicide if he doesn't get his way, or has he attempted suicide multiple times?
- Does your MIAC exhibit risky behaviors? For example, does he steal from you, shoplift, steal cars, use illegal drugs, sell illegal drugs, engage in promiscuous sexual behaviors, turn to prostitution to pay for a drug habit, or break into or damage your home or car?

- Does your MIAC harm himself by cutting, burning, or scratching, or does he have an eating disorder? Dangerous examples include continuous cutting that requires stitches; burns from a lighter, curling iron, or cigarettes; scratching and picking at the skin causing numerous scabs and infections; refusal to eat and insisting that food is poisoned; or purging after meals.

Try to remember that your MIAC's harmful behaviors are a manifestation of his disease and not a personality flaw. I have this quote on the wall in my kitchen, so I can read it daily. "Your child is suffering as much, if not more than you are, and this is not how he would choose to behave if he weren't mentally ill."

When your child experiences a severe thought disorder, he's afraid, incoherent, and he can't act with any amount of reason. The only thing he can understand is that he wants the pain to stop and will do anything to make that happen. Unfortunately, your MIAC rarely has the coping skills necessary to alleviate his extreme discomfort in a positive way. If you can remember that your precious child lies underneath those terrible behaviors, then it may help you to release the trauma of his actions.

Your child is suffering as much, if not more than you are, and this is not how he would choose to behave if he weren't mentally ill.

The mind relives what the heart can't erase. Nightmares and flashbacks are common after experiencing trauma but should improve over a short time. If you continue to replay the events over and over without any improvement, you should seek out a professional and have an evaluation to determine if treatment would be helpful. A diagnosis of PTSD is nothing to be ashamed of and, in my opinion, is reasonable considering what parents of some MIACs deal with daily.

It can take weeks and sometimes months after a traumatic event for PTSD symptoms to appear. There are several therapies and coping strategies available that can help diminish or resolve your symptoms. Know that PTSD is treatable, and the earlier you begin treatment after a traumatic event, the better the outcome. Please don't think that because your child caused your trauma that you don't need to take care of yourself. You don't deserve to be treated badly by anybody, not even your child.

My doctor asks me, "What's going on?"

I explain, "I've got a few aches and pains, and my stomach hurts."

Today, all doctors ask if you feel depressed, have thoughts of hurting yourself or others, or feel frightened for your safety in your home, but ten years ago, that didn't happen.

"How's your family?" he asks, and I give a cursory description of my son's mental health diagnosis.

I don't get into the craziness of my life and don't even think to tell him how it affects me mentally and emotionally because I've already listed my physical symptoms.

I tell him, "It's upsetting having a child diagnosed with such a severe disease."

He doesn't ask me how I'm holding up or if there's anything I need. Instead, he tells me, "Even people with Down's syndrome can bag groceries."

What? How can a medical doctor be so ignorant? He doesn't know the difference between a low IQ and MI?

I look him in the eye and say, "My son was normal and had a full life ahead of him, and now he doesn't, and the worst part is he knows what he's lost."

I leave feeling worse than when I came in and think to myself that it's time to find a new doctor.

The following week I visit my rheumatologist, who monitors my fibromyalgia. I tell her about my recent flare-up and what's going on at home. Because I'm on a low-dose antidepressant for my muscle pain, she increases the amount.

Again, my mental health isn't addressed. My medication is increased in an attempt to alleviate my physical pain. The doctor doesn't suggest that maybe the emotional stress is causing my physical symptoms, and I don't know enough to recognize the connection. I head home with a prescription that does nothing to address the underlying cause of my pain.

In three weeks, I've seen two doctors and taken my son to see his psychiatrist, and not one of them considers that I might be struggling. Not one of them sees the despair in my eyes, how nervous and jumpy I am, or notices the weariness of my walk. It's like I'm invisible. Some wounds aren't visible; they're buried deep within your heart. It's not a physical injury but one that pierces your soul.

Situational Depression and Anxiety

Depression can be a normal reaction to an abnormal situation. Situational depression and anxiety are very common in parents, especially moms, who care for a MIAC. They can sneak up on you, and one day, you feel lost and broken, not sure if or how you can go on.

You keep it to yourself because it's difficult to find people who understand. You want to talk about it. Damn it. You want to scream! You want to yell. You want to shout about it, but all you can do is whisper, "I'm fine." You bottle up everything. You hide your emotions. You pretend to be okay. You know it's not healthy, but you don't want to be a burden, and you don't want people to worry about you. You feel like you've lost something but have no clue when or where or what. Then one day, you realize that what you've lost is yourself in the drama of your child's illness.

> *. . . one day you realize that what you've lost is yourself in the drama of your child's illness.*

Just because it's called situational depression doesn't mean it will go away on its own or that you don't need professional support. Your child's MI will be an ongoing stressor that you'll need to handle for years to come, so it's imperative that you do whatever's necessary to heal yourself. If you expect your MIAC to acknowledge, seek, and accept help for his mental illness, then you need to take the same advice for yourself. You can't manage your child's care if you're too depressed or anxious to function. Listen to your family and friends when they suggest that you might benefit from counseling. They might see how much you've changed when you cannot.

There are many common signs of depression. Do any of these resonate with you?

- Does your irritability cause small things to frustrate you?
- Do you miss the big picture because your focus is on small problems?
- Do you experience feelings of sadness? Are you unable to have fun or find enjoyment? Do you no longer enjoy sex? Or have you lost interest in normal, daily activities?
- Do you spend your nights worrying, or do you avoid life by sleeping excessively?
- Has anxiety caused loss of appetite or overeating, restlessness or a short attention span, or decreased concentration?
- Do you have angry outbursts, feel helpless, or lash out at others?
- Do you have physical pain caused by repressed emotions, have you lost energy, or do you cry for no reason?
- Are you having thoughts of suicide or death?

If you're experiencing some of these symptoms, you may be depressed. If any of these behaviors become ongoing, it can lead to deeper problems because you aren't addressing your emotions and haven't found a constructive way to work through them. Depression isn't a choice; it's a response to an unmanageable situation. It's not a sign of weakness or a sign of failure to feel overwhelmed and depressed by the prospect of caring long-term for a chronic, severe MIAC. It's common to get stuck in the inertia of your child's disease.

Anxiety

Listen to Deepak Chopra when he says, "The best use of imagination is creativity. The worst use of imagination is anxiety." Anxiety can be described as overwhelming feelings of fear, worry, or apprehension that are extreme to the point that they affect your daily life. Anxiety is the most commonly diagnosed mental illness, but many people choose not to seek professional help and continue to suffer. Untreated, ongoing anxiety typically gets worse over time because the brain turns these new patterns of behavior into habits. While it's normal to have occasional anxiety around stressful situations such as before giving a speech, before a medical procedure, or waiting for test results, it's *not* typical to experience anxiety over small, mundane things. Anxiety is induced when you're unable to control circumstances and are unwilling to accept that reality, which is why it makes perfect sense that caring for a MIAC causes uncontrolled feelings of anxiety.

The symptoms of anxiety are similar to depression, but in addition, anxiety provokes a fight-or-flight response including:

- Feeling on edge
- Having nervous energy
- Tense muscles
- Shortness of breath
- Increased heart rate and stomach acid
- Excessive worry
- Extreme or irrational fears that inhibit normal life
- Panic attacks

"Anxiety and depression are flip sides of the same coin," says therapist Nancy B. Irwin, PsyD. It's possible to be only depressed or only anxious, but you might also experience a combination of the two. If you aren't certain whether you fall into one or both of these categories, you could ask a close family member or friend for their opinion. People outside your situation can often be more objective in their observations of your behaviors. Depression is when you don't really care about anything. Anxiety is when you care too much about everything. Having both equals misery.

I've been dismayed by the lack of regard and resources available for the moms of MIACs. By ignoring the elephant in the room, the medical community discounts the enormous impact mental illness has on the family caregivers of MIACs. Millions of lives are lost to serious MI every year, and that number is at least doubled when including the impact MI has on the parents of these unfortunate individuals.

As a caregiver, you're never in control of what happens around you, but you're always in control of what happens within you. Choose to make your mental health a priority. Skills to cope with depression and anxiety include:

- Making healthy lifestyle choices
- Eating well-balanced meals, not skipping meals, and avoid binging on unhealthy snacks
- Limiting alcohol and caffeine
- Exercising daily
- Getting enough sleep
- Breathing slowly and deeply
- Laughing frequently
- Doing something you enjoy
- Volunteering in your community

Engaging in the above will minimize your focus on your problems. Remember nobody's perfect, accept what you can't control, learn what triggers you, and remove yourself from the problem to clear your thoughts. Finally, remind yourself to be grateful, cultivate a positive attitude, and reach out to family and friends when you feel overwhelmed.

Mindfulness

Begin by practicing mindfulness. It means paying attention to your thoughts, feelings, and bodily sensations moment-by-moment. The intent is to let everything come and go without judgment.

Let everything pass through you. You don't need to cling to your emotions or overanalyze them; just notice them. Mindfulness allows you to slow down and enjoy everything in your day instead of rushing to get to the end. You can stay on task and accomplish things and still be mindful and present. Practice mindfulness while washing the dishes by focusing all your attention on how the soap smells, what the bubbles feel like on your skin, the sound of squeaky, clean plates, and the look of sparkling glasses. If your mind wanders to problems, gently guide it back to the task at hand. Your body and mind will thank you for this break from constant stress.

The following tips will help you add mindfulness into your day:

- Focus on breathing deeply. Make your exhales twice as long as your inhales to create relaxation and do the opposite to increase your energy.
- Focus on your senses. What do you see, hear, smell, taste, feel/touch or intuit/what does your gut tell you? This forces you to stop the endless internal dialog and stay present in the moment.
- Sit quietly and count. Count your breaths, rosary beads, things you're grateful for, friends and family, steps when taking a walk—just count.
- Practice listening to the voice in your head. If you hear a negative thought, turn it into a positive one and repeat it three times.
- When going to sleep, lie down and tense, then relax each muscle group from your toes up to your forehead. Hold the tension for the count of three and then completely relax. Notice how your body feels before and after.
- Meditate by chanting one positive word over and over for five minutes. Change the word each day. This is a great exercise for when you're not at home and feel overly stressed by a situation. You can even chant silently.
- Sing along or dance to music you love. You don't need to be a good dancer; simply get caught up in the music and drown out your thoughts.

- Do what you're doing with intention. You don't have to make it a special event to practice mindfulness. Pick any activity and focus without distraction.

Mental Tricks to Manage Anxiety

Managing your anxiety doesn't need to be complicated, but you need to be consistent and determined to create lasting changes. Here are some tips for managing anxiety that have helped me:

- *Think of your anxiety as a parasite and name it.* Think about your anxiety like it's a foreign object attached to you. For example, I named my anxiety Leonard, and I like to think of him as a slug or vampire who sucks away my energy. It's easier for me to get rid of my nervousness when I can visualize pulling Leonard off me and flinging him away.
- *Define your anxiety triggers and determine how they affect you.* Do you experience butterflies, feel like you're walking on eggshells, have a need to pace, experience shallow breathing, or have a roller coaster sensation in your belly? What does the anxiety look like—a tornado, a thunderstorm, like you're stepping off a building or walking a tightrope? When are you most likely to feel anxiety—when you face potential conflicts, feel a loss of control, make a difficult decision, need to stand up for yourself, are dealing with irrational situations, need to set boundaries for yourself, or are enforcing rules and consequences for your MIAC?
- *Imagine yourself in battle with your anxiety.* Have go-to strategies for each situation that causes your anxiety to flare. What are your weapons? Can you breathe deeply, meditate, count, walk outside, call a friend, play with your pet, dance to your favorite music, take a long hot shower, or soak in a bubble bath? Consider your anxiety an invader, and remember that you have the tools to fight it. When you practice using your tools, they'll quickly become new skills that you can use whenever you're feeling anxious. "It's only

in sorrow that bad weather masters us; in joy, we face the storm and defy it," says author Amelia Barr.

I didn't recognize that I was depressed. I was still highly functional but moved through life from memory and habit, devoid of any joy. My world was dark and scary, my view pessimistic. I accomplished the bare minimum each day, nothing more. My actions were directed toward numbing myself out. My spouse at the time was so deep in denial about my son's illness that he went to great lengths to avoid me, so he didn't have to deal with what was happening.

My enormous anxiety manifested as intense neck pain and IBS. Again, I didn't stop to connect that what was happening with my son had impacted my physical and emotional health. I was so focused on helping him receive treatment that it never occurred to me that I might also need support. I couldn't see the damage the disease inflicted upon me.

Spirituality

I've experienced depression and anxiety many times. I believe that my physiology is more sensitive to stress, and until I learned this, I didn't do enough to maintain my mental health. Many times, I wondered why I never felt really good. I always had either a headache, a stomach issue, or shoulder and neck tension. My stress always settled in one of those areas. When it became too much, I would feel depressed and anxious. This often occurred when I was in situations where I felt powerless and vulnerable: growing up with an alcoholic, OCD, depressed, and anxious dad, and a perfectionist OCD mom; in my first marriage to a man who was verbally and physically abusive; during my second marriage when my ideas and feelings were discounted; when my mom became sick, and I was designated power of attorney; when both my daughter and son developed cancer within three months of each other; and when my son started to exhibit irrational, paranoid delusions.

Unfortunately, I never learned positive ways to handle stressful circumstances. I didn't have any tools to navigate a life-altering MI diagnosis. In the months after my son's diagnosis, I took a higher dose of my fibromyalgia medication until I felt more stable, and then I reduced it when I experienced side effects.

I realized my depression and anxiety were normal given the circumstances, even though others didn't think so. After all, my son hadn't died, so why was I so distressed? I read every book I could that addressed personal growth and spirituality. If I couldn't change what had happened, I needed to adopt new ways to handle stressful events, or they just might do me in. That might sound a little dramatic, but my life would definitely be less joyful if I hadn't gotten a grip on my emotional well-being.

I consider myself spiritual, which means I believe in a power greater than myself, but I don't align with all the rules associated with organized religions. As I began to understand spirituality, I gained greater insight into more productive ways to deal with my son's diagnosis and the emotions tied to his dismal prognosis. By focusing on my inner world, I was able to get a handle on the ups and downs of day-to-day life. I began to believe that everything happens for a reason and that even the most difficult circumstances could show me how to be a better person, how to be more accepting, how to judge less, how to trust more, how to allow things to unfold, how to love more, and how to struggle less. Seeing the world from a bigger perspective makes my problems seem small.

It's been a few years since I've felt depressed or anxious, and I believe that's because I let go of my expectations and codependent habits. My intention is to live in the moment, not dwell on the past or worry about the future. One of my favorite sayings is, "Worrying is praying for the wrong outcome."

Whenever you begin to feel overwhelmed, ask yourself if you can control the outcome, if this will matter on your deathbed, and how you want to feel in this situation. It's helpful to step back and view the issue from the eyes of an observer, which helps move your emotions aside to give you a clearer picture of what's actually happening. There will be times when you react before thinking things through, but mostly you'll be able to slow down and ask yourself:

- Why is this happening?
- Is this really about me?
- Can my actions change the outcome?
- Is it my place to step in?
- What are my emotions telling me?
- Am I sad, afraid, angry, frustrated, or lonely? Did someone else's behavior cause me to feel this way, or did I choose these feelings because of my own perspective?

You get to choose how you feel, and doing so will give you a sense of power in your life. Not power over others, but in how you want to experience your journey.

The more you trust that life is inherently good, the less depression and anxiety you'll feel. Look for the silver lining. Choose to be optimistic in the face of disaster. Choose to move past the emotions of your MIAC's diagnosis and live the best life you can.

I'd like to add a disclaimer here: I'm talking about getting over *situational* depression and anxiety. There are many other types of depression that aren't easily overcome. Some are lifelong issues that require ongoing treatment. If you were already depressed or anxious before your MIAC's diagnosis, the added stress of dealing with the illness could cause you to become even more distressed. Please seek professional help if you can't cope and are struggling on a daily basis.

> I'm afraid, so afraid. I don't know what to do or where to turn. B is acting psychotic for the second time this year, and he's hospitalized again. My head feels like it's being squeezed in a giant vise, my stomach is a washing machine on spin cycle, and my lungs won't expand enough for me to take a full

breath. I don't know what to do, where to turn for advice. My family doesn't understand the severity of what's happened. I need to find a place to care for him when he gets out of the lockdown unit. I need to look for information about mental illness and schizophrenia. I need to look for services in my area. I need to look for books on the subject. I need to find answers. What I can't see in the middle of this expanding catastrophe is that I need help too.

I'm excited that I find a support group that meets in two days, and I sign up. The day arrives, and I'm not sure I have the energy to go, but I make myself get in the car and drive to the meeting. It's my first NAMI F2F meeting, and the number of people there is overwhelming.

The first thing the facilitator says is, "Welcome. This class will be about you, not your ill relative. I'm going to give you information on mental illness, but most importantly, I'll show you how to take care of yourself during this chaotic time."

This class is what I've needed for so long, and I'm so glad I decided to come.

Find a Support Structure

Many moms who care for a MIAC are unwilling or unable to ask for or seek support. No matter if you think you're coping well or know you're struggling, it's important to speak with a professional. Receiving advice, guidance, and support earlier rather than later can help keep your life on track. Just like a yearly physical exam and dental checkup, an annual visit to a mental health professional will help you recognize potential pitfalls that could affect your mental and emotional well-being.

There are several reasons why we may put off seeking help. Do any of the excuses below sound familiar?

- Fear of rejection: You're afraid that your family's and friends' opinions will be negative. What if they decide to abandon you?

- Embarrassment: You feel uncomfortable sharing personal thoughts and feelings with someone you don't know. You're embarrassed that this situation has happened to you. You're embarrassed for your child.
- Perfectionism: You're used to being able to handle problems, and this feels so messy and out of control. What will happen if you appear less than perfect to those close to you?
- Guilt or shame: You feel awful that you waited for your life to get this bad before seeking help. Mental health is a private matter that your family doesn't talk about. It should be kept secret. You feel guilty that your health may impact your ability to care for your MIAC.
- Low self-worth: If you were smarter or stronger or made better choices, maybe you wouldn't be in this position. Others don't have these problems because they're better than you.
- Futility: You've tried therapy and medications before, and they didn't work. Your life is miserable, and nothing can change that. You don't think you should feel better when your child continues to suffer.
- Hopelessness: Nothing will make you feel better, so why try? You don't have the motivation to feel better. You can barely make it through the day, so you can't add anything else—like therapy—to your plate.
- Self-blame: You have mental health issues, so it must be your fault that your child's sick. You feel horrible for passing on a defective gene. It's your fault that your MIAC struggles.
- Struggle to describe what you experience: You don't know how to articulate what you're feeling. You're lost in a void and can't find the words.
- Feel like a failure: It feels like you've personally failed a test because you don't know how to be an adult and deal with your problems without becoming overly emotional.
- Sympathy quota has expired: You've struggled for a while, and your family and friends must be getting tired of your drama. You need to pull yourself together and stop leaning on others.

- Too tired of fighting: You've spent so much time and energy fighting to get your child help that you don't have any fight left for yourself. You're too exhausted to care anymore.
- Want to keep the focus on your child: All your attention needs to stay on care and services for your MIAC. You can't divert focus away from your child, or something terrible might happen.
- Financial strain: You don't have the money to seek help for yourself. All extra money needs to be used to care for your MIAC.
- Lack of time: Your schedule is already overbooked. You don't have time to squeeze in additional appointments with doctors.

There are many ways to seek help when you feel like you've lost your way, and not all help needs to come from a professional. You can talk with a family member, a close friend, your pastor, or look in your community or online for a support group. Talking through your problems can ease your burden and offer a different perspective. Being part of a group of moms who are going through similar circumstances can help you feel less isolated. Reading online blogs or posts from people who struggle with the same issues can help you sort through your feelings. The first step is always the hardest, but it moves you a bit closer to a balanced, happy life.

The benefits of seeking mental healthcare far outweigh the initial fear of treatment. Overcoming your biggest struggles leads to the most substantial personal growth. It's like the rainbow after a storm. When you change the way you respond to difficulties, it can be extremely uncomfortable, but growth can only happen when you step into the unknown. What you've been doing hasn't worked, so it's time to try something different. Many of you will find that staying stuck in your old dysfunctional ways seems easier than trying something new.

You can find help in unexpected places. I found it in a women's empowerment group, a personal development workshop, a business coach's wise words, a monthly consciousness-raising discussion group, the occasionally inspirational post on social media, and through online blogs about all sorts of life struggles. I eked along inch by inch, pulling myself out of the chaos until one day my head was above water, my feet were on solid ground, and I could stand up and move toward the light of a brighter future.

Nobody ever suggested that I could put myself first, and I'm sure if they had, I would have thought it was too selfish. I didn't know what I didn't know, so I struggled for years. Real self-care is when you create a habit of putting your needs first. It includes creating personal boundaries, recognizing your worth, and giving as much love to yourself as you do to others. A self-care routine should include actions that address all areas of your life: physical, emotional, mental, spiritual, relationships, career, free time, finances, and family life.

> *Real self-care is when you create a habit of putting your needs first. It includes creating personal boundaries, recognizing your worth, and giving as much love to yourself as you do to others.*

My journey toward health was long and twisted, but I'm so grateful I stuck with it. It didn't happen overnight, but it did happen because I decided I wanted my life to be better. I'm here today, healthy and happy, because of the new choices I made. Everything new led to the balanced life I have today.

I'm not the person I was before my son became sick, but I am a better person because of what I've been through. MI forced me out of my comfort zone and into the storm. I had the choice to be sucked under and allow my life to be washed away or try anything and everything to move myself to higher ground. Some days it seemed easier to sink to the bottom, but then I would see a glimmer of hope in the distance. If I had decided to remain stuck, my son's journey would have been similar. He strives to have the best life he can because he follows my example.

When I face uncomfortable feelings or chaotic situations today, I have many reliable habits to help me through them. Most of what helps me is the strength that comes from within. The more inner work I do, the more stable, peaceful, and calm I feel regardless of what happens around me. I understand what I can control and what I can't. I feel so much more powerful because I know I have choices instead of feeling trapped by circumstances. I'm blessed to be able to create peace, happiness, and balance in my life in spite of B's mental illness.

Ward Hessig encourages us by saying, "Courage is not being fearless—it's acting in the face of fear." Stretch yourself to act courageously, make the effort to move beyond the heartache, and decide you want more in your life, despite your child's illness.

Visualization Journey

Sit in a comfortable, quiet place. Close your eyes.

Breathe in and out slowly to the count of three several times until you feel yourself begin to relax.

Visualize walking through a beautiful meadow. You hear the insects buzz, smell the sweet grass, and feel the sun on your shoulders. You walk for a few minutes and enjoy the serenity and calmness of the meadow.

Suddenly you see clouds begin to form. Lightning flashes, thunder booms overhead and shakes the ground under your feet. It looks like a storm's coming, so you head into the nearby woods for shelter as it starts to rain big, fat drops.

The canopy of trees protects you from the rain, but the darkness makes it difficult to see where you're headed. The ground is covered in leaves. It smells wet and earthy. With your next step, you realize you've walked into a pool of quicksand.

Your breath comes faster, the hair stands up on your neck, and your stomach clenches with fear. What will you do?

You call on your higher power to provide you with an escape. Overhead you notice four branches appear in the semi-darkness. One is gold, one is silver, one is bronze, and one is copper. Which one should you grab? Does one offer you a better chance of rescue? Your brain churns as you try to make a decision, the right decision.

Your guardian angel appears by your side and quietly whispers in your ear, "Choose a branch, any branch. It doesn't matter which one. But if you don't choose, you will be sucked under. Just choose."

"The best choice," your angel continues, "is to simply make a choice. Indecision will be the end of you, so any choice is better than death." You close your eyes and reach up to grab the nearest branch.

Immediately, you're pulled from the quicksand and placed on firm ground a safe distance away. You sit cradled in your angel's arms and cry silent tears of relief and gratitude.

Softly, your angel tells you, "It didn't matter what you chose; I would have saved you. It isn't about the best choice, but about making a decision to want something different. You have the power to decide to change your future. All you need to do is decide to choose what's best for you."

Your guardian angel hands you a golden heart-shaped locket. It's engraved with your name on one side, and the other side has the phrase *Choose to love yourself. Choose to live.* This is yours. Keep it close to you always. Whenever you feel afraid, are unable to make a decision, or are unable to move forward, take out this locket as a reminder that you are worthy, you deserve good things, and you can reach for what you need.

With a kiss on your forehead, your angel leaves you comfortable in the soft, fragrant moss. You rest a little longer, holding the precious locket close to your heart. Stay here as long as you need.

When ready, open your eyes and journal any messages, words, symbols you received. You may decide to buy yourself a golden locket and have it engraved with this message or one of your own. A physical symbol is a great reminder to practice self-care each day. Or you might decide to write a message to yourself on a small stone that you carry in your pocket. Whatever you choose, know that you have made the right decision.

Courage in the Face of Fear

We are sisters
Shackled by fear
We look for strength
We find answers
We share a common goal
We are sisters

Fear manifests as unpleasant feelings triggered by a real or imaginary perception of danger. Causing anxiety and loss of courage, fear creates intense reluctance to face or deal with a situation or person. The fears that parents of a MIAC feel are tied to the unknown. Everything about a new mental health diagnosis is unchartered territory. You don't know anything about the disease, you don't know anything about available treatment options, you don't know who to turn to for help, support, or advice. You don't know how to deal with, care for, and cope with the demands of a MIAC. You aren't afraid of making a choice but afraid that your choice won't lead to the desired outcome. Your fear isn't about finding the best care but that your MIAC will refuse it or that it will be ineffective.

We're taught from an early age to fear the unknown, that there's strength in having everything figured out, and that it's good to be in control. In horror films, the fear is not knowing what the monster looks like, what it's going to do, or when it will unexpectedly pop out. Mental illness is indeed a monster, one that nightmares are made of. It shows up out of the blue, turns your child into someone you don't recognize, and has you tiptoeing around your own home, hiding from your MIAC. Fear fills your days and nights. Fear that he won't take his meds, fear that he'll relapse, fear that you can't find treatment, fear he'll be shot by the police, fear he'll be put in jail for his crazy antics, fear he'll harm you, fear he'll harm himself, fear you'll go bankrupt from your attempts to help, fear your family won't understand, fear about who will care for your child when you're gone. Fear is your constant companion.

As a parent, you want to do what's best for your child, especially when he struggles or suffers. Finding help is a daunting task at a time when you're completely overwhelmed with attempts to stay on top of your MIAC's care.

The following reputable organizations may be able to help:

- **AMHF** American Mental Health Foundation
- **BRF** Brain & Behavior Research Foundation
- **CAMH** Center for Addiction and Mental Health
- **DBSA** Depression and Bipolar Support Alliance
- Department of Health and Social Care - GOV.UK
- **JED** The Jed Foundation
- **MIND** for better mental health
- **MHA** Mental Health America
- **NAMI** National Alliance on Mental Illness
- **NHS** National Health Services
- **NIMH** National Institute of Mental Health
- **SAHM** Society for Adolescent Health & Medicine
- **SAMHSA** Substance Abuse and Mental Health Services Administration
- **WFMH** World Federation for Mental Health
- **WPA** World Psychiatric Association

All of these—and there are many, many more—offer research, resources, disease-specific information, treatment center options, therapies, and/or support groups. But I wanted more—something to help *me* walk through the storm without getting washed away. I wanted and needed more than an umbrella. I wanted a step-by-step manual or process to help me sail through the difficulties associated with the care of a child with a severe mental illness, but I couldn't find any guidebooks to navigate this daunting journey. I wanted information and education, so I could better understand what was normal, what to expect, and how to treat my MIAC. I wanted hospitals, clinics, and doctors to offer information instead of just answering my uneducated questions. I wanted to be able to get my MIAC the care he desperately needed without having my hands tied by the HIPAA laws.

There's a huge amount of information online, but its focus is on identifying mental illness symptoms, not how to help the parents of MIACs. I wanted a one-stop spot with specific examples, suggestions, and guidance to help me deal with an adult experiencing a debilitating thought disorder and all that goes along with that diagnosis. I wanted my needs met, as well as those of my MIAC.

I wanted something to help me walk through the storm without getting washed away.

Immobilized by the fear of making the wrong decisions about my son's care, I felt lost. Doctors talk about med compliance and symptom relief, but they don't offer options about practical struggles, and they rarely provide definitive answers about what will work. Their treatments involve medications and/or therapies that address the MIAC's symptoms but offer nothing for the parents who care for these extremely sick young adults. I could find no studies that offered advice on how to survive life with a MIAC, day in and day out, how to handle the roller coaster of emotions, irrational delusions, threatening behaviors, paranoia, and general discord. I desperately needed a class to teach me how to deal with ongoing chaos, unending crisis, and an adult who has the mental and emotional maturity of a teen.

I understand the reasons behind the practical information that pertains to medical care for those with a mental health diagnosis, but as a parent with no formal education in mental illness, how was I supposed to make informed decisions? I've spent years of trial and error trying to get the best care possible for my MIAC. It would've been so much easier to have a plan to follow instead of guessing what would be best in each situation. There are family care plans for other diseases, guidelines of expectations, and probable prognosis. I was simply told my son would remain chronically ill and never be well enough to make important decisions for himself. What exactly did that mean? I needed more information! Not only for his care but also how to traverse this new reality without becoming a casualty myself.

Nobody understands the battle parents go through as they try to access quality, affordable care for their MIAC as they deal with a system that ties their hands. They're forced to interact with untrained and uneducated police departments and schools, deal with hospitals that will only keep a MIAC if they're a threat, deal with lack of outpatient treatment facilities, housing, day programs, fight for disability, government assistance, and insurance coverage. That's just the logistics of caring for a MIAC. What about all the behaviors that go with the disease? Where's the help for the ongoing turmoil? What about all the symptoms that medications don't fix? If I'll be running a mini-psych ward in my home, I need to be educated and supported, not left alone to find my way out of the shadow society has placed over my child and me.

I'm not a fan of traditional support groups. I prefer to attend classes or workshops that offer advice and information. Don't get me wrong; support groups can be a great way to feel that you aren't alone in your struggles, and many people like the connection and community, but I want more. The few in-person groups I attended were more about sharing your story with occasional advice gleaned from another parent's experience. The online groups were similar, with many parents using it more as a place to vent their frustrations. I understand the importance of a safe place to air your heartache and grievances, but I believe it's beneficial to also have access to educational materials. To know what behaviors to expect, what's normal for MI, what's a red flag for relapse, the best ways to approach and handle situations, and where to find local resources and professional support. I also wanted information about what was normal for me to experience as a mom of a MIAC, strategies to keep myself sane, and how to go about having a life of my own.

What would I want this guidebook to look like? It would address the parent's perspective and their needs and concerns. It would not be about the MIAC's disease, but how parents can come to terms with and deal with such a debilitating diagnosis. It would walk you through the stages of loss, grief, denial, frustration, understanding, acceptance, and give advice on how to move on with your own life. It would focus on how *you* feel while caring for a MIAC instead of how to deal with your child's problems. I believe more needs to be provided—more education, insight, and advice to the moms on the frontlines of this battle, who are not only trying to get help for a MIAC but also trying to hold themselves and their families together, trying to maintain a sense of normalcy, trying to hold on to their jobs, trying to care for other children, trying to maintain a relationship, trying to create a calm and peaceful home environment, trying to have time for themselves, and trying to make it through each day with a positive attitude. Resources are needed so they can do more than just try.

I found a tremendous amount of information through NAMI.org. They offer support, workshops, and list resources on their national and local websites. Unfortunately, like most of the sites that offer information and services, just because they're listed doesn't mean they have availability, take your insurance or Medicaid, or are located near you. Everything sounds great when you read about it, like community clubhouses, but in reality, as good as they are, there are currently only three hundred clubhouses located in thirty countries. Most resources talked about have extremely limited access due to the sheer number of people who seek out these services. I can't even begin to explain the frustration in reading about promising treatment strategies only to find out they are still only theory or that availability is so limited it could take years to get an appointment.

Search for books on mental illness, and you'll find hundreds. But most are from the ill person's perspective, are for clinicians and doctors, discuss societal views, report on the abysmal conditions of the imprisoned MI population, offer therapies, review the science behind brain disorders, or explain practical advice for treatment and care. Being selfish, I wanted a book about what moms, dads, grandparents, siblings, and friends suffer from with the diagnosis of a severe MIAC, which is the main reason I decided to write this book. *The purpose of this book is to offer mothers of MIACs a blueprint that allows you to have a happy, balanced life of your own while caring for a mentally ill adult child.* This important area has been ignored, avoided, and hidden for too long. I'm tired of my child's disease and my struggles to deal with it being kept a secret. Until all of us stand up and allow others to see what mental illness does to us, nothing will change. It's time to step out of the storm and into the light.

I sit in the ER on a hard, metal folding chair, cold, shaky, and alone. My son is completely out of his mind. He doesn't know where he is, how he got here, or who I am. The doctor asks him if he works.

"Yes," B says, "I have a full-time job, I live in my own house, and I have a wife."

None of this is even remotely true. He's been in his room nearly catatonic for the last six months. I called the police to transport him to the hospital because he refused to go with me. I'm so scared. I'm forced to sign an affidavit before they'll treat him.

Can't they see how sick he is? He's delusional, paranoid, skeletal. What more do they need to see to agree that he needs to be here? I wait. I wait for hours, hours that feel like days. I wait for a psych evaluation to determine if B is sick enough to be admitted.

"Get her off me. There is a little girl sitting on my chest. Get her off."

"There's nobody there," I say quietly.

"Yes, there is!" he screams. "It's M!"

He thinks his grown sister is here threatening him. He makes up a rap song with the words he hears over the intercom, laughing hysterically. He stands on the bed, dancing and singing at the top of his lungs. I wrap my arms around myself and try not to fall apart. If I didn't see this with my own eyes, I wouldn't believe it. This can't be my son. He looks absolutely demented.

In the wee hours of the morning, the doctors finally determine that "Yes, B is sick enough to be transferred to the lockdown psych ward."

Up to this point, he hasn't shown any awareness of where he is or what's happening, but when they ask him to get in the wheelchair, he starts to yell.

"You can't take me to the psych ward! I won't go! You can't make me go!"

Two very large male attendants wheel him away. Now I can cry. I head to my car feeling lost, disoriented, and wrung out. Two hours later, I call to see how it went.

The nurse in the psych unit says, "I'm sorry I can't tell you if he's here or not due to privacy laws."

Apparently, when he got to the ward, after being deemed incompetent, he was asked if he wanted anyone else to have access to his health information, and being paranoid, he said no. I've just involuntarily committed my child to a locked psych ward, and now nobody will talk to me.

What kind of convoluted system does this? How can they ask him to sign anything when he doesn't even understand that he's sick? They've basically twisted a privacy law into something that impedes a parent's ability to be involved in their MIAC's care. The HIPAA law was designed to protect personal health care information and offer privacy to individuals. Unfortunately, the law can be and is often misconstrued by hospitals and care providers. There are loopholes in the law that give doctors and staff leeway with cases where the patient is too impaired to make decisions for their own care. The law isn't intended to isolate patients from their families, and it expects professional caregivers to exercise good judgment when a patient is incapacitated. The hospital can notify and speak with family when it's determined to be in the best interest of the patient. I've experienced this type of cooperation and have also resorted to threats of legal action if they released my son without informing me.

When I was asked if anyone else in my family had mental health challenges, I had no answer. It wasn't until my son became ill that we began having conversations about things that had been kept in the closet. I'm the first in my family to openly discuss mental illness. Once I started talking, all kinds of family stories emerged, and it became clear that we had a history of depression, anxiety, OCD, and hoarding.

My parents' and grandparents' generation never talked about mental health. It turns out we have a lot of mild MI, and I mean a lot, but no incidence of schizophrenia, which is my son's diagnosis. I never heard anyone in my family discuss my dad's depression and alcoholism, my aunt's nervous breakdowns, or my mom's anxiety. They all focused on physical health, not realizing that mental health needs to come first. So much suffering, so much silence, and so many avoidable misunderstandings. This secretiveness prevented my family members from receiving much-needed help.

Would it have helped to know some of this history when my child was younger and exhibited odd behaviors? Who knows? I do know that doctors don't like to label or diagnose a child until they're into their teens because of stigma and also because children behave differently than adults until their brains are fully developed. As I look back and know what I do now, my son did show early signs of schizophrenia but not the normal recognizable symptoms associated with the disorder. Would earlier treatment have made a difference in his overall prognosis? Maybe, maybe not, but we don't get a redo in life. My hope is with more education and information available to parents, that mental illnesses can be caught earlier, and treatments can begin before the brain is irreplaceably destroyed by the disease.

I readily explain my son's illness to anyone who has questions. Anyone who asks about my children hears his story. Some say that's a breach of his privacy, but if I shared his cancer or muscular dystrophy diagnosis, would they think the same? I still have some family members who choose to stay in denial about their own children's mental well-being, but that's their choice. I won't be one of them. It discounts the hardship and struggles of our loved ones if we deny or dismiss what they experience. It also prevents them from getting appropriate help—help that could make their lives more manageable.

> *My hope is with more education and information available to parents, that mental illnesses can be caught earlier, and treatments can begin before the brain is irreplaceably destroyed by the disease.*

For a population that already deals with discrimination, stigma, and disability, to act as if their illness doesn't exist, to remain silent, is a slap in the face. Society as a whole won't see this illness for what it is—a legitimate disease—until we, as parents and family members, step up and share our stories. We must be the voice for those who aren't able to speak on their own behalf. We must be advocates for better care, for better understanding, for better lives for our MIACs.

I am honest to a fault but have no problem fabricating stories to enable my son to receive hospitalization. With MI, it's sometimes necessary to lie to find the resources for my MIAC. I'll claim innocence and ask for forgiveness later. I'm now a rule-bender and know all the ins and outs of talking to staff, relaying valuable information to his psych doctors, and coercing social workers and case managers into providing necessary information, support, and care. I'm a strong advocate for my MIAC and see it as my purpose to share advice and knowledge with other moms who seek help and advice. My credentials don't include any degrees in mental health, but my lived experience is just as valuable—perhaps more.

The bottom line for me is to make sure that my MIAC receives the care he needs if it's at all within my power. My job as his mom is to ensure his safety, so all my choices revolve around that. It makes those hard decisions easier by using that as a marker for what needs to happen. For every choice I have to make on his behalf, I weigh if it will improve his health, add value to his life, or make a difference in the overall quality of his life.

If your MIAC acts delusional and erratic, behaves aggressively, refuses to eat, hasn't slept in weeks, uses illegal drugs or alcohol, hallucinates, threatens suicide, or tries to harm you, then he needs to be evaluated and hospitalized. You can't handle those symptoms alone. These are circumstances when you should seek professional help and involuntary commitment. I understand that sometimes your MIAC will refuse help, but if possible, it's your responsibility to get him treatment. If you've exhausted every avenue available for care with no positive result, and if he still refuses all help and denies he's sick, then it may be time to make some really hard choices about where he will live, how much you'll provide for him, and how much contact you'll have with your child.

This will be the hardest decision you'll ever have to make, but many times the courts can and will intervene when the family steps back and your child is a menace to themselves or society. Involuntary outpatient services, Medicaid, subsidized housing, and SNAP (Supplemental Nutrition Assistance Program/food stamps) are more attainable when a MIAC doesn't have family support. AOT (Assisted Outpatient Treatment) and ACT (Assertive Community Treatment) are orders granted by civil courts for individuals who have difficulty engaging in rehabilitation. These options are court-supervised treatments that enforce medication and therapy compliance. They're mandated to prevent relapse and deterioration in those with severe mental illness.

ACT is designed to teach coping and life skills and to reduce hospital stays and jail time. Forty-three states have some form of AOT, but unfortunately, few implement it as it's intended. As of this writing, I was unable to find data on the implementation of ACT. Every state or county follows and interprets mental health laws differently, so depending on where you live will depend on the availability of services. It's a huge problem everywhere to find, access, and receive adequate mental health services for those with the most severe mental illnesses.

I decided if I couldn't find what I searched for, that I would create it myself. I'm now in the process of putting together online women's groups specifically for moms of MIACs. My goal is to create the structure for these groups and train facilitators/moms to build a community of support in their cities and neighborhoods. My website, www.SistersintheStorm.com, includes helpful links, downloadable transformation material, blog posts, online workshops, professional services, updates on government policy, and support options for maintaining your mental health. I don't claim to be an expert in those areas, and laws and regulations change all the time, but it will give moms a place to start in their conversations with doctors, hospitals, and the police in their city and community. Having information reduces fear. Informed parents are the most effective advocates for their MIACs and compel societal change.

It takes courage and determination to stand up and demand the care and services your MIAC deserves, but if you don't do it, who will? With practice, you can move past the fear of making a wrong decision because, in reality, any choice you make is better than making no decision at all. To move forward through this disease is the goal. Hopefully, you'll be able to maintain a quality of life for yourself, find appropriate care for your MIAC, and make a difference in how society views mental illness as you continue on this journey of perseverance and hope. It takes courage to be vulnerable, determination to find answers, and a boldness to challenge the status quo for MI treatment. Together our voices and stories will make a difference. Together we will find the strength to face each day. Together we will change the way mental illness is viewed. Together we will create a better future for our MIACs.

Let Karen Salmansohn inspire you with her words of encouragement, "Your mission: Be so busy loving your life that you have no time for hate, regret, or fear."

Go wholeheartedly forward, seeking happiness and fulfillment. Don't let anything or anyone stop you from living your best life.

Visualization Journey

Sit in a comfortable, quiet place. Close your eyes.

Breathe in and out slowly to the count of three several times until you feel yourself begin to relax.

Visualize yourself entering a meeting room. In the center is a large conference table.

Take a seat at the head of the table because, in here, you're in charge.

Today you will conduct interviews to see who will help you face your fears.

Below is a list of candidates. Each is an archetype (collective, universal energy that acts as guardian and ally). Choose one or more that resonates with you.

Choose from the archetypes listed. Use your intuition.

ARTEMIS—Child of Nature. Emotionally sensitive and independent.
HERA—The Companion. Loyal, tenacious, emotional, offers practical support.
MORRIGAN—The Crone. Wise woman, compassionate, offers transformational healing, assists with death and endings.
KALI—The Destroyer. Highlights personality aspects that no longer serve, destroys illusions, and helps people reach their potential.
ATHENA—The Diplomat. Mediator, understands both sides of conflicts.
EOS—The Femme Fatale. Reminds you to be honest, asks why you stay in a relationship, what you're emotionally connected to.
ISIS—The Goddess. Offers wisdom, nurturing, guidance, grace, and power.
NIKE—The Heroine. Awakens inner strength and power to overcome obstacles.

MA'AT—The Judge. Balances justice with compassion, sets realistic and fair boundaries, encourages people to take responsibility for their actions.

APHRODITE—The Lover. Enables passion and selfless devotion to a person, music, art, nature, or yourself.

PERSEPHONE—The Maiden. Brings purity and innocence, where the soul dreams.

ARIANRHOD—The Mother. Life-giver, source of nurturing, devotion, patience, and unconditional love. Shares the ability to forgive and provide for her children.

MARY MAGDALENE—The Divine Feminine Leader. Gathers resources, evokes feelings, offers wisdom and love.

Choose the goddesses who will help you battle your fear. Decide who will sit closest to you. How will they be positioned around your conference table? This is your high council, the women who will offer you their unique strengths and support.

Sit at the table with them. How do they make you feel? Do you feel empowered? Who do you feel closest to? Ask them about dilemmas you struggle with. Ask open-ended questions. Sit quietly and wait for them to answer. Sample questions: What is causing my fear? What can I do to feel less afraid? What do I get when I stay fearful? Write down any messages you receive.

Remember that, over time, you may want to repeat this exercise because your archetype goddesses may evolve as you grow and change yourself.

When ready, open your eyes and journal any messages, words, symbols you received. Remember, you can always go inside and ask for guidance from your archetype goddesses. You may want to do more research about the specific goddess you chose.

Find Happiness in Acceptance

We are sisters
We deny our reality
We want to fix our MIACs
We search for hope
We find understanding and happiness
We are sisters

"Happiness can exist only in acceptance," said George Orwell. And yet, having an adult child who's been diagnosed with a serious mental illness is a heartbreaking tragedy that's hard to accept. It takes years to work through, acknowledge, and move past the sadness and despair.

I played several types of mind games in an effort to avoid the pain and misery of admitting that my child would never be well. These included denial, repression, projection, displacement, regression, rationalization, reaction formation, compartmentalization, and intellectualization. I used these defensive mechanisms to cope with something I believed was too big, too disastrous, too gut-wrenching, and too overwhelming to handle. Below are the common evasion strategies.

Denial

Denial is the opposite of acceptance. In the early stages of mental illness, denial is a common strategy used to avoid a reality that's too painful to confront. Denial, an emotional coping mechanism, is the number one way to avoid confronting a personal problem or unpleasant situation. You may engage in distractive or escapist strategies to reduce the stress related to a circumstance you prefer to ignore. For example, you might choose to disbelieve the doctors' diagnosis of mental illness and think your child simply has a behavior problem that can be fixed with punishments, bribes, threats, or rewards.

Repression

Repression is when you reject painful or disagreeable ideas, memories, emotions, or situations. You may bury feelings about your child's illness and refuse to acknowledge that he's sick or that his situation is having a negative impact on you. You ignore everything about your MIAC and keep living as if nothing has changed. You brush everything under the rug in hopes that it will magically go away.

Projection

Projection is when you push undesirable feelings or emotions onto someone else rather than admitting or dealing with them as your own. You may accuse others of the feelings you don't want to accept in yourself. You might accuse your spouse of being angry and unable to deal with your MIAC when in reality, you're the one who struggles with your own impatience and inability to come to terms with your child's illness.

Displacement

Displacement happens when negative feelings are transferred from the original source of emotion to a less threatening person or event.

For example, you might blow up at your spouse over something insignificant after an altercation with your MIAC. Instead of confronting your mentally ill child, you berate your spouse for forgetting to take out the trash when the real issue is your child using and selling heroin in your house.

Regression

Regression is when a traumatic event causes you to revert to a less mature way of handling a problem. An example would be to have temper tantrums or hide out in your room even though you stopped these behaviors as a young teenager. The stress of caring for a MIAC can cause you to act out, binge eat, or abuse alcohol because you don't have the skills to cope with what's happening.

Rationalization

Rationalization is an escape to avoid the real reason something happens, and it involves fabricating a logical or seemingly rational explanation that's more tolerable than the truth. An example would be to insist that your child simply needs more time to mature because he was born a preemie instead of recognizing that he has a mental illness. Another rationalization would be to insist that his aberrant behaviors are caused by something he experienced as a child and not a brain disease.

Reaction Formation

Reaction formation is when you deny reality and support the opposite position. For example, you may speak against the mentally ill because you don't want to associate yourself with that group of people. You might blame or judge those with MI for using their illness as a cop-out. You insist that it's not really an illness but an excuse for poor behavior.

Compartmentalization

Compartmentalization is used to avoid mental discomfort. You do it when you stuff your emotions away into a tiny corner of your heart and refuse to acknowledge what's really happening. For example, you might segment your life into separate realities based on how you want it to look. Your coworkers and friends don't know you have a MIAC who lives with you and wreaks havoc in your home. You keep each aspect of your life separate. What you don't talk about seems less real.

Intellectualization

Intellectualization is when you use reason to block confrontation with an unconscious conflict and its associated emotions. You remove yourself from the uncomfortable feelings and look at everything from a mental standpoint only. An example would be to only discuss the broad consequences of mental illness instead of how it affects you. This allows you to avoid the personal consequences and emotions associated with having a mentally ill child. You view what happens from the standpoint of an observer or educator instead of a participant.

Acceptance

Intuitive coach and author Kirra Sherman suggests, "Acceptance means to embrace what is, without resistance. The acceptance isn't about agreeing with an event outside of you, but in how the event makes you feel. Acceptance doesn't have to mean you like it, support it, or choose it, you just need to realize that you can't change it."

Every parent who cares for a MIAC has to progress through several stages of acceptance and will experience many emotions to get to the other side of the diagnosis and prognosis. There's no set time it should take or will take to go through the phases, but each one is important if you want to reach your goal of personal happiness. It doesn't matter the order. There's a progression, and each step builds toward the next. I like to think of these phases as gates or doorways that you need to pass through to get to your destination: happiness in acceptance. Acceptance isn't about liking a situation. As Elizabeth Kubler-Ross & David Kessler say in *On Grief and Grieving; Finding the Meaning of Grief Through the Five Stages of Loss,* "It's about acknowledging all that has been lost and learning to live with that loss."

Emotional Gates of Acceptance

From Rejection to Welcoming What Is

Initially, you want to reject that mental illness is the real problem with your child. Maybe the problem is drugs, hanging out with the wrong friends, not trying hard enough, being lazy, or any number of reasons that sound better than a serious brain disorder. You can't imagine that possibility. It's foreign territory, incomprehensible, and shadowed by darkness and stigma. This is the last thing you expected to happen to you and your family. As a parent, you did a good job raising a fun, intelligent, lovable child who's capable of success and independence. You may feel like rejecting your child because he isn't living up to the expectations you have for him. If he would just shape up and try harder, you could get beyond all this nonsense and get back to your old life.

Eventually, you come to the point where you yearn for an answer to the madness; you want to put a name on the illness that's turned your child into someone unrecognizable. If it can be named, it has to have a treatment, a cure. Surely once you have a definitive diagnosis, things will start to get better, get back to normal. You welcome a diagnosis as a starting point toward recovery. That is, until you're shocked with the understanding that this is mental illness.

You may feel like rejecting your child because he isn't living up to the expectations you have for him.

From Disbelief to Belief

When you finally have a diagnosis after weeks, months, or years of searching, there's a deep, kick-in-the-gut feeling of disbelief. This can't be real. The doctors must be wrong. They need to run more tests, do more evaluations, recheck all the information. You can't wrap your mind around the idea that your healthy child has a thought disorder, a damaged brain. You may think that you'd rather he have diabetes or even cancer because you understand those illnesses. There are treatments for those diseases, society doesn't look upon those illnesses as a personal failure, and nobody with a tumor ever denies they have a serious illness.

Instead, you're stranded on an island of disbelief, all alone with your uncontrollable thoughts of imminent doom. You aren't prepared to deal with what comes next. Nothing can prepare you for the chaos and turmoil of caring for a MIAC. You know deep in the recesses of your broken heart that you have to come to terms with this diagnosis if you're to help your tormented child, but it feels like your entire being is made of glass, so fragile you may shatter into a million glittering pieces. Shattered memories, shattered dreams, shattered hopes, shattered lives. A kaleidoscope of broken glass. But your spirit is resilient. Just like a tree, life's storms help you grow deep roots.

> *You know deep in the recesses of your broken heart that you have to come to terms with this diagnosis if you're to help your tormented child . . .*

When I got to this point, I began reading everything I could get my hands on, attended a NAMI Family to Family twelve-week program, and I researched mental illness online. I slowly came to understand more, slowly trusted the doctors more, slowly came out of hiding, slowly began the arduous task of sweeping up the remnants of my shattered life, and I slowly pieced myself back together bit by bit. I'll never be the person I was before this happened. This new me is covered in scars and held together with hope and tenacity. As I gained more knowledge about severe MI, I began to rebuild my coping skills, rebuild my equilibrium, rebuild my ability to be a supportive mom to my seriously ill adult child, and rebuild my life. My acceptance of his diagnosis came in tiny glimpses and small *aha!* moments until I could finally fully integrate the sheer horror of what had taken over my child and believe his diagnosis.

From Needing to Fix to Accepting That There Is No Fix

When you can acknowledge to yourself and others that your child has a mental illness, you'll enter the phase where you believe that with enough effort on your part, there's a way to fix him. With enough perseverance, you can find the perfect doctor, the perfect treatment, the perfect therapy, the perfect combination of meds, the perfect solution to make your MIAC well. While you've accepted the *diagnosis,* you haven't made peace with the *prognosis*. There must be a cure for this dreadful illness; after all, most diseases have cures or treatments that enable people to have fulfilling lives. In your new normal, you spend countless hours on research, visit new doctors, try alternative therapies, and change medication combinations. Or you plead, beg, and pray that your child will agree to get help, see a doctor, admit that he's sick. Nothing works. Henry Wadsworth Longfellow wisely stated, "For after all, the best thing one can do when it's raining, is to let it rain." Some things can't be fixed.

> *While you've accepted the* diagnosis, *you haven't yet made peace with the* prognosis.

Your MIAC is still stuck in the grip of delusions, irrationality, anxiety, and paranoia. While you spend all your time and energy trying to fix your broken child, he spends just as much energy trying to persuade you that there's nothing wrong with him and that you're the one who's crazy. Round and round you go, dancing to the tune of desperation and delusion. Ever so slowly, small cracks form in your resolve and intention until one day your armor crumbles, and you're exposed to the brutal truth: *your child won't get better.* There's no magic pill or treatment. All you can do is call a truce.

Now, when you're at your most vulnerable, you begin to accept the fact that you don't have the power to heal your MIAC, that you never did have that power, and that it's time to deal with reality. Admitting that no amount of effort can fix your child is a bitter pill to swallow. Would you have tried less if you'd known the outcome? Or was it necessary to go through this trial and error, the push and pull, this charade of disbelief to get to the other side of acceptance?

From Despair to Hope

When you admit that you can't fix your child, it doesn't release you from feeling the despair of a young life lost. It's easy to slip into despondency and sadness. Where before you kept yourself busy looking for answers, now all you have is empty time, time to examine what you might have done wrong, time to feel the grief of losing a child, time to think about all the horrific situations that could arise, time to think—too much time to think.

Despair feels like you've lost everything and there's no way to make it right again, but that's defeatist thinking. So let's break this down. What exactly do you mourn? Is it the life you had planned for your child to have? Realistically, that was never a given, never a guarantee. That was just a fantasy that you created that lived and breathed only in your imagination. How hard is it to let go of a hypothetical future?

Even if your dreams for your MIAC were only figments floating around in your head, it doesn't mean that something real hasn't been lost. Every parent dreams of their child having a life that's happy, successful, and free from struggles. How do you let go of what could have been and embrace what is? How do you come to terms with the difficulties your child will endure when you're unable to make it better?

For me, these answers came from a place deep inside, a place where I'm connected to the presence of Spirit, the place I go to surrender my pain and sorrow, where I feel part of something that's bigger than myself, where I recognize that there's a divine order to everything, where my despair is transformed into hope that things unfold exactly as they are supposed to. I don't need to know what will happen next. I don't need to have all the answers. All I need to know is that everything will be okay, in spite of my child's mental illness. Joseph Campbell, an author of comparative religion works, thoughtfully reminds us to "Find a place inside where there is joy, and the joy will burn out the pain."

Your life won't look anything like you thought it would, but what you dreamed about wasn't real. What you lost is just an illusion, a daydream, a wish. What you lost only existed in your mind. Can you change the way you look at this and reconcile your shattered dreams to support your MIAC's new reality? This is a hard lesson to learn—that nothing is guaranteed and that in order to find peace, you must accept what's in front of you now. Oh, how you want to kick, to scream, to flail at the injustice of it, but that won't make a bit of difference. You want to disavow God and pretend like you have all the answers, but the truth is you need to believe in something more powerful than yourself to make it through this tragedy. You need to believe in a bigger picture, in a sacred plan, and believe that regardless of your MIAC's disability or disease, it's all part of a grand scheme. You need to believe that everyone matters, that everyone contributes, that everyone is a perfect soul in an imperfect body with a damaged brain, that everyone is here with a special purpose. Maria Erving, transformational teacher and energy healer, reminds us, "Argue with life, and you'll suffer. You can either react to it from ego or respond to it from a place of Spirit."

... the truth is you need to believe in something more powerful than yourself to make it through this tragedy.

From Resistance to Holding Space

Why is change so difficult? Why do you resist and cling to what was when you know deep down that you can't change what's happened? Resistance keeps you from feeling vulnerable, out of control, uncertain. Everything feels different, and different is uncomfortable. You're concerned about your competence to handle this change. It overwhelms you, and your normal life feels threatened. Being a creature of habit makes you feel safe, but when tragedy appears out of the blue, your natural inclination is to hunker down and resist. It's your unconscious way of stating, "I don't like this. I don't want this. I want things to go back to the way they were before this disturbing disease took my child." Unfortunately, you don't always get a heads up that something terrible is about to happen, and there's nothing you could have done to stop this disease from destroying your MIAC's mind.

In essence, your adult mind understands that nothing will ever be the same again, but the child inside you stomps her foot and says, "No!" Resistance is your unconscious refusal to face what seems too devastating to handle, but the more you push against the truth, the more anguish you feel. Resistance is really an internal battle between what should have been and what is. Resistance is a normal phase you go through when you face any catastrophic event. It gives you time to assimilate this outlandish new reality that's sabotaged your ordinary life and thrown all rules and normalcy to the wind. Resistance buffers you from the harsh reality of severe MI; it allows you time to acclimate yourself, adjust your expectations, and learn how to cope with your MIAC. Your goal is to do as Eckhart Tolle recommends: "To offer no resistance to life. To be in a state of grace, ease, and lightness" with everything that occurs.

You may want to stay in this phase and permanently resist what happens to your child, but this will destroy relationships and cause further hardship for you and your MIAC. Take a week, a month, or a year to get your bearings and then move on. It's time to open yourself to the reality of your child's illness and hold space for him as he learns to live with MI. When you hold space for your child, you walk along with him without judgment. You simply share his journey.

By accepting your child's diagnosis and prognosis, you help your MIAC come to terms with it as well. How do you do this? By being the observer of what occurs instead of reacting emotionally, letting go of the outcome, and accepting what happens with understanding. It takes practice to simply hold space for another without any attempts to fix, but the end result is more peace in your life. "The more important an activity is to your soul's evolution, the more resistance you will feel," says author Steven Pressfield.

I can hear your protests: "This just isn't possible. My child refuses to admit he's sick." Or maybe you're not in contact with your MIAC, but I'll argue that yes, it's possible and even vitally important if you're to have any chance of living a good life. You can accept, acknowledge, and hold space for your child—whatever the circumstances. When you let the resistance go, you open the door to feeling more compassion, empathy, and understanding that MI isn't your child's choice but a tragic misfortune. Bad things happen to good people all the time, and if you can change your perspective to see everything from a place of neutrality, then life is so much sweeter. Just because a situation *seems* bad doesn't mean that it is in the overall spiritual picture. Doesn't everything serve in some way? Is it possible to change your mindset to see every event or situation as a gift designed to further spiritual development and growth? If you can't control the outcome, then what's the benefit of holding on to resistance? What you gain by letting go is far greater than anything you'll receive by continuing to resist.

When you let the resistance go, you open the door to feeling more compassion, empathy, and understanding that MI isn't your child's choice, but a tragic misfortune.

From Judgment to Understanding

Judgment means to quickly form a biased or personal opinion about someone or something. You don't even realize how many times and how many ways you judge others throughout each day. Your opinions are based on your parents' views of the world, personal experiences, and societal norms. What you see as bad or improper behavior might be perfectly acceptable in another culture or ethnic group. You judge people for everything: how they dress, their sexual preference, and the foods they eat; whether they're successful, have manners, or if they're upstanding citizens; their hobbies and friends, how they treat others, whether they have no children or too many children, how they drive, where they live, if they smoke, drink, use drugs—the list goes on and on. The point is that you judge others all the time. It's a subconscious way for you to boost your self-esteem by looking at others as *less than*. When considered like this, it seems a rather self-serving and very hurtful way to deal with differences. Mother Teresa reminds us, "If you're judging people, you've no time to love them."

Judgment isn't love. Feeling sorry for another isn't love. Condemnation isn't love. Demands that your child live up to your expectations isn't love. Requests that your MIAC shape up, act rationally, or behave according to your rules isn't love. Judging your child's choices does nothing but put a wedge in your relationship, create hurt feelings, distrust, and disrespect. Nobody likes to be judged, criticized, or forced to comply with someone else's rules. It's futile to think that judging your child will change his behavior. As a parent, you've placed judgments on your MIAC in an attempt to persuade him to correct irrational behaviors. Nobody likes to be judged or criticized for something they have no control over. If criticism was an effective tool, you would have seen results long ago. I love this anonymous quote: "Never look down on anyone. Only God sits that high."

It's futile to think that judging your child will change his behavior.

How do you stop judging and begin to show understanding? How do you show your child love when you don't like his choices? As you learn more about the symptoms and behaviors of severe MI, you'll see that the things you don't like are part of the disease and are not your child. When you can see that your MIAC is doing the best he can, then you'll see every behavior through a lens of compassion. It isn't differences that divide us, but our inability to recognize, accept, and understand those differences.

Offering compassion and understanding is the greatest gift you can give your MIAC. To have a disease that's draped in discrimination and stigma is more than anyone should have to bear. Adding your judgment makes the struggle even more tragic. No other disease causes you to blame and condemn the ill person. You may not like or condone your MIAC's behaviors or choices, but you can accept that it's the best that he's capable of, given his illness. Just because it doesn't look like *your* best doesn't mean he's not trying. He's doing what he can within the limitations of a severe thought disorder. Your acceptance won't change your child's condition, but it can change how he feels about himself and how you interact with him.

> *Your acceptance won't change your child's condition, but it can change how he feels about himself and how you interact with him.*

Every adult child wants his parents' approval and acceptance, and that doesn't change when he becomes ill. When you can offer understanding and empathy, you make him feel valued, appreciated, and loved. This boosts his self-worth and makes his journey a little easier. It's not your job to like what's happened to your child, but it is your job to understand that he doesn't choose to be mentally ill, he doesn't choose to behave irrationally, he doesn't choose to be violent, he doesn't choose to be homeless, he doesn't choose to be an addict, he doesn't choose to be delusional, he doesn't choose to be paranoid, he doesn't choose to self-harm, and he doesn't choose to commit crimes. Nobody would ever choose to be mentally ill. The disease takes your child. The disease makes these poor choices. A MIAC doesn't have the ability to choose better, but you do, so choose to accept what you and your child can't change. Accept that you judged your child in the past, but you know better and will do better now. "There is no greater disability in society, than the inability to see a person as more than their disease," says Robert M. Hensel, disability activist and poet.

From Anger to Forgiveness

I'm stronger now because I've learned to turn heartbreak into peace, hurt into love, and anger into forgiveness. Tom Gates, author of *Wayward: Fetching Tales from a Year on the Road,* says, "It's a lot easier to be angry at someone than to tell them you're hurting. . . . Anger is just a cowardly extension of sadness."

After your adult child is diagnosed, it's normal to feel angry at the circumstances and even at him. You're angry because you can't fix it, can't control your MIAC's actions, can't make society understand, can't turn back the clock to happier times. You're angry because you can't do anything to make your child's life better. It's easier to feel red-hot anger piercing your heart than to admit that you're aching so badly that you don't know how to survive this bleak turn of events. Anger always blankets pain.

It's easier to blow up at the irrational behaviors exhibited by your MIAC than to admit you may have done something to cause this, admit that you don't have the answers, admit that your child will never be well again, admit that you're not sure you have what it takes to go on this turbulent journey with your child. You may even feel resentment and anger at your child's aggressive or violent behaviors toward you and your loved ones. You're angry that your MIAC doesn't try harder to be better, to get well, and that he seems to be unable to pull himself out of the chaos of his disease. You're angry at a society that refuses to treat MI as a legitimate illness. You're angry that your family and friends don't understand what you live with. You're angry that there aren't enough hospital beds, treatments facilities, or psychiatric doctors to handle the number of people who struggle with MI. You're angry that the hospital will only treat your MIAC if he's a threat to himself or someone else. It's so much easier to be angry than to be broken and grief-stricken. You feel too vulnerable to do anything more than hide behind your shield of outrage and bitterness.

> *It's so much easier to be angry than to be broken and grief-stricken. You feel too vulnerable to do anything more than hide behind your shield of outrage and bitterness.*

At some point, you need to let go of the anger and forgive yourself, forgive your MIAC, forgive your family and friends, and forgive a society that views mental illness as a behavior problem. Anger makes you feel strong, whereas your pain seems too private, too personal, too vulnerable to share with the world. You can turn the energy behind your anger into fuel for advocacy. I use it to initiate conversations, to educate others, and I used it to write this book. I want something more, something better to come out of my son's illness, and my anger won't create the changes I search for.

It's midnight, and I sit in a small room with my son and an intake nurse. B's evaluation is taking forever to complete, and my soul is tired. I just want to go home before the snow starts.

"You're the crazy one. You're not even my mom," B says.

I hear this every time he becomes psychotic. "Well, B, if I wasn't your mom, I sure as heck wouldn't have sat in this room with you for the last four hours, would I?"

"They're going to kill me, and it'll be all your fault."

B rages on about how I won't help him get the implants out of his head, how I poison his food, and . . . I stop listening.

I don't need to listen because I've heard it all before. I play with my phone and tune out what he says. I know that this is the voice of his disease and not my son. My son is lost and alone, trapped beneath a tidal wave of psychosis. I understand that an imposter has taken control of B's brain, refusing to release the tight grip it has on his sanity.

At the start of my son's illness, I was angry when he talked to me like this, but after years, I now understand that he isn't thinking rationally, and I know he'll apologize when he's better if he remembers the event. I could be angry because he refuses to use any of the tools he's learned when he feels paranoid, but while he can recite what he needs to do, he's not able to initiate any of those behaviors. I rarely feel angry now that I realize the majority of his actions and behaviors are out of his control. His disease is his puppet master and causes him to live in a reality that only he experiences.

On the rare occasion he does try to push my buttons or manipulate me, I walk away rather than engage. I forgive him, for I know if he could do better, he would. I forgive myself for not being able to offer more help. I still work to release the anger I have at how MI is viewed by society. Nobody chooses to be mentally ill, and so I choose to lay down my anger and live from a place of ongoing forgiveness.

Last week, my son decided to cut implants out of his head, so as I write this, he's in the hospital again, and I fight the urge to be angry at this horrific illness. I know it will do no good. I want to lash out at the randomness of its victims, but my gut-wrenching anger is still with the doctors and social workers who don't have a plan or a clue how to help him, who ask *me* for suggestions. Our mental healthcare system is so broken, so inadequate, so flawed. As soon as he's no longer a danger to himself, my son will be released, terribly paranoid, delusional, and no better than when he was admitted. I need to forgive those who have devoted their lives to caring for the mentally ill because I know they, too, want a better system. Anger won't create change. Anger won't make my son well. Anger won't fix an inadequate healthcare system. Anger won't remove the stigma and discrimination. Anger won't bring my son back to me. So I will use my anger as fuel to propel me toward improved advocacy and education and forgive myself for hoping against hope that this will be the last visit to the lockdown unit in the psych ward.

From Working Against to Working With

In most cases, the event that occurs isn't difficult; it's the emotions that you attach to the event that hold you hostage. You become so attached to what's happened, so intent upon pushing away the trauma, so set on moving past what's happened that you can't figure out how to deal with your MIAC within the confines of his disease. You spend so much time trying to make a damaged brain behave rationally instead of trying to understand your child's limitations. Only after you accept what your MIAC's capabilities are can you move forward and work *with* instead of *against* what's undeniable. You have to stop pushing and pulling your child in an attempt to modify his behaviors; the reality is you need to modify your expectations.

MI is like a river. You can't change the direction of the current, you can't control whether it floods, and you can't prevent it from drying up. All you can do is go with the flow.

> *You spend so much time trying to make a damaged brain behave rationally instead of trying to understand your child's limitations.*

What does it mean to work *with* instead of *against* something? If your MIAC can't handle money, stop trying to teach him. Instead, put a plan in place to manage his money for him. If your child can't maintain a household, stop the badgering, and hire someone to clean for him. If your MIAC is delusional, quit trying to reason with him. If your child's aggressive, walking on eggshells won't make him passive. Do what's necessary to ensure your safety and his. Stop bailing your MIAC out of situations that could initiate changes in his behavior. If your child is incapable of keeping himself safe, have him placed in a care facility if at all possible.

Your MIAC is being held hostage by a thought disorder, and no amount of force or hope on your part will enable his brain to function normally. That doesn't mean you give up on your child; it means you give up thinking you can coerce him into compliance with your plans for his future. We can thank Iyanla Vanzant for this wisdom: "Acceptance doesn't mean you agree with, condone, appreciate, or even like what has happened. Acceptance means that you know, regardless of what happens, there's something bigger than you at work. It also means you know that you are okay and that you will continue to be okay."

From Playing the Victim to Connecting to the Warrior Within

The role of victim is a coping strategy you fell into because life seemed too difficult, and you felt you had no control over the outcome. Many moms of MIACs play the victim in order to receive sympathy. But if you act like a martyr, you give away the power to solve your problems—or the opportunity to learn new ways to deal with your emotions. Your refusal to make choices that are in your own best interest keeps you stuck in unpleasant situations. When you play the victim or martyr, you act like you deserve admiration, praise, or sympathy because you're being treated badly by your MIAC. Because MI is a silent disease, it's understandable why many moms end up playing the pity card.

You garner a lot of power when you pretend to be a victim. It allows you to avoid responsibility, gain attention, receive sympathy, and feel important, but it also takes away your ability to create solutions and find workable answers to what causes you pain. Signs that you grasp a victim mentality rather than handle your problems effectively include:

- Blaming others for your miserable feelings
- Making every problem a catastrophe
- Reliving past victim experiences
- Being closed to other perspectives
- Taking no responsibility for what happens in your life

You may enjoy feeling sorry for yourself as you share your tragic stories and blame others for how you feel. But your refusal to make choices to improve your life and to stay powerless won't work in the long run.

If this sounds like you, then you're not alone. It's easy to fall into the victim/martyr trap when you have a MIAC. Unfortunately, MI is not a disease that warrants much sympathy or understanding from others, and you may be relying on unhealthy behaviors to feel heard. Neither you nor your child will benefit from this victim mentality. Even if there are no right meds, perfect therapies, or incredible new treatments to fix your child's brain, you can choose to be responsible for your life and your happiness.

Becoming a victim of your MIAC's disease is a waste of two lives. Your child would never want you to throw away your contentment because he has an incurable illness. Don't add that burden to your already troubled child. You're the only one accountable for your life, and you should live it to the fullest, regardless of the circumstances your child faces.

Becoming a victim of your MIAC's disease is a waste of two lives.

"No one saves us but ourselves. No one can and no one may. We ourselves must walk the path," says Buddha. You can move out of this role by following some of the steps listed below:

- Use "I" statements when you talk with others. Instead of "You make me feel . . . " try "I feel _____ when this happens."

- Visualize yourself as a survivor. A victim pushes against what's happened to them, while a survivor embraces the event and moves on. Don't relive an unpleasant event. Live in the here and now.
- Practice gratitude by finding things to be thankful for every day.
- Be responsible for your own life. Notice what you get from others when you play the victim, figure out where you learned this behavior, and decide if you're ready to let it go.
- Perform an act of kindness. When you help others, it takes the focus off yourself and your problems.

If you see yourself in some of these examples but find it difficult to break the cycle, you can always ask a professional for additional help and insight. Show yourself compassion as you work to change these patterns. It takes time to create new habits. To give up being a victim doesn't mean you don't care what happens to your child. It means you don't allow what happens to define your life. It doesn't negate the horror of your MIAC's experience, but it makes it *his* experience, not *yours*. You're a bystander in your child's storm, so you don't need to throw yourself in the water with him. Make yourself responsible for living your life to the fullest because it's the best gift you can offer your MIAC. Show him by example how to move on in spite of tragedy. This is one of the most valuable gifts you can give your child.

From Silence to Sharing

Reverend Dr. Jeff Hood says, "Distance doesn't separate people; silence does." You've made it through all the gateways to acceptance, and now it's time to step up and advocate for your child. One way to have the most impact is to tell your story. If enough of you break your silence and openly talk about what you and your MIAC go through, then slowly, we'll begin to see a difference in how mental illness is addressed. Your acceptance is the key to creating acceptance within society. It does your child a huge disservice to only whisper his stories behind closed doors. We talk about our children's cancers, learning disabilities, broken bones, digestive issues, and MI should be no different. We perpetuate the stigma and discrimination by our unwillingness to share our struggles.

Fred Rogers spoke eloquently when he said, "Anything that's human is mentionable, and anything that is mentionable can be more manageable. When we can talk about our feelings, they become less overwhelming, less upsetting, and less scary." Let's start talking.

> *We perpetuate the stigma and discrimination by our unwillingness to share our struggles.*

Mental illness can be talked about as easily as appendicitis or kidney problems. Education is the key, information is the doorway, and your voice puts a face to a physical and biological disorder that manifests as irrational behavior. When you choose not to disclose your MIAC's illness in order to protect his privacy, this perpetuates the stain of this disease. You can share your troubles without revealing personal details. You may be worried that sharing his story will impact his future job options, but let's be realistic; those with severe MI are rarely well enough to hold a job. We don't ask a diabetic to use his mind to control his high blood sugar, and it's just as ludicrous to expect someone with MI to control his malfunctioning brain. Speaking up for your child when he's unable to do so for himself is the best way you can honor his struggle. I want my legacy to be that I created an opening for moms of MIACs to be seen and heard.

You've worked hard to get to where you are today, so now what? How do you create a balanced life while caring for a MIAC? So much of your time has been devoted to your child that you're not even sure who you are, what you want, where to begin, or if it's even possible to have a life of your own. You've forgotten what it's like to dream, to set goals, and you've forgotten how it feels to be peaceful and joyous. It's time to pull yourself out of the chaos and head into the light of a well-lived life.

Visualization Journey

Sit in a comfortable, quiet place. Close your eyes.

Breathe in and out slowly to the count of three several times until you feel yourself begin to relax.

Visualize yourself dropped at the entrance of a boxwood garden maze. The lush green shrubs are all around you, eight feet high. A sign states that if you can find your way to the end, you'll find true happiness. You just need to make it through the Emotional Gates of Acceptance.

You take a deep, cleansing breath and head into the maze.

You come to the first gate on the path. Do you choose "Rejection" of what you experience, or do you "Welcome" whatever is on your path?

The second gate asks you to choose to "Believe" in yourself and that each experience you face is for your highest good. Or you can choose "Disbelief" and hang out at this gate until you're ready to move ahead.

Gate three is all about your decision to "Fix" what's wrong in your life or accept what isn't "Fixable." It's time to come to terms with your lack of control over the outcome.

The fourth gate gives you the option of choosing "Hope" or "Despair." Hope knows that you'll have greater good than bad in your life and will move you closer to happiness, while despair will keep you trapped in unfulfilled dreams.

You'll meet "Resistance" at gate five. You can let go of your expectations and move on to "Holding Space for your MIAC," or you can stick around and push against what is, but this will only drain your precious energy.

You're halfway through the maze. Now is the time to really get to work, so you can finish before it gets dark.

Gate six gives you the opportunity to give up "Judgment" of yourself and others and embrace the "Understanding" that we're all doing our best.

Here comes the seventh gate, and it's a doozy. Should you continue to hold "Anger" in your heart, or is it time to offer the gift of "Forgiveness" to all who will benefit?

Gate number eight teaches you to "Work with" what occurs instead of "Working against" what you can't change. Pushing just tires you out. It's time to stop the struggle and use your efforts wisely. Define your boundaries and stay within them as you move ahead. You're so close—just two more gates. I know you can do it.

The ninth gate is a tricky one. You'll need to let down your guard, get comfortable with vulnerability, and learn a new way to deal with stress and heartache. It's time to stop "Playing the victim" and connect with the "Warrior within." Grab your sword and let out a triumphant yell to let those coming behind you know that's it's possible to find your way to the end of this maze of emotional growth.

Gate ten is where you declare your victory and move from "Silence" into "Speaking your truth" and give mental illness and your child's journey a voice.

You have reached the end, and "Happiness through Acceptance" is now yours.

Take a deep breath and notice how happiness feels. What does it smell like, sound like, look like? How does it make you feel deep down inside? Can you feel the expansion?

You can choose to grab it and hold on tight. Or, at times, you may feel the need to go through a few of the gates again if struggle returns.

Relish the delight, euphoria, and pleasure you feel at this moment.

When ready, open your eyes and journal any messages, words, symbols you received on your journey through the gates. What additional emotions did you experience along the way? Which gate was the most difficult to get through? Which one was the easiest? What have you learned about yourself?

Pull Yourself from the Rubble

We are sisters
We take back our lives
We reignite our spark
We move forward
We create a better life
We are sisters

You were taught by your mother and society that your wants and needs should always come after those of your children, but that assumes your children grow up to be capable, independent adults. What happens when your child is diagnosed with a chronic mental illness? Psychologists now understand that taking care of your needs is an essential part of your mental health. You need to stay physically and mentally strong if you're going to survive unscathed and be an effective advocate.

How do you decide what's important to you? How do you have your own life without feeling selfish and guilty? Where do you begin?

After years of being immersed in your MIAC's life, you may not know how to decide what you want. I understand. It's daunting to look at the shambles of your once-happy life and see nothing but emptiness and heartache. I'm here to tell you that it's not only possible to have a life of your own, but you can have a life that's filled with joy and purpose. It takes perseverance, time, energy, courage, and self-love, but you deserve it and are worth it. The only requirement is a burning desire to have more, experience more, and be more than just the mom of a MIAC. This is no easy feat, but you've been to hell and back, so I know you have what it takes to move forward and live your best life possible. "Loving yourself isn't vanity, it's sanity," encourages Andre Gide, French author and winner of the 1947 Nobel Prize in Literature.

I've never liked conflict and learned as a child that when I asked for what I wanted, my needs were rarely met. It was easier not to ask than be continually disappointed. If I didn't ask, I wouldn't get hurt. It's not surprising that my husband (not my son's father) wasn't emotionally available during my son's initial diagnosis and illness. This forced me to look at what I needed to do to make it through the shock, the devastation, the despair, the chaos, and the turmoil that MI dropped in my lap. An unbidden horror, my love for an adult child with severe MI became a catalyst for inner reflection and change. Up to this point, I hadn't taken the time to figure out what was best for me. I'd always compromised my feelings and choices, but no more. I needed to be strong for my child, and I could only do that if I could stand solidly in what was right for me.

My husband declared that he wouldn't be emotionally available for me as I learned about, grappled with, and resigned myself to my son's debilitating illness.

He asked, "Is that a deal-breaker for our marriage?"

I didn't need to think about it twice. My answer was decisive. "Yes, that's a deal-breaker."

I could have decided to stay and deal with my son all on my own, but I knew that even if my husband wasn't involved with decisions and care, he would critique my choices and still expect me to weigh his opinions. It's my belief that if you're not willing to walk with me and extend emotional support, then you don't get to offer advice or criticism. I knew I would have to make difficult decisions and decided it would be easier to do so on my own. Taking care of my MIAC, as well as myself, was going to take most of my time, and I didn't want to hold on to a spouse who preferred to be only a friend with benefits. So, I took a stand and refused to let anyone steal my joy.

That choice was easy to make, while many others would prove much more difficult. I felt intense guilt at the thought of putting my needs and wants before those of my MIAC. Good moms aren't supposed to be self-centered. How can I possibly be happy when I know my son suffers and struggles every day? What kind of mother would I be to enjoy myself when he can't? Wasn't it my duty to be miserable right along with him?

A dear friend, Mike Kitko, offered this advice: "Your son will never have the quality of life you or he would want, but does it improve anything if you also live a miserable life? What if you lived a better life, your very best life, to honor the life he won't have?"

I was stunned by the simplicity and integrity of his statement. My choice to be miserable hurts everyone. I now follow the advice of author and speaker Mandy Hale: "It's not selfish to love yourself, take care of yourself, and to make your happiness a priority. It's necessary."

I try to live every day with joy and enthusiasm. In my opinion, it hurts my son to see me sad because of his illness, and he already has enough to deal with. I believe I cause him harm if I don't live my life. We don't all get the opportunity to have a wonderful life, but if we do, we need to show our appreciation by filling it with as many happy memories and joyful experiences as we can. The best way to celebrate your child is to live all out with heartfelt gratitude that you have another day and can make choices that fulfill you. This may seem indecent or crass, but does living a miserable life change your child's prognosis? If things were reversed and you were sick, you would wholeheartedly want your child to have a phenomenal life full of adventure, success, and love. Isn't that what your MIAC would want for you? If not, recognize that it's his disease talking and not his heart.

I give thanks for these great words from Neale Donald Walsh, author of *Conversations with God*, "Life begins at the end of your comfort zone." There are three Cs in life: Choice, Chance, and

Change. You must make a choice to take a chance if you want anything in your life to change.

When your life unravels overnight, it's difficult to know how to put the pieces back together. Do you keep them all or throw a few out? When you're so focused on your child's care, there doesn't seem to be enough room for your life. I wasn't ready to throw in the towel and give up on a life for myself, so I started adding in things that I'd enjoyed doing in the past. I didn't know what I wanted for myself, and I didn't know where to begin, but I knew I was ready to move forward and begin to find my way. I listed all the areas I considered important for building a quality life. Then I created a snapshot of what I wanted in each area.

When you do this exercise, I recommend you use a separate sheet of paper for each area and list everything you want in that part of your life. Now is the time to dream, imagine, and visualize what you want your life to look and feel like. No idea is too ridiculous or too far-fetched. Just remember that it's your energy that will get you there, one small step at a time. Don't forget to include a list of what you don't want as a reminder not to fall back into dysfunctional habits. "Your present circumstances don't determine where you go, they merely determine where you start," states motivational speaker, Nido Qubein.

Below is a list of specific life areas with examples of what's important to me in each category in order of importance to me. Over time, the order has changed as my inner growth priorities have evolved. When I began this journey, my career, environment, and financial security topped my list, but now my choices for personal comfort and well-being have moved to the top. At this time, I have no desire to be in a romantic relationship, but if that changes, I'll move that category up.

The lower the number of the category, the more time and energy I focus on that area. The higher numbers are on the back burner for now. For example, my career is going well, and I enjoy my work, so I don't devote much thought or energy to changes in that area.

1. Emotional Well-being

- I don't want my days crammed full of things to do.
- I don't want to feel tired and stressed.
- I want time for things I enjoy.
- I don't want to feel like my life is a job or my job is my life.
- I want to feel relaxed and stress free.

How I feel is important to me because that's what creates the foundation for how I deal with the rest of my life. If I'm miserable, sad, or angry, it affects my outlook and perspective, as well as my ability to deal with my MIAC's stressful situations. My emotional well-being is based on adequate sleep; downtime to relax, meditate, and read; quiet time to reflect and ground myself; and time spent in nature. I make it a priority to schedule time for myself because if I don't, I can easily become overwhelmed and frustrated by the smallest things. I require a lot of alone time to recharge and work through my feelings.

- What do you need to let go of for your emotional well-being?
- Where does this fall in your list of priorities?
- What can you add to your life to improve your emotional health?

2. Spiritual/Faith

- I don't want to feel judged by religion.
- I want to feel supported.
- I don't want to see God as vengeful.
- I don't want to feel diminished by a higher power.
- I want to feel connected to everything.

I've evolved and expanded, and my faith and spirituality have run the spectrum. I was raised Lutheran, living in an all-Catholic neighborhood, always being made to feel like the outsider, the heathen. As a young adult, I continued to attend church on and off but never really felt connected to the rigidity and judgment being pushed on me to conform to a particular dogma.

For a while, I thought I was an atheist, not wanting to believe anything preached. All I saw was war and destruction caused by opposing religious views. None of this felt right to me. It didn't ring true deep down in my soul. From there, I moved into being an agnostic, believing there was something greater than me but not defining it. Until finally, my son's illness pushed me into spirituality.

Where religion, atheism, and agnosticism didn't give me the answers I searched for, spirituality felt like coming home to a truth bigger than myself. I believe that there's a spirit source greater than me that I can tap into whenever I need support or understanding, which has seen me through the heartache, confusion, and turmoil of my son's diagnosis and prognosis. My connection to Source is what I lean on when I feel lost and alone. It's always with me at my core, ready and waiting to provide comfort and love. It has shown me that I have all the answers and that everything I need is already inside me. All I need to do is get still and listen. What I love about spirituality is the way it can look and feel different to each individual person. There's no strict adherence to doctrine, no denunciation of differing opinions or philosophies, no judgmental stance of black or white ideology.

Is my way of believing for everyone? Of course not. And that's the best part; you get to choose to believe whatever feels right in your heart regardless of what anyone else thinks. My relationship with God/Spirit/Source (whatever term you use) is mine and mine alone. It's personal and intimate, and it provides me with peace, reverence, awe, and acceptance that everything happens for my highest good.

My spirituality has allowed me to receive whatever appears in my life and see it as a gift. I may not understand how or why immediately, but over time, everything that's happened to me has moved me closer to God, to a place without judgment, to a life well lived regardless of my son's disease. My hope for each of you is that you also find a similar place deep inside that upholds you in times of grief, supports you in times of crises, and gives you a feeling of profound undying love and compassion in your darkest moments.

- Have your beliefs been helpful in your dealings with your MIAC?
- How has your faith assisted you in accepting this illness?
- Do you need to focus more on expanding your beliefs?

3. Personal Development

- I want to always continue to improve myself.
- I don't want to limit the time I spend on personal growth.
- I don't want to live without goals or aspirations.
- I want to be a different person today than I was a year ago.

I believe our purpose in life is to grow ourselves into the best soul living in a human body that we can be. My personal development is tied to knowledge and spirituality. I function better if I understand myself and how the world and I are connected. Inner reflection is more important to me than physical health because it's how I understand who I am, explains why I do the things I do, and gives me insight into how to move past what causes me trouble and heartache. I get quiet so I can hear my intuition. Talking with others on the same path helps me realize that I have control over my perceptions, my thoughts, my judgments, and how I live my life. Without inner work, you stay stuck in old patterns, don't understand yourself, and act like a victim rather than being the author of your own story. Time spent each day working on yourself is never wasted.

- How do you feel about self-improvement?
- What does personal growth look like for you?
- What are your goals for one year? Five years? Twenty years?
- Are you able to make goals that don't include your MIAC?
- At what age are you too old to work on personal development?

4. Family and Friends

- I want to have time for friends.
- I don't want my family to get pushed to the bottom of my priorities.
- I don't want my friends to think I don't care because I'm too busy.
- I want to spend quality time with my grandkids.

I didn't grow up in a close-knit family, but now I make the effort to stay in touch with them and check in to see how they're doing, even if they don't do the same for me. It feels good to know what's going on in their lives and see if I can be supportive in any way. I know deep down that they care but aren't good about staying in contact. My friends and I are in touch more frequently, as I see them as my soul family. We have similar interests and enjoy spending time together, in person or digitally.

- What does your family mean to you?
- How do you stay connected with family and friends?
- Do you initiate get-togethers, or do they?

5. Social Activities, Hobbies

- I don't want to participate in or watch sports (except for my grandkids' activities).
- I want to visit museums and gardens instead of shopping.
- I don't want to spend time scrolling social media or watching TV.
- I want to travel. That's a hobby for me.
- I don't want to be so busy that I have no time for entertainment.

I have a long list of things I love to do, and I don't quite understand people who have no interests or hobbies and then complain about being bored. I've always made time to do the things that feed my soul. I love all kinds of books, cooking, being in nature, creating SoulCollage® cards, participating in online classes, taking local workshops, having lunch with friends, hanging out with my grandkids, having conversations with my daughter, and visits with my son. I could go on and on.

It doesn't matter what you enjoy doing, as long as it's not illegal. Just make time and do it. My mom always complained that she didn't have time to sit on her patio and read, but she chose to spend her time doing things she didn't enjoy and never made time for fun. It makes me sad, but it's a reminder to include leisure activities in my schedule. I want things that nourish me, give me a more positive attitude and better coping skills for the difficult times, and remind me that life isn't all bad but is filled with moments of both pain and joy.

- What hobbies have you decided you don't have time for?
- What activities feed your soul?
- What will you add to your life to bring more happiness?

6. Health and Fitness

- I don't want to be sick, weak, or tired.
- I want to be healthy and strong physically, mentally, and emotionally.
- I don't want to be old before my time.
- I want to be able to continue to do the things I enjoy.

I take responsibility for my health by making and eating healthy meals. I drink a lot of clean water, walk, meditate, do simple yoga stretches, and make sure I get plenty of quality sleep. I believe that health and disease are created by what I put into my body, how I release emotional toxins, and my attitudes about life circumstances, much more than by my genetics. I view my body as a sacred vessel and a home to my soul. It's my duty to treat it with respect and appreciation.

Our bodies have a great way of letting us know when we're out of alignment and need to readjust our focus. I don't hold anyone else responsible for my health. Physical, mental, and emotional health are intricately linked to the quality of life, and I want to do everything I can to have a great life, free of disease and discomfort. I recently started working with a personal trainer two days a week to increase my core strength and balance. She is showing me things I can do at home to stay fit as I age.

- What does health look like for you?
- What do you do to stay healthy and fit?
- Do you take full responsibility for how you feel?

7. Recreation, Fun

- I want to have time for fun.
- I don't want to be too miserable or too serious to enjoy life.
- I don't want my child's illness to impact my ability to play.
- I want a schedule that includes downtime and relaxation.

Each of us has a different idea of what we consider fun, how we relax, what we do as a distraction, which hobbies we enjoy, and how much time we devote to recreational activities. I enjoy time spent with my children and grandchildren and time with friends and family. I like to walk in nature and visit museums. I love to read, be creative, work in my flower garden, attend sisterhood circles, anything to do with crystals, essential oils, oracle cards, enlightened conversations, and travels to near and far destinations.

I made a choice to fill my life with activities I enjoy doing in spite of my child's illness. I savor those downtimes, relish the silliness of life, and embrace simple, fun activities. My choice to make time for amusement is good for my mental and emotional health. "There is no fear when you're having fun." says American novelist Will Thomas.

- How do you rate having fun?
- What do you do in your downtime?
- Do you feel guilty enjoying yourself when your child is sick?

8. Financial Security

- I don't want to live paycheck to paycheck.
- I want to live comfortably.
- I don't want to feel like I have to deprive myself.
- I don't want to spend all my discretionary income on my MIAC.
- I want money for fun activities.

Money is not a top priority for me. It serves a purpose and is the means to an end, but I see money as merely a tool. I don't believe money makes you happy, and I don't want to work extended hours to increase my paycheck. I choose to live conservatively. I'm a minimalist, and I carefully consider any purchases. If something doesn't add value to my life, then I don't need it. For example, I live in a very small condo, don't own a TV or subscribe to cable, and rarely eat out. Those are my choices, and they offer me the disposable income to travel, which I absolutely love doing. My security comes from within, so this area isn't important. I understand that no amount of money will make my child well or add to my happiness. "The goal isn't more money. The goal is living life on your terms," says Will Rogers, who lived a life full of fun and adventure.

- How do your finances make you feel?
- Is the amount of money you have tied to your feelings of safety?
- How much do you spend trying to make your MIAC's life better?

9. Career

- I want to work in a stress-free environment.
- I want a flexible schedule.
- I want to work less than forty hours per week. Right now, I work twenty-five to thirty hours.
- I don't want to be an employee.

- I want to stay home in bad weather.
- I don't want to work with complaining coworkers.

I've worked in the same field for almost twenty years, and I enjoy my job. When my son first became sick, I was an employee at a large company with fixed hours. About a year later, I made the decision to resign and started working for myself in the same field. Being a sole proprietor, I have more flexibility in my schedule, can take off on a minute's notice, and create a relaxing, peaceful place to spend my working hours. My work became an oasis in the storm, a place to get away from what happened at home, and it offered much less stress than being an employee. In the next two or three years, this category will move up to the top as I decide what to do when I get closer to retirement. My advice is to design your workspace to support your mental and emotional health, do something you love or at least like, and remember it's only a way to earn money and not your whole life.

- What do you want in this area?
- Where does this fall in your list of priorities?
- What would you need to change to love your job?

10. Mental/Intellectual Stimulation

- I don't want to become mentally stagnant.
- I want to be well read and well rounded.
- I don't ever want to stop learning.
- I want to be informed.
- I don't ever want to think I know it all.

I love to learn new things, have discussions from opposing viewpoints, and stay open-minded to different possible perspectives. As a child, I asked so many questions, always wanting to understand how something worked or why it happened the way it did. This quality has helped me understand and cope better with my MIAC by allowing me to always look for answers and alternative solutions regardless of what popular belief dictates. I continually read, evaluate, and question mental healthcare, therapies, and medications. Keeping my mind fresh keeps me young and stimulates healthy brain function. Refusing to entertain new or different ideas limits your opportunity for growth and satisfaction. I love the new word game I recently downloaded to my phone; it offers constructive play while waiting at appointments.

- How do you stimulate your mind?
- How do you feel about learning new information?
- Are you stuck in your old way of thinking?

11. Relationship/Significant Other

- I want to be accepted for who I am.
- I don't want to be a friend with benefits.
- I want a partner in fun and hard times.
- I don't want to be a housekeeper, cook, or maid to another adult.
- I want a best friend who wants to spend time with me.

Having a romantic relationship is not high on my priority list right now. I'm happy and content with my life, I'm busy doing things I enjoy, and I don't have time to date. I feel complete without a significant other. I might change my mind someday, but for now, I enjoy my life as it is. I grew up hearing that women should marry and compromise their lives for their spouse's comfort and convenience, and that ideal doesn't fit with my reality. I don't think you need to be in a relationship to have a fulfilled, satisfying life. There was a time when I thought I needed a spouse to support me financially, but not anymore. I've created a rewarding life for myself, and until I feel the need to share it with someone, I'll continue to appreciate living on my own.

- How does your relationship add or detract from your happiness?
- Does your significant other support you caring for your MIAC?
- If you're not in a relationship, how does that affect your well-being?

12. Physical Environment

- I don't want to feel like I have to keep up with the Joneses.
- I want my home and business to be relaxing and inviting.
- I don't want my surroundings to feel uncomfortable or stiff.
- I don't want to compromise my style for conformity.
- I want my home to be welcoming.

I'm comfortable living almost anywhere. I've moved many times during my life and have always been able to make wherever I am feel like home. I have little attachment to material things or possessions, but I do like my living space to contain live plants, lots of light, and good smells.

It's important for your home and work environment to be comfortable, welcoming, and peaceful to you, regardless of what anyone else thinks. I feel most serene when my home is clean, clutter-free, and warm. My condo will never be featured in a magazine, and that's okay because it gives me what I need—a place to relax and unwind. I have added personal pictures and memorabilia, books, a fountain, and a couple fairy topiary gardens, soothing music, decorative pillows and baskets, a small dog, and two cats. It's my nirvana, my oasis from stress and the noise and chaos of the rest of the world. I'd love to add a soaking tub because baths on a cold winter night are so relaxing.

- What makes your house feel like home?
- Does your home feel like an oasis? If not, what changes can you make?
- How can you make your house into a sanctuary?

I regularly evaluate my blueprint to see if I'm on track to achieve what I desire in each area of my life. I look to see if the decisions I make bring me closer to what I want or throw me off course. At the start of a new year, I pull out my lists and review what's worked and what hasn't.

As I evolve and grow, my list of priorities changes as well. What I thought I wanted or needed ten years ago is completely different from what I want and need now because I'm a different person. My goals and aspirations have become more personal and less materialistic. Where in the past I thought a new purse or a set of earrings would make me feel better, I now realize I need to go on an inner journey of self-discovery to find the things that make my life good. That doesn't mean I don't ever buy myself anything, but that immaterial things mean so much more because they don't break or lose their sparkle.

Keri Russell, actress and dancer, spurs us on with this pertinent quote: "Sometimes it's the smallest decisions that can change your life forever." Once you have your list of wants, it's time to decide where to begin. Adding in small changes will create lasting transformation. This will be a slow process, one step forward and two steps back, until one day you realize your once-miserable existence is now better.

The categories I shared above evolved over several years of trial and error. It's all about living a life that suits you and not worrying about what others think, as long as you don't harm another and live in a way that supports your best life. It's not your job to decide what someone else's life should look like. They get to decide what's best for themselves.

Even if your MIAC makes poor choices, until he's a threat to himself or others, it's his choice. I decided a long time ago that my son could choose to be homeless, an addict, or even refuse medication, and I would still have a good life. My being happy doesn't negatively impact my child's decision-making or inhibit his ability to get better, so why should I be miserable? You deserve to be happy and healthy. Choose to be.

> *My being happy doesn't negatively impact my child's decision-making or inhibit his ability to get better . . .*

It may seem like an insurmountable task to start over in life. Maybe you think that you're too old to begin again. The first step toward something different, toward something better, is always the hardest. To completely change your life feels overwhelming, so just do one thing differently. This will take time, diligence, and courage. It's time to begin, although there may be many days you want to give up. As you see small signs of success, you'll be emboldened to make more changes.

I'll let you in on a little secret: Your changes won't affect your MIAC's illness at all. It won't make him better or worse. It won't make him less delusional or paranoid. It won't keep him drug free. But it will allow you to accept his disease as his reality, not yours.

Moving on with your life allows you to stop trying to control every aspect of his life and to accept that you can only control yourself and your life. That doesn't mean you don't step in when your MIAC's spiraling into another crisis, but you don't become trapped in the chaos. Live your life and deal only with what presents itself and be thoughtful about what you want. Be grateful that you have the ability to choose what your life looks like. You can have a wonderful life and feel blessed every day. Become the CEO of your life, the owner of your destiny, and the leader in your quest to be joyous. Remind yourself every day that you're in charge of your happiness. Don't allow anything outside of yourself to change that. As you create a life that feels good on the inside, it will turn into experiences that look good on the outside.

> *Remind yourself every day that you're in charge of your happiness.*

It feels so good to be free of your shattered life. Breathe deeply and feel the peace and calm of a life restored. You've got an action plan, so now let's create a massive amount of joy. I'm here as a walking, talking example that it's possible to have a life filled with satisfaction, fulfillment, and happiness.

Are you ready for the final step? You've worked so hard to get here; don't stop now. It's time for the icing on the cake, to claim the joy that's rightfully yours.

Visualization Journey

Sit in a comfortable, quiet place. Close your eyes.

Breathe in and out slowly to the count of three several times until you feel yourself begin to relax.

Visualize yourself walking through a gigantic grocery store of life. Every aisle holds a category that will enrich your life. Each has more options to choose from than you can imagine.

The aisles run in alphabetical order, but you can choose which is most important to you. Take a cart, and let's begin.

Aisle one is "Career" options. What do you want to change or enhance about your job? Whatever comes to you, put it in your cart.

Next is "Emotional Well-being." What do you need in this area of your life? What will strengthen your well-being? What positive emotions would you like to add to your cart?

"Family & Friends" is in aisle three. What do you need to upgrade your relationships? What qualities would make you a better friend and family member? Does this area need any booster items, or do you need a product to erase a bad behavior?

Aisle four is "Financial Security." What would you do with financial security? How much money do you need to have freedom of time? What needs to change to augment your finances? Do you need to make more or spend less?

Aisle five offers items that benefit your "Health & Fitness." What do you need to increase your health? What would help you raise your level of fitness?

The aisle for "Mental/Intellectual Stimulation" has so many interesting items to choose from. Do you like books, music, jigsaw or crossword puzzles, sudoku, or maybe a visit to a history museum?

"Personal Development" fills aisle seven with a multitude of options, which include emotional, spiritual, physical, social, and moral choices—everything needed to create a better you.

Aisle eight has items to enhance your "Physical Environment" from artwork, plants, comfy linens, music, kitchen gadgets, and sunken bathtubs.

Here comes "Recreation & Fun," the aisle for the child in you. What do you enjoy doing in your free time? How much amusement can you fit in your cart? Don't forget to pick up a few happy childhood memories.

"Romantic Relationships" is an important category with every option imaginable to upgrade your existing relationship or create space for a new significant other in your life. Choose what the perfect relationship looks like to you. Pick up tools to boost the relationship you already have or find options to repair one that's not working.

Aisle eleven includes "Social Activities & Hobbies" and is great fun to browse. What do you enjoy doing in your spare time? How many hobbies are too many? What else do you enjoy—movies, theatre, museums, bars, dancing, concerts? Do you have a collection, like to travel, work with your hands?

And last, but not least, aisle twelve has everything to do with "Spirituality & Faith." Choose items to reinforce your current beliefs or learn about something new. The choice is yours. Books, meditation, gospel music, a new church, prayer circle, Bible study, and more.

Now that your cart is full of everything to make your life better, open your eyes and journal any messages, words, symbols you received. Make sure to make a list of the things you want to add to your life and assign an order of importance to each category.

Joy Is an Inside Job

We are sisters
Bound by our journeys
Stronger together
We live with sorrow
We choose to be joyful
We are sisters

This chapter is designed to help you create more joy in your life, and it offers you a step-by-step process to experience more contentment, more balance, and more enjoyment. The process requires determination, consistency, a desire to be defined as more than only the mom of a MIAC, and an eagerness to embrace the best life has to offer. Joy is yours. It's your choice, it's your birthright, and it's within your grasp. All you need to do is allow it into your mind, your heart, your soul.

Amanda Gore's blog in the *Huffington Post* from December 10, 2014, lists "The 12 Timeless Secrets to Creating a Joyful Life," which are hope, forgiveness, gratitude, compassion, reverence, generosity, energy and vitality, listening, laughter, love, cheerful enthusiasm, and inner peace. In the following pages, I'll explore the meaning of each word and include a guide for a daily intention, an actionable to-do list, a short meditation, and a suggestion for a small talisman that will remind you of the lesson.

You can address one topic each month or skip around. Do whatever feels right for you. As you embody these attitudes and practices, the benefits you gain will be numerous. Hopefully, these practices will become habits, will encourage you to look at life's ups and downs in a healthier way, and will spark a renewed sense of purpose and determination to live your best life.

Joy is yours. It's your choice, it's your birthright, and it's within your grasp. All you need to do is allow it into your mind, your heart, your soul.

Hope

Hope is an optimistic state of mind that's based on expectations of a positive outcome. Can you still have hope without a positive outcome? Can you continue to be hopeful if you don't get the results you want? Could hope cause you to believe that every experience—good or bad, beautiful or ugly, wonderful or horrific—is part of a grand, unseen plan? Dr. Martin Luther King, Jr. reminds us that, "Only in the darkness can you see the stars."

Hope is the desire or belief that everything will be okay. It allows you to cultivate a positive attitude about the future even though your child is mentally ill. Being hopeful also means you have faith—faith in something more than yourself, faith to see the world as inherently good, faith you'll find a rainbow after the storm. Hope allows you to move forward after a tragedy, gives you a reason to try again, and fills your heart with love and light in spite of imminent catastrophe. It offers a positive mindset, the ability to strategize, and the courage to face setbacks and failure. The benefits of hope can be felt through better health, a happier disposition, and a renewed sense of faith in humanity.

An *intention* activates your receptivity. It's a visualization of what you want, and it moves you from victim to chooser. Intentions are personal, a way to align your energy with your attitude and purpose. Intentions are heart-driven and tie your thoughts to your actions through a repeated phrase or word. You can use the intentions here or create ones of your own. Write them down, put them somewhere you can see them often, and read them daily, hourly if needed. Deepak Chopra says, "Intentions compressed into words enfold magic power."

A gentle reminder: Your intentions are to create what *you* desire in your life, not what you want to happen in your MIAC's life. If you try to create intentions to change your child's choices or behaviors, you will be disappointed.

Intention for Creating Hope

Just for today, just in this moment, I will fill my heart with hope, belief, and optimism that I may see my future filled with light.

Activities to Do

- Connect with someone positive who makes you feel happy.
- Make a list of the good things in your life.
- Be like a tree. Watch how a tree perseveres in all kinds of weather and conditions, day after day, year after year. Trees come back each year after losing it all, and they always reach toward the sky.
- Watch children play and laugh.
- Read about someone who has overcome terrible adversity.
- Listen to the *Live Inspired* Podcast with John O'Leary, or read his book *On Fire: The 7 Choices to Ignite a Radically Inspired Life.*
- Plant a paperwhite flower, put it on a sunny windowsill, and watch it bloom.
- Listen to uplifting music or gospel hymns.
- Volunteer at a local pet rescue.
- Attend a prayer group.
- Deliver meals to the elderly.

Meditation for Hope

> Close your eyes and take a few slow, deep breaths.
>
> Visualize a beautiful, pink light in the distance.
>
> This radiant light is Hope; its approach is soft and gentle.
>
> Watch as this pink glow moves toward you.
>
> As Hope gets closer, it expands into a large orb, large enough to enfold your entire body.
>
> You can feel the warmth as you're surrounded by this delicate pink light.
>
> Stop, breathe deeply, pull Hope deep into your heart space.
>
> Hope is now a part of you. From this day forward, anytime you feel lost or desolate, picture your heart filled with the quiet strength of this iridescent pink light.

Talisman

Purchase a small rose quartz crystal heart to carry with you or to wear on a chain as a constant reminder that Hope lives within your heart.

Forgiveness

Forgiveness doesn't want you to forget, condone, or excuse angry or resentful feelings toward your MIAC, but to instead make an informed, deliberate decision to willingly release those feelings, whether the other person deserves it or not. Holding on to pain harms you and has little to do with your child. Forgiveness allows you to move forward without contempt or a desire for revenge. Paul Lewis Boese wants us to know that "Forgiveness doesn't change the past, but it does enlarge the future."

A MIAC creates many circumstances that beg forgiveness, so make a conscious choice to let go. In many cases, your child can't control his actions and would never choose to behave in such a way if not for his disease. Forgive your child for his poor choices, aggressive behaviors, derogatory words, addictions, crimes, and mostly for becoming mentally ill. It'll be your redemption and will open the door for you to move on with your life. It may also be necessary to forgive family, friends, coworkers, and spouses for not understanding the way mental illness manifests and the toll it can take on an individual. Release your anger toward a society that refuses to see brain health through the same lens as physical health; release your resentment toward a broken healthcare system and the inadequacy of available treatments and doctors. It's crucial if you want to have a life filled with joy and contentment.

You are a more effective advocate if you accept rather than confront situations. When you grant forgiveness, you lighten your heart, brighten your mood, and move forward, released from past hurts. Heartfelt thanks to Robin Sharma, a Canadian writer, for the reminder: "Forgiveness isn't approving what happened. It's choosing to rise above it."

You are a more effective advocate if you accept rather than confront situations.

Intention for Creating Forgiveness

> Just for today, just in this moment,
> I will let go of my anger and resentment,
> grant everyone forgiveness,
> accepting they have done their very best.

Activities to Do

- Recall a time when you were the offender, and understand your intent wasn't to harm. This can help you accept others' mistakes.
- List the benefits you'll gain if you grant forgiveness.

- Volunteer at a homeless shelter or soup kitchen.
- Let go of your expectations of your MIAC. Expect nothing.
- List your expectations. You might be surprised how many you have and how unrealistic they really are.
- Pray for the person you want to forgive. Ask God to bestow upon them immense happiness.
- Write a letter to your child, then burn it. Visualize the smoke dissolving your hurt.
- Focus on the things you like about your MIAC.
- Imagine the roles are reversed. How would you feel? How would you want to be treated?
- Read *The Choice: Embrace the Possible* by Dr. Edith Eva Eger.
- Collect rocks of various sizes. Assign a resentment to each stone and then, in a vacant field or lake, throw each as far away from you as possible.
- Change the ending of your story to include your forgiveness and how you now feel about the incident.

Meditation for Forgiveness

Close your eyes and take a few slow, deep breaths.

Visualize yourself sitting in a field.

Imagine small sticks laying on the ground in front of you. Each stick represents a hurt, resentment, or anger you've held on to (if you don't know how many there should be, just intuit a number and go with it).

One by one, break each stick into two or three pieces and throw them into a large pile to your left.

When finished, imagine a bright star coming down and blasting the pile into smithereens. Poof! Your hurt, anger, and resentments are gone.

Offer a prayer of thanks, take a deep breath, and feel the lightness in your heart. You can perform this ritual any time you feel the need.

Talisman

Purchase a box of toothpicks. Whenever you feel like you're holding on to something, break a few toothpicks, place them in a ceramic saucer, and burn them. Send your resentments up in smoke. You can also perform this ceremony with larger sticks or tree branches and a fire pit. Remember to give voice to what you're releasing.

Gratitude

Gratitude is feeling thankful, a readiness to show appreciation, and to act with reciprocity. Is it possible to feel grateful for things that have nothing positive or good to add to your life? Is gratitude just being thankful for a gift, a compliment, and a helping hand—or is it more of an attitude, a way to consider everything that happens to you? Perhaps it's possible to not only see gratitude as an emotion but to make it an ongoing mood and incorporate it into your personality. Gratitude is the flip side of misfortune, and you have the choice of which side you choose to see. Quoting the fabled Aesop, "Gratitude turns what we have into enough."

Did you know that when you practice gratitude, it increases the dopamine production in your brain? This encourages your brain to want more and makes you want to do the same things again. The more you're grateful, the more you'll find to be grateful for.

Gratitude can relieve stress, minimize fear, and open your eyes to the good all around you. It improves your physical, mental, and emotional health, enhances empathy, and promotes better sleep. It's called practicing gratitude because it takes practice to get good at it, but with work, you can make it a valuable habit in your quest for a joyous life. Melody Beattie, an author of self-help books on codependent relationships, suggests, "Gratitude makes sense of your past, brings peace for today, and creates a vision for tomorrow."

Intention for Creating Gratitude

> Just for today, just in this moment,
> I will fill my heart with gratitude, thanks, and grace.
> For there is much good in my life.

Activities to Do

- Purchase a gratitude journal and write in it each night before bed.
- Make a blessings jar. Write what you're thankful for on small slips of paper every day. Each month empty the jar and read about how good your life has been.
- Keep track of how many times a day you can say "thank you" to others for the little things they do.
- Notice whenever you have a negative comment, and try to flip the narrative to positive. This takes practice but offers many rewards.
- Organize a closet and recognize how much you have.
- Read the book *The Power of Vulnerability: Teachings on Authenticity, Connection, and Courage* by Brené Brown.
- Donate to your favorite charity. If you don't have one, do some research and find one you love. Some of my favorites are NAMI.org, stlfoodbank.org, charitywater.org, and crisisnurserykids.org.
- Handwrite a thank-you note to someone who made your day special or helped you.
- Say grace before each meal for the bounty you have.
- Thank someone who never gets thanked. Examples: your postal person with a homemade muffin, the delivery driver with a bottle of water, your trash person with a gift card for coffee, the nurses in the psych ward with a fruit basket, your kind neighbor with a bouquet of flowers. I challenge you to see how many people you can add to this list.

Meditation for Gratitude

> Close your eyes and take a few slow, deep breaths.
>
> Imagine you're in the presence of God/Spirit/Source.
>
> Offer thanks for your family, your friends, the earth, the sun, the moon, the stars, all who inhabit this world, those who have harmed you, those you've harmed, difficult situations, unresolved drama, heartache, and anything or anyone else you'd like to include. Don't forget yourself.
>
> Ask your higher power to lavish your gratitude upon everyone included in your prayer, even those you've forgotten.
>
> Take a moment to breathe and feel your blessings of gratitude fall upon your shoulders and wrap you in warmth. Feel the spaciousness in your chest and the smile on your lips.
>
> Thank you, thank you, thank you.
>
> Amen.

Talisman

Purchase or make your own gratitude charm. You can find many beautiful, inexpensive choices online. Wear it on a bracelet or use it as a keychain to remind you daily that gratitude is a choice.

Compassion

Compassion shows sympathetic pity and concern for others through thoughtful words or actions. Compassion takes you away from thoughts of yourself and puts your focus on recognizing and reducing the suffering of others. With compassion, you put yourself in your MIAC's place, feel his struggles, and have a strong desire to take away his pain. You can learn to increase your compassion by showing affection, concern, and generosity toward your child instead of anger and animosity. Thomas Merton, a scholar of comparative religion, shares his thoughts: "Compassion is the keen awareness of the interdependence of all things."

Practicing compassion improves your health as it strengthens your immune system, normalizes blood pressure, reduces stress and depression, and can even extend your life. It creates the opportunity for better relationships, heightened levels of happiness, and increased social connections. Put yourself in your MIAC's shoes. It's a great lesson in understanding what he struggles with and offers you the option to respond with compassion rather than to belittle or humiliate him. Compassion won't change his behavior, but it changes the way you see and respond to it.

> *Practicing compassion improves your health as it strengthens your immune system, normalizes blood pressure, reduces stress and depression, and can even extend your life.*

Intention for Creating Compassion

> Just for today, just in this moment,
> I will fill my heart with compassion, kindness, and charity, blessing each person I see with a warm, heartfelt smile.

Activities to Do

- List your MIAC's positive qualities.
- Discover characteristics that you share with him.
- Look underneath his behaviors for the hidden emotions.
- Read *Tattoos on the Heart: The Power of Boundless Compassion* by Roman Catholic priest Gregory Boyle.
- Offer to do a favor for someone you don't like.
- Volunteer or donate to a battered women's shelter.
- Visit a nursing home in your area and talk with a resident who doesn't receive visitors.
- Ask your pastor if there's a family in need that you can help.

- Write a letter to a prison inmate.
- Volunteer at a soup kitchen.

Meditation for Compassion

>Close your eyes and take a few slow, deep breaths.
>
>Imagine your MIAC standing in front of you. Look at his face until his body disappears and all you see is his eyes.
>
>Stare deeply into his eyes until you see all the way down into his soul. What color is it?
>
>See past his behaviors, past his words, past his attitudes.
>
>See the spark of God that lives buried under his humanness.
>
>Visualize yourself pulling his soul into a loving embrace.
>
>Whisper into his ear, "I understand you, I accept you, I love you."
>
>Feel the transference of his appreciation in your soul. What color is your soul?
>
>Soak in this feeling of compassion. When you give it away, it comes back to you.

Talisman

Purchase a small candle the color of the soul you touched or the color of your soul. Whenever you need to offer or receive compassion, light your candle and remember that the spark of God is in everyone.

Reverence

Reverence is a feeling or attitude of deep respect and awe. It creates warmth in friendships and family life and holds relationships together. Usually tied to religion, reverence honors the uniqueness of each person. It looks for the good in everyone, finds something to admire, realizes that we all embody aspects of God regardless of outside appearances. Gary Zykav, a spiritual teacher and author, provides understanding: "Reverence is an attitude of honoring life. Reverence automatically brings forth patience. Reverence permits non-judgmental justice. Reverence is a perception of the soul."

How does reverence relate to you and your MIAC? Why is this an important quality to develop? How will being more reverent make you happier? Once you can accept your child's behaviors and actions as symptoms of a serious brain disease and are able to appreciate and defend what he struggles with each day, only then will you be able to hold him in reverence. The ability to see your child's strength, the ability to admire his tenacity, and the ability to honor his courage is reverence in action. It's the capacity to see beyond the disease and admire the determination it takes for him to get up and try to live the best life he can each day. Reverence looks for the individual hidden beneath the disease and offers consideration and courtesy instead of judgment and condemnation. Reverence looks through the eyes of God and knows everyone has beauty and deserves to be treated with dignity.

Intention for Creating Reverence

> Just for today, just in this moment,
> I will fill my heart with respect, awe, and reverence
> for every person and circumstance I encounter.

Activities to Do

- Spend a few minutes each day in stillness and silence.
- Challenge yourself to look for the beauty hidden in everything.
- Spend time in nature. Visit a botanical garden, walk through a garden shop, neighborhood park, or local floral shop.
- Find a way to give back to your community.
- Develop a spiritual practice that feeds your soul.
- Read *Reverence for Life: The Words of Albert Schweitzer*, Harold E. Robles (editor).

- Lovingly wash someone's feet. Take time and care.
- Say a prayer each morning that you be reverent toward everyone you encounter.
- Visit a veteran's monument or cemetery.
- Collect donations for your local homeless shelter.

Meditation for Reverence

> Close your eyes and take a few slow, deep breaths.
>
> In front of you are several pairs of eyeglasses, each with a different colored lens. Choose the brown lenses first. How does the world look tinged with brown? Does everything and everyone look dull, dirty? Does it seem sadder without all the vibrant color?
>
> Try on the other colors, one at a time.
>
> How do you feel when you see the world as all green? Or blue? Or orange? Or red? Or violet? Or black? Or yellow? Do you feel shortchanged looking at a monochromatic world? Does it feel strange and alien? What do you feel is missing by viewing the world through only one color?
>
> The last pair of glasses are brilliantly clear. When you put these on, you see everything and everyone, as they are, all the beauty and all the ugliness, revealed in dynamic color.
>
> Can you enjoy, appreciate, respect, and revere the immense diversity you see when your vision isn't clouded by the prejudices that have colored your vision in the past?
>
> Look around and cherish the richness and depth.

Talisman

Purchase an inexpensive pair of glasses with colored lenses and place them on your nightstand. Each morning put them on before you get out of bed as a reminder of how your judgments stop you from seeing people through the lens of reverence.

Generosity

Generosity is a personality quality that describes someone who's happy to give their time, money, food, or kindness to others in need. It's the eagerness to share what you have with those less fortunate. Being generous encourages you to see others in a more positive light and creates a feeling of community, a feeling that we're all connected. Giving to others also has the added benefit that it makes you feel good about yourself, is a natural confidence booster, and helps banish self-hatred. Generosity decreases feelings of isolation and depression and opens your heart to the abundance in life. Francis of Assisi tells us, "For it is in giving that we receive."

Generosity can also be defined as being benevolent with your judgments, showing compassion toward others, and being able to offer sympathy instead of judgment or criticism. When you offer the generosity of your spirit, of your attitude, of your words and actions, it allows you to see what a magnanimous world you live in.

How can you be more generous toward your MIAC? Not in terms of spending more money or more time, but more generous with your opinions of his actions, with the way you interpret his words and behaviors, with how you describe his struggles. Generosity takes place in the heart, not the mind, and offers you a chance to embrace your child's misfortune with dignity and grace. Generosity is the most natural outward expression of an inner attitude of compassion.

How can you be more generous toward your MIAC?

Intention for Creating Generosity

> Just for today, just in this moment,
> I will fill my heart with attention, encouragement,
> and benevolence, that others may feel the essence
> of my generosity.

Activities to Do

- Handwrite a note to someone and tell them how they've made your life better.
- Give to someone with no strings attached.
- Pay something toward student lunch debt at a local school.
- See how many random people you can help by holding a door, helping carry groceries, reading stories in an after-school program, helping an elderly person pump gas, etc.
- Thank everyone you come in contact with. "Thank you. I appreciate . . ."
- Buy a coworker lunch, coffee, or share a snack with a friend.
- Give your place in line to a stranger.
- Offer to help a friend clean or watch their children.
- Read *The Giving Tree* by Shel Silverstein.
- Check out Charity Navigator's top twenty organizations that give 99 percent of the money they receive to their cause. Pick one or two and donate a few dollars.

Meditation for Generosity

Close your eyes and take a few slow, deep breaths.

Imagine yourself in a beautiful meadow, where the sun is hidden behind rain clouds.

In front of you is an ornate bowl inscribed with the message *Give, and you shall receive.*

Visualize yourself placing items in the bowl: coins, a thank-you card, time, attention, encouragement, acceptance, a donation, or anything else you'd like to share with others.

How does it feel to give so freely? Notice that the more you put into the bowl, the more the sun begins to shine. Feel the warmth on your shoulders.

The more you resist, the more the sun hides behind the clouds. You feel a few raindrops.

Reflect on the way you feel when you give freely and when you want to hold on to what you think should be yours. Do you notice how the universe conspires to bless you when you give willingly? Give, and you shall receive.

Talisman

Purchase or make a small stained-glass suncatcher to put in your window or hang on your car mirror as a reminder of what you receive by being generous.

Energy and Vitality

Spiritual teacher Sonai Choquette sagely suggests, "As with everything in nature, if your life isn't supported by a grounded source of energy, it will wither and lose its vitality." To be energetic is described as being filled with action and purpose. A lively and spirited outlook on life makes you more energetic. Someone who is by nature energetic typically has a positive attitude, is always willing to pitch in and help, and takes time out for self-care. Vitality is the capacity to live and grow, maintain physical, mental, and emotional health, and be excited about all aspects of life. It means you wake up each day feeling capable and energetic. Vitality is the ability to survive and continue a meaningful or purposeful existence after experiencing tragedy or setback. Someone who exhibits vitality is infused with positive energy, has good health habits, and practices balance between work and play.

Vitality isn't just about staying active and strong; at its core, vitality is the enthusiasm to get up each morning ready to face whatever happens. It's a purpose and direction. It's your life force. It's that spark of light deep inside that makes you uniquely you. Energy is the byproduct of connection with your inner essence, living life full out with courage and fortitude, and seeing life as an adventure rather than a burden. Living with vitality increases your optimism, reduces physical ailments, and improves your mental well-being.

Energy is the ability to do all the things you want to do, and vitality is doing them cheerfully. It's not about running yourself ragged, but rather taking care of this human body housing your soul.

Intention for Creating Energy and Vitality

> Just for today, just in this moment,
> I will add in more movement, sleep, and healthy foods.
> I will connect with my soul's essence.

Activities to Do

- Incorporate fifteen minutes of exercise into your day. ABE for Fitness videos on vimeo.com offer short bursts of activity you can do anywhere, any time.
- Practice mindful breathing. To feel more energized, breathe in for a count of eight and out for a count of four, twice a day for five minutes.
- Cut out one soda a day and add in eight ounces of water.
- Spend a few minutes each day meditating with the free app *Insight Timer*. It offers short, guided meditations for sleep, relaxation, and anxiety reduction.
- Getting rid of clutter is a great way to change the energy of your environment, and the best part is it's contagious. What can you let go of?
- Try a new activity, take a class, or start a new hobby to stimulate your mind. Try something you've always wanted to do.
- Go to bed and get up at a regular time. Get enough quality rest.
- Spend time outdoors. The sun is a wonderful mood enhancer.
- Read *Goddesses Never Age: The Secret Prescription for Radiance, Vitality, and Well-Being* by Christiane Northrup, M.D.
- Limit your exposure to digital media, TVs, cell phones, and computers. They can zap your vitality and nab your energy.

Meditation for Energy and Vitality

Close your eyes and take a few slow, deep breaths.

Imagine yourself barefoot in the grass. It feels cool and lush.

Wiggle your toes and plant your feet solidly. See yourself as not just standing on the ground but becoming part of it.

Visualize a tree trunk growing from your torso, going straight down into the earth, down, down, down, until it reaches the center crystal iron core.

Let your tree trunk grow a root that wraps three times around the core. Feel yourself grounded and snug to the earth.

Imagine energy coming up through your trunk and filling your body. What color is the earth energy? Any color except brown or black is beneficial.

Allow the energy to run up through your body until it sprays out the top of your head and enfolds you in beautiful light three feet in all directions. Enjoy the feeling as the earth energy clears away any toxic emotions.

Now move your focus to the sun. Imagine a single vibrant beam of golden light coming all the way down into the top of your head and merging with the earth energy.

As they blend together, allow this combined energy to flow out the top of your head and fill your entire home with colorful golden light, cleansing the negative energy and leaving behind a feeling of positivity and peace.

Spend a few minutes and enjoy the feeling of energy flowing through you, coming in through your feet and out the top of your head. How does this make you feel? Do you feel blessed, renewed?

When done, thank Mother Earth and the Sun for the energy they shared with you.

Talisman

Choose a battery. Any size will do. Carry it with you as a reminder that you can renew your energy at any time. Decorate it if you want with the colors of your earth energy.

Listening

Listening isn't a passive activity. It takes great skill to be attentive. The qualities of a good listener include giving undivided attention, maintaining eye contact, and repeating back what you've heard to make sure you don't misinterpret what's said. Focus on the person talking instead of what your response will be. This allows you to observe body language, look for the emotions under the words, and show that you value what's being shared. Mindful listening decreases selective hearing and requires patience and practice. A good listener doesn't offer a quick fix or unsolicited advice. Listen to self-care coach Cheryl Richardson: "People start to heal the moment they feel heard." Feel that statement in your heart and soul. You have the power to offer this beautiful gift.

> *The qualities of a good listener include giving undivided attention, maintaining eye contact, and repeating back what you've heard to make sure you don't misinterpret what's said.*

Listening makes you a better friend, spouse, and parent, and it gives you the opportunity to be fully present with another as they share their thoughts, reality, and vulnerability. It can help you develop tolerance, see new opportunities, and solve problems. Active listening boosts your confidence and leads to better understanding. It makes you a good communicator if you can listen to your MIAC with no agenda, ask questions for clarification, and wait until he's finished talking before you formulate a response. Effective listening encourages your child to feel valued, accepted, and understood.

Hearing, but not listening, is the main cause of confusion, arguments, and hurt feelings. "We think we listen, but very rarely do we listen with real understanding, true empathy. Yet listening of this very special kind is one of the most potent forces for change that I know." I offer gratitude to psychologist Carl Rogers for this profound reminder that we can all do better.

Intention for Listening

>Just for today, just in this moment,
>I will quiet my mind and open my ears to listen
>with patience, understanding, and clarity.

Activities to Do

- Face your MIAC and focus on his words.
- Keep an open mind. Don't predetermine your opinion.
- Put your phone on silent and leave it in another room, turn off the TV and radio, remove all diversions.
- Practice discriminative listening by looking past the words to find the underlying message.
- Make a list of everything you notice while listening to your MIAC. What he's feeling, if there's a hidden agenda under his words, if is he able to clearly articulate his thoughts. What is he really trying to say?
- Learn to ask open-ended questions to gain better understanding.
- Practice ten minutes of meditation each day to increase your ability to quiet your brain and become a mindful listener.
- Be aware of your body language. Do you look bored, angry, passive?
- Read *Practicing the Sacred Art of Listening: A Guide to Enrich Your Relationships and Kindle Your Spiritual Life* by Kay Lindahl, founder of The Listening Center.
- See if you can go for an entire day without TV, radio, phone, and computer. How did it make you feel? What did you learn?

Meditation for Listening

> Do this meditation outside.
>
> Close your eyes and take a few slow, deep breaths.
>
> How many sounds do you hear? Birds, traffic, people, trains?
>
> The longer you sit and listen, the more you'll be able to hear the more subtle sounds. Insects, the trees whispering, squirrels, the wind.
>
> How does it make you feel to listen to the sounds of nature?
>
> Do you hear with just your ears, or can you hear with your heart?
>
> How do the sounds differ if you try this exercise during the day, as opposed to after dark?

Talisman

Purchase an ornamental stone large enough to use as a paperweight. Apply the word LISTEN to it with paint or stick-on letters. Place it somewhere that you'll see it every day—on your desk at work, the kitchen windowsill, or the bathroom counter.

Laughter

Laughter is the expansion of a smile, the bubbling over of positive emotions. It relieves stress and physical tension, keeps you relaxed for up to forty-five minutes, and increases your resistance to disease. Even the words used to describe different forms of laughter like guffaw, giggle, snicker, and chortle make you want to chuckle in amusement. A good laugh lightens your burdens, inspires hope, keeps you grounded, releases anger, and leads to forgiveness. Indeed, laughter is good medicine. It improves your mood, decreases pain, and diffuses conflict. A good sense of humor has even been shown to help you live longer. I love German author Thomas Mann's visually inspired quote: "Laughter is a sunbeam of the soul."

How do you bring more laughter into your life? Practice smiling, count your blessings, and spend time with fun, playful people. If you need even more ideas, watch a funny movie, read the comics, ask others to share their favorite jokes, host a game night, play with a pet, spend time with a child. Kids love to laugh and find the most mundane events hysterical. I remember my five-year-old twin grandsons laughing until they snorted—over a burp!

Laughter is contagious and is guaranteed to lift your spirits. Laugh with friends, laugh with coworkers, and don't forget to laugh at yourself. Don't take things too seriously. Be silly and laugh at the absurdity of life. Laughter reminds you to make playfulness part of your day.

Is it possible to add laughter to your interactions with your MIAC? My son and I have some of the best laughs over the ridiculous symptoms of his disease. Kudos to W.E.B. DuBois, civil rights activist and author who gives us permission to share our joy. He said, "I am especially glad of the divine gift of laughter: it has made the world human and lovable, despite all its pain and wrong."

Intention for Creating Laughter

> Just for today, just in this moment,
> I will look for reasons to smile and laugh,
> to fill my heart and life with joy.

Activities to Do

- Remember a funny movie you enjoyed and watch it again. I love *Planes, Trains and Automobiles* starring Steve Martin and John Candy.
- Attend a comedy show or watch a standup comedian on TV.
- Try a "laughter yoga" class. You can find several videos online.
- Watch young children play. Their giggling is infectious.
- Read the book *Crowded in the Middle of Nowhere: Tales of Humor and Healing from Rural America* by Dr. Bo Brock.
- If you watch TV, include less news and more funny sitcoms.

- Spend time playing with a pet. If you don't have one, borrow a friend's dog or cat for a few hours.
- Make a scrapbook of funny things family members say and do.
- People-watching can be quite entertaining. Try the mall, airport, or a busy grocery store.
- Play charades, Twister, or try a hula hoop.

Meditation for Laughter

Close your eyes and take a few slow, deep breaths.

Remember back to a time when you were a small child. When you played, laughed, aand were happy, laughing so hard your belly hurt and you could hardly breathe. Smile and laugh along with that memory.

Recall how laughing made you feel.

Did it relax you? Did life seem better? Did you feel more connected to those you giggled with? Did it make you forget all your problems?

Now try to remember the last time that, as an adult, you laughed that hard. If you can't remember, it's been way too long.

It's time to bring back that happy, funny child.

It's time to see the comical side of life.

It's time to be less serious, to lighten up, to laugh until you cry.

Talisman

Purchase a Joke-of-the-Day calendar.

Love

A mother's love is the strongest love there is, as long as it's true love and not ego-based love. Your child isn't in the world to take care of you, make sure you're happy, or fulfill your hidden agendas. It's not your MIAC's responsibility to be who you want him to be, to conform to your rules and morals, or fill an emptiness in your heart.

You often hear that a mother's love is unconditional. While you think that you'll love your child that way, it rarely happens. Life hands you the tragedy and chaos of a severe mental illness, and it becomes difficult to love with no strings attached. You think when you demean, belittle, or shame your MIAC that you show him love because you want his behaviors to change, but this isn't so. It's hard to have unconditional love when you care for your MIAC. Helen Steiner Rice, a writer of religious and inspirational poetry, has a unique understanding of mothers who care for MIACs: "A mother's love is patient and forgiving when all others are forsaking. It never fails or falters, even though the heart is breaking."

> *You often hear that a mother's love is unconditional.*
> *While you think that you'll love your child that way,*
> *it rarely happens.*

Love is not what you say. Love is what you do. We confuse many things for love, and they aren't authentic love. Love isn't pain, it's not fear, it's not attachment, it's not possessiveness, and it's not addiction. Love is the opposite of what many of us were taught to believe. Love allows your child to be who he is. Love doesn't try to fix or change. Love holds lightly, love offers personal sovereignty, love doesn't expect anything in return, and love is granting your MIAC happiness, however that may look. Love doesn't control, demand compliance, or have conditions, and there are no agendas. Love doesn't threaten to withhold itself, make promises, or allow abusive behavior. Love gives freedom, wants happiness, and is without boundaries. From ancient Chinese philosopher Lao Tzu, "Being deeply loved by someone gives you strength, while loving someone deeply gives you courage."

Love isn't just for family, friends, and romantic relationships; love is a way of being in the world. A combination of intimacy, compassion, and commitment, love is when you choose to be at your best even when your child isn't. Ego-based love wants what's best for you, while spirit-based love wants what's best for everyone. Love is the highest form of vibration. It can change the energy of a person or circumstance, and it offers healing, acceptance, and power.

Love is a choice, and giving love to others improves your physical, mental, and emotional health and creates greater happiness in both the recipient and the giver. Love isn't just a feeling; it's a lifestyle. Seeing every person, event, and circumstance through the lens of love creates more authentic relationships, more compassion for others, and less conflict and struggle within yourself.

Intention for Creating Love

> Just for today, just in this moment,
> I will see my heart filled to the brim with the
> pure white light of love and tenderness.

Activities to Do

- After a stressful encounter with your MIAC, replay the event from his point of view. Walk in his shoes. Try to see and feel from his perspective.
- Work on loving yourself unconditionally. Offer yourself the same love you give to others. It's not as easy as it seems.
- Practice pausing before responding. Figuratively put on your "love" glasses.
- Try doing what's best for your MIAC if it doesn't infringe on your boundaries—not what you think is best—by asking what he needs from you.
- Allow your child to face the consequences of poor choices.

- Be unattached to others' decisions because your happiness comes from inside yourself. Your child's choices shouldn't impact your love for him or how you feel about yourself.
- Observe how animals love their owners unconditionally. They don't hold grudges, have expectations, or ask them to change.
- Read *Love: What Life Is All About* by Leo Buscaglia.
- Look at pictures of your MIAC as a baby and small child, and remember that what you love is trapped behind the MI.
- Give more hugs. Thirty-second hugs add to everyone's well-being.

Meditation for Love

Close your eyes and take a few slow, deep breaths.

Imagine yourself lying on your back on a beautiful sandy beach. Hear the waves against the shore, see the gulls flying overhead.

Feel the warmth of the sun on your face.

Visualize a single golden ray of sunlight coming down from the sky, penetrating your chest, and going directly into your heart.

You can feel your heart expand with the golden energy of love.

Enjoy the sensation of tenderness, respect, and appreciation as it fills you.

Imagine giving your child a hug and transferring this golden love light into his heart, which boomerangs back into yours.

Watch the light trace the eternal infinity symbol as it passes between the two of you, back and forth.

Take a mental video of this experience to return to whenever you want or need to be reminded what true love feels like.

Talisman

Purchase a small infinity symbol as a reminder that love flows free, never ends, and needs to be shared. In my online search, I found some beautiful stones carved with a heart and infinity symbol intertwined that can be custom engraved.

Cheerful Enthusiasm

Henry Ford endorses cheerfulness like this: "Enthusiasm is the sparkle in your eyes, the swing in your gait." Being cheerful is having a positive perspective, a belief that everything happens for a reason, and that you'll be okay regardless of what life gives you. People who are cheerful exhibit lightheartedness, optimism, and hopefulness.

Enthusiasm is defined as a lively interest in a person, activity, or life. Gordon Parks, photographer, writer, and musician, says, "Enthusiasm is the electricity of life." It's what pushes you to take action and moves you forward toward goals. It means cultivating a good attitude and receiving satisfaction from performed activities and pursued dreams.

Choose to live with cheerful enthusiasm. It's a great way to guarantee you'll get the most out of life. It allows you to tackle whatever happens with readiness, determination, and zest and allows you to see the silver lining in every event. With cheerful enthusiasm, you do everything with an eager willingness.

What if you don't feel cheerful or enthusiastic? Is it possible to cultivate more joy and lightheartedness? Can optimism and eagerness toward life be learned? The good news is both enthusiasm and cheerfulness are contagious, so hang out with people who exhibit both, and you'll be able to add more of it to your life. Fake it until you feel it. Act as if you're absolutely excited about a project you don't feel like doing. It'll make you find reasons to justify your feelings. Gratitude increases cheerfulness; activity enhances enthusiasm. Life is better when you choose to look at the positive instead of assuming the worst will always happen. Our words prophesy our reality. Take thought leader Ray T. Bennett's advice and "Believe in your heart that you're meant to live a life full of passion, purpose, magic, and miracles."

Intention for Creating Cheerful Enthusiasm

> Just for today, just in this moment,
> I will fill my heart with cheerful excitement
> and joy that I'm alive another day.

Activities to Do

- Jump on a trampoline or have a pillow fight.
- Take a Zumba class. Dance and sweat your way to optimism.
- Make a list of everything good that's happened this week.
- Clean out your junk drawer. It feels good to get rid of clutter.
- Stay away from energy vampires or people whose negativity drains you.
- Practice saying no to commitments that don't fill you with joy. No explanation is required. Simply say, "Thanks for asking, but I'm not able to do that at this time."
- Read *Enthusiasm Makes the Difference* by minister and author Dr. Norman Vincent Peale.
- Find what arouses your enthusiasm and do more of that. Is it art, nature, books, sports, learning a new skill, cooking, or a yoga class? What makes you feel light and joyful?
- Be mindful of everything you do. It creates an attitude of enthusiasm.
- Get enough sleep, eat healthy foods, and drink water. These create the perfect pallet for cheerful enthusiasm. It's easier to be happy when you feel good.

Meditation for Cheerful Enthusiasm

> Close your eyes and take a few slow, deep breaths.
>
> In your mind's eye, go into the very center of your being, the place of your soul essence. I like to imagine this place deep in my womb or abdomen space.

Notice there is a tiny spark of light at the very core of your being.

See how everything is connected to this spark: your veins and arteries, your tissues and ligaments, your organs and bones. Everything is created from this small spark of life.

Ask your soul essence to show you what color cheerful is for you. Ask what color enthusiasm is.

Visualize those two colors as they blend together and move up through the center of your body, filling you with vibrant-colored sparks of light, like your own internal fireworks show.

These sparks of color are the keys to becoming more cheerful and living your life with enthusiasm. They turn on your ability to get more from everything you experience.

Move these colors up into your heart space.

Know that you can tap into these colors anytime you need to.

Remember, you hold the key to how you experience life.

Talisman

What color is cheerful? What color is enthusiasm? Purchase keys in those colors or with a theme that makes you happy and reminds you that life is better with cheerfulness and excitement.

Inner Peace

Inner peace is a deliberate state of mental and spiritual calm despite stressors. It means you have enough knowledge and understanding to keep yourself strong and resilient in difficult situations. Inner peace has been described as the harmony of mind, the tranquility of spirit, or inner serenity, and it's acquired by going inward and connecting with your soul and intuition. When you spend the time to cultivate calmness, quietness, and contentment, you're better able to transcend difficult situations, tragic circumstances, and everyday conflicts.

Inner peace allows you to see beyond what happens and become the observer of an event. It doesn't mean you don't care what happens; it means you know what you can and can't control. You also understand that feeling stressed won't change the outcome. In the midst of life's many storms, you have the ability to stand firm in the center of your own peace and know that all will be okay.

Inner peace is one of the most important life skills to cultivate when you care for a MIAC. It's your inner support system in times of crisis, chaos, anxiety, and turmoil. Serenity comes from a strong bond with your higher power, feeling grounded in reality, and knowing what's within your control. Inner peace allows you to weather any storm with grace and fortitude, knowing that it will end and the sun will come out again.

When you struggle and suffer because you want things to be different, inner peace is the ability to accept what is without fighting to make it what you think it should be. That doesn't mean you don't offer advice and support, but rather you discern when it's time to step back and let things unfold naturally. Inner peace comes from believing that there's an order to things, that something larger than yourself is in control, and that certain experiences serve a higher purpose, even if you can't see what that might be.

Inner peace is one of the most important life skills to cultivate when you care for a MIAC.

Inner peace and serenity feel like a superpower. It's the capacity to trust what you don't know, to believe what you can't see, and to appreciate that everything happens for a reason. It's letting go of expectations, accepting that there's very little you control, and welcoming what has occurred as if you'd asked for it. Inner peace takes you back to when you were a small child living in each moment and enjoying whatever happened to be in front of you with no thought about what would come the next minute or next hour. It's not about being happy in every circumstance but receiving it with a peaceful heart, mental clarity, and the insight that God has everything under control. Achieving inner peace takes a huge burden off your shoulders because it allows you to lay down your troubles and look for the beauty and perfection hidden all around you.

Intention for Creating Inner Peace

> Just for today, just in this moment,
> I will go within, find my strength, and fill my heart
> with calmness, serenity, and peace.

Activities to Do

- Read *The Power of Now: A Guide to Spiritual Enlightenment* by Eckhart Tolle.
- Listen to *The Art of Living: Peace and Freedom in the Here and Now* by Thich Nhat Hanh with a free audible.com trial.
- Spend time outdoors without your phone. Sunrise and sunset are especially peaceful.
- Practice being an observer before you decide if or how to respond.
- Spend a few minutes each day in stillness and quiet. Listen to your intuition. What advice does it give you?
- Visualize everyone in the world connected by an invisible web of love.
- Remember, everyone is doing their very best every day based on their abilities and circumstances.
- Go out of your way to show kindness to others, including strangers. Keep score of how many times a day you can be an ambassador of kindness.
- Don't take anything personally. Everything is a reflection of the person who said or did it and has nothing to do with you, even if it's done to you. Observe, don't react.
- When confronted with a difficult decision or circumstance, think about what the worst-case scenario would be and then decide the probability of that actually happening. Fear is a

figment of your imagination running wild. Your worst fears rarely occur.

Meditation for Creating Inner Peace

> Close your eyes and take a few slow, deep breaths.
>
> Imagine yourself walking down a long, dimly lit hallway.
>
> At the end of the hall, you see a small wooden door. You can see a light shining from underneath, inviting you to enter.
>
> As you get closer, the door swings open, and you see the most peaceful room. It's lit with rose-colored lamps, the air is scented with jasmine and lavender. The walls are painted a tranquil aqua. Soft music plays.
>
> You enter the room and immediately feel an overwhelming sense of peace and serenity. The floor is covered in fuzzy lounging pillows, and you make yourself comfortable.
>
> Sit with your eyes closed and feel the tranquility seep deep into your body, filling you with a calm stillness.
>
> Feel yourself enfolded in a giant hug of love, acceptance, compassion, and comfort. Sink into the feeling of peace.
>
> You know everything is right in the world. You know everything will be okay. You know this is your inner sanctuary and you can return any time you need to.
>
> This is where you connect to your deeper self, your soul self, your inner peace.
>
> Stay as long as you like. Fill your heart with love and light.

Talisman

Purchase a copy or write out the Serenity Prayer. Hang it in a place where you can see it daily. Read it every time you walk past.

"God, grant me the SERENITY to accept the things I cannot change, the COURAGE to change the things I can, and the WISDOM to know the difference."

Visualization Journey

Sit in a comfortable place. Close your eyes

Breathe in and out slowly to the count of three several times until you feel yourself begin to relax.

Visualize yourself walking outside in nature. An angel guide will take this journey with you, will be by your side all the way. Let's begin.

You come to a rose garden. You can choose to see and enjoy the fragrant blooms, the velvety petals, and the soft colors of the rose blossoms. Or you can choose to see the thorns. Which do you choose?

Walking on, you enter a forest of evergreens. You can choose to enjoy the fresh pine scent, the smooth feel of the needles, and the shade the trees offer. Or you can choose to see the mess of the fallen, dead branches. Which do you choose?

Next, you come to a meadow full of sunflowers. You can choose to smile at their bright yellow faces, marvel at the height of the stalks, and be amazed by the fact that such a magnificent flower came from such a tiny seed. Or you can choose to see the flowers that are bent over, drooping, or have died. Which do you choose?

There's a stream near the meadow. You can choose to listen to its gurgling song, watch it meander around rocks, and enjoy feeling the cool water on your feet. Or you can choose to see the algae collected near the rocks, worry about slipping, complain about the unevenness of the bottom. Which do you choose?

Further on your journey, you approach a beach and see the ocean lapping at the shore. You can choose to laugh as the powdery sand squishes between your toes, enjoy the warm water tickling around your ankles, and breathe in the salty breeze as it ruffles your hair. Or you can choose to worry about jellyfish stinging you, complain about the sand getting into your shoes, the sun in your face. Which do you choose?

Your last adventure is a hike in the mountains. You can choose to marvel at the sheer size of the mountains, the breathtaking beauty of the multi-colored rock formations, and the way you feel protected and safe as you climb. Or you can choose to moan about the lack of vegetation, the loose gravel underfoot, how tiring it is to climb. Which do you choose?

As your journey comes to an end, your angel guide reminds you that you always have a choice in how you see the world. You can recognize and be grateful for the beauty that's all around you. Or you can choose to see everything through a veil of darkness and disappointment. You have the ability to change your reality by the way you choose to see it.

Nature reminds us that life is messy. You can focus on the disorder, or you can choose to see the beauty, wonder, and awe.

When ready, open your eyes and journal any messages, words, symbols you received. What did the places you visited smell like? Could you feel yourself right there in the middle of the woods, near the stream, climbing the mountain, smelling the flowers, and enjoying the bounty that nature has to offer?

Choose wisely, dear one. Choose wisely.

I leave you with a prayer that your life be filled with peace, balance, and joy.

We are sisters
We walk arm in arm
Heart to heart
We share our stories of hope and promise

We are sisters
We reclaim our lives
We restore our faith
We recover our joy

We are sisters
Advocates
Defenders
Champions for justice

We are sisters
We inspire change
We encourage reform
We reduce stigma and discrimination

We are sisters
We love unconditionally
We honor our children by living with joy
We become a light in the storm

We are sisters

Resources

Throughout this book, I've mentioned a number of resources—books, organizations, and websites—that can help you in your journey to joyful fulfillment. You'll find these and more on my website: www.SistersInTheStorm.com/resources.

Acknowledgments

This book could not have been written without the support and encouragement of Nancy Erickson—aka The Book Professor—coach, editor, and owner of Stonebrook Publishing, who not only walked me patiently through each chapter but also made order out of my hodgepodge of words. I'm amazed and grateful for how she formatted the book into bite-sized pieces, perfect for struggling moms to ingest. Thank you so much for your hard work and dedication to seeing my dream of helping other moms come to fruition.

My heartfelt appreciation to all the moms who were brave enough to share their stories of heartache and loss, to my personal coach Courtney Blaine Brophy who encouraged me to fulfill my purpose and be a guiding light for struggling moms everywhere, and to my dear friend, Mike Kitko, who pushed me out of my victim mentality and gave me the courage to share my story.

About the Author

Not only has Linda Hoff survived the storm, but she has also created a life of balance, joy, and purpose for herself and her mentally ill adult child (MIAC). In her debut book, *Sisters in the Storm,* Linda shares her struggles, heartache, and lessons learned over the last ten years as she navigated through her son's unexpected schizophrenia diagnosis.

Linda shares a home on the outskirts of Saint Louis, Missouri, with a friend and fellow mom of a MIAC, two dogs, and two cats. She visits her son regularly and loves to spend time in nature, traveling, reading, and enjoying time with her four grandchildren.

CPSIA information can be obtained
at www.ICGtesting.com
Printed in the USA
LVHW110725260422
717138LV00005B/61